BECOME A
TOP CONSULTANT

BECOME A
TOP CONSULTANT

How the Experts Do It

Ron Tepper

JOHN WILEY & SONS

New York • Chichester • Brisbane • Toronto • Singapore

This publication is designed to provide accurate and
authoritative information in regard to the subject
matter covered. It is sold with the understanding that
the publisher is not engaged in rendering legal, accounting,
or other professional service. If legal advice or other
expert assistance is required, the services of a competent
professional person should be sought. *From a Declaration
of Principles jointly adopted by a Committee of the
American Bar Association and a Committee of Publishers.*

Library of Congress Cataloging-in-Publication Data:

Tepper, Ron, 1937—
  Become a top consultant.

  Includes index.
  1. Business consultants—Case studies.
I. Title.

HD69.C6T46   1985   658.4'6   85-12066
ISBN 0-471-81706-6

Printed in the United States of America

10 9 8 7 6 5 4 3 2 1

To Janet, the consultant's consultant

Preface

Webster defines consulting as giving advice and providing counsel. Thousands of companies throughout the United States pay millions of dollars each year to consultants for that advice.

With the rapid growth of high technology, consulting is an industry that will grow as quickly as—or more quickly than—any other in the coming years. It is an expanding industry and offers incredible opportunities for those with the background and skills.

What kind of skills and background? In many cases, consulting requires no more than the ability to be analytical and a problem-solver. Consultants are good listeners. They are not high-pressure salespeople, nor do they jump to conclusions. They think carefully about problems before they offer potential solutions.

These are skills that most in business already possess. Many of the consultants operating today have a business background. A good percentage worked for companies in a variety of positions—some were engineers, lawyers, accountants, psychologists, insurance salespeople, personnel directors, trainers, sociologists and laymen. These people are filling needs in every industry. At the same time, they are building successful businesses and their own financial independence.

This book examines 10 of the most successful consultants in the country. We look at them from the perspective of how they got into business, what qualifications they have, how they built their practice, what pitfalls they found and solved and, most important, how others, desiring to get into the consulting field, can duplicate their success.

These 10 are in industries ranging from management consulting and data processing (information systems) to sales training, "headhunting," civil and electrical engineering. They have many common characteristics and substantially different backgrounds.

Some thought they could never succeed. Others believed they could never convince a client to utilize their services. Some have a multitude of college degrees; others simply were graduated from high school.

Each shows readers how they can build a practice part-time (or full-time). They detail the methods they have used and show professionals how to establish a practice with minimum capital.

Several things they share have made them successful. One is specialization. In some way, all of them specialize. Because of specialized services their businesses have grown rapidly and competition has had a minimal impact.

They also share another characteristic—none has ever advertised to build a business. They have developed consulting firms (and six figure incomes) without ever spending money on advertisements.

Their personalities are as divergent as their professions. One spent 25 years as an electrical engineer working for a large company. His career was a disappointment. Despite his talents, he was passed over for promotion. He felt trapped. He never imagined he had the ability to own his own business. Nor did he ever even dream that his own company would one day hire him as an independent consultant. Today he not only owns his own firm but he has offices in two states and his services are in demand nationally. Anyone, he says, could do the same.

Another was an information systems/data processing specialist who had spent an equal amount of time working for various firms. A talented, successful individual, he occupied a position of high responsibility. Yet his dream was to open his own business, and he did. In less than eight years, he has built a firm with a national reputation and more than 40 employees.

A third was a high school graduate and college dropout. A man who drifted from one job to another until he focused on a goal of becoming an investment advisor. His story is not only remarkable but is illustrative of what others have the capability of doing when they set their minds to it.

A fourth was even considered "unemployable." As a last measure to find a job he went to work for a personnel firm and developed a technique that has made him one of the highest paid headhunters in the country.

Another was a government employee who spent years working in the engineering department with little remuneration. During those years, he learned the ins and outs of city hall—a skill that has made him one of the highest paid government/land consultants in the industry.

The 10 were selected not only because of their achievements but because of their fields, backgrounds, and their ability to show others how to duplicate their success. They are:

LARRY NICKELS. Quiet, soft-spoken, a loyal employee of Allis-Chalmers for 25 years. Nickels was an electrical engineer with expertise in power electronics. His skills were taken for granted. More than anything, Nickels wanted to get out on his own and show people—throughout the country—how capable he was.

The opportunity finally arose when a friend not only convinced Nickels to go into business but showed him how he could build a clientele without ever selling.

JOSEPH IZZO. One of the foremost data processing experts in the country. Izzo, whose immaculate appearance matches his thoughtful approach to problems, was a key executive with one of the largest information system consulting firms in the country.

Despite the well-paid job, Izzo had a dream of going into business. With careful planning, he made the move. Today, his firm is considered one of the premiere information systems' companies in the United States and his problem-solving ability is unrivaled.

ARNOLD VAN DEN BERG. An inspiration for anyone thinking about entering the consulting field. Van Den Berg, a positive thinker with a penchant for research, entered one of the most competitive consulting fields imaginable (investment) and built a highly successful firm through a unique approach that can work, says Van Den Berg, for anyone willing to put in similar time and effort.

LARRY SENN. A careful, deliberate management consultant who was never sure if his academic background (BA, MBA, Doctorate) was good enough. Senn found an interesting way to start part-time and, at the same time, his innovative ideas as to specialization enabled him to carve a niche in a competitive industry despite a shaky economy.

FRED PETERS. Casual, relaxed, straight-to-the-point, Peters entered business because he had no other choice. Without the benefit of training, he developed a recruiting technique for a specialized group of employees that has made him invaluable to personnel departments.

The former Ohio University football player is a prime example of the opportunity in the personnel field. His methods, which he describes in detail, are easily duplicated and his industry is one of the most promising in the coming years.

HUGH HOLBERT. Gregarious, outgoing, a former real estate salesperson who was tiring of the grind. He saw a need that no one was filling. He took the most difficult path of any consultant—he went to law school, graduated, passed the bar exam and started practicing part-time in one specific industry. His knowledge of that industry enabled him to become one of the highest-paid attorneys in the field and switch from part-time to full-time within a year.

ED PEARSON. Like most civil engineers, Pearson is analytical and observant. He watched his industry change and he changed with it. He built a firm and a clientele in building—an industry that is as volatile as the economy. Yet, Pearson has succeeded. Among his clients are some of the largest building firms. His is another business that offers prospective consultants an opportunity in a field that continues to grow.

TOM HOPKINS. If it wasn't for his love of sales training, Tom Hopkins could have been a politician. He's quick, an excellent speaker and a consultant who got into business almost by accident. Despite his success, Hopkins had to overcome adversity to establish his company. For three years, he worked as a trainer without compensation. Today, he makes $17,500 a day in a field that is in need of consultants and beckons to part-timers.

JACK SPAHN. A former government worker, Spahn is outspoken and through his pragmatic approach to problems he has been able to build an unmatched clientele. Spahn walks the corridors of city hall and represents clients in a variety of development cases. His expertise and experience have made him the highest paid consultant in the field. For those working in city hall or other governmental agencies, Spahn's is an ideal practice to emulate.

HANK ZDONEK. He's busy and always on the move. He saw a way to build business that seldom occurs to accountants and carved a special clientele at the same time. His part-time techniques are fascinating and his thoughts on fees and client relationships are valuable lessons for present—and potential—consultants in any field.

RON TEPPER

Torrance, California
September 1985

Acknowledgments

This book would never have been possible were it not for the time and effort of many people. First, my sincere thanks to the 10 consultants who generously provided countless hours of interview time so this book could be put together in a thorough, accurate manner.

Second, to Michael J. Hamilton and Marilyn Dibbs at John Wiley & Sons, the two people who spent almost as much time on this project as I did. A special thanks, too, to Michael, who provided many of the ideas and the thrust for the book.

Last, but certainly not least, to Janet, my wife, who patiently endured the long hours I spent away from home while writing, and then, without hesitation, volunteered to read and critique this book. Without her help, assistance, and guidance, this book would not have been possible.

R.T.

Contents

CHAPTER 1

HOW TO DETERMINE YOUR MARKET

Los Angeles in the sixties. The real estate industry was booming. Tracts were being built throughout Southern California, interest rates were relatively low, and opportunity was high.

Thousands of people were flocking to the industry in hopes of hitting it big. One of those hopefuls was a young, aggressive, dark-haired California native who had visions of becoming the number-one salesman in the real estate field.

For Tom Hopkins, there were some surprises ahead. After three months in the field, Hopkins found that selling wasn't as easy as he had thought. He looked at his commission check. $40. Hardly enough to live on, let alone qualify him as a salesperson after 90 days.

Perhaps selling wasn't for Hopkins after all. That was one of the thoughts that crossed his mind. Hopkins was ready to quit, when he decided to give sales one more shot. He had heard about a seminar that was being conducted by one of the leading salespeople in the country. It would take almost every dollar he had to attend, but why not give it a shot? And he did.

What Tom Hopkins learned in that seminar not only turned his sales career around but also opened his eyes. He looked around at the hundreds of others in the room, all salespeople and every one of them there for help.

Suddenly, Hopkins saw an opportunity and a giant market. Sure, he thought to himself, selling is a great profession, but look how many salespeople are unprofessional and need help when it comes to selling. What was even more amazing to Hopkins was that salespeople knew they needed help and were willing to pay for it. The hundreds in the room were evidence of that.

At that moment, Tom Hopkins decided that one day he was going to be a sales trainer. He could see the need. It was in front of him. It would take time, but one day Hopkins would get there.

Today, of course, Hopkins is one of the most successful sales training consultants in the country. He is evidence of the adage that if you have something that people need, there is no end to the sales potential. But the first rule with any service (or product) is to test it. Find out if people want it before you try to sell it.

Hopkins could see the need by the attendance in the room that day. Within a short time, he saw additional evidence that convinced him there was tremendous opportunity for a sales trainer. The same is true of the other nine consultants in this book. Each in their own way tested the waters first and determined there was a market for their services before they entered the field. And in this chapter, each describes the simple techniques they used for testing.

Testing, researching, and forecasting needs is not as mysterious or as difficult as it may seem. For example, market areas fall into three general categories—retail, service, and manufacturing.

The retailer will find his customers, his market area, does not go much beyond a five-mile radius. In other words, customers will not travel farther to get to the retailer (unless he has some unique product they cannot get elsewhere). Eighty percent of the retailer's customers will fall somewhere within that five-mile zone.

The service business—the field consultants are in—extends far beyond retail. A consultant may service an entire city, state, or his services can even go across country.

FIVE PRACTICAL RESEARCH KEYS

To determine how big the consultant's market (and potential) is, only five steps are required: (1) knowledge of the (consulting) profession you want to enter; (2) time for some research; (3) the ability to listen, observe, and analyze; (4) some common sense; and (5) a vision of the future.

None of those five require any special training. For example, back in the 1970s an entrepreneur named Chase Revel forecast that roller skating would become a national craze. Within a year after he published that prediction, roller skating was popular indeed.

How did Revel know? He simply read an item in a trade paper that mentioned roller skate manufacturers had had the largest increase in orders and sales in 20 years. He called several of the manufacturers to determine where the orders were coming from. They told him most came from stores in and around colleges.

He visited several local colleges and noticed roller skates were being used; he went to the beach and saw a roller skate rental shop opening. Over the next few weeks, he watched roller skaters on the streets and could see the numbers increasing.

On the basis of his research and observation, Revel made his prediction. Some laughed at it but within six months he was proven correct and hailed as a genius for his forecasting ability.

Revel says there was nothing magical about his roller skating forecast or any of the other trends he's predicted (he was also the first to predict the antique and bicycle crazes and the emergence of skateboard parks and computer stores).

FREE RESEARCH INFORMATION

Before any consultant jumps into the fray, he or she should examine his or her market; do a little research. This doesn't mean you have to hire a market research firm. On the contrary, with a few telephone calls and some legwork, you can get all the information you need. The first place to call is the market research department of your local metropolitan newspaper. Market research departments have invaluable information on every industry in the newspaper's area. They compile statistical data on household incomes, average home values, average number of people in each family, how many households have two breadwinners, industries that are moving into the area (and industries that are moving out) plus a myriad of other data.

These departments compile the information for potential advertisers. They make it available at no cost. It is part of the newspaper's service—and a part of the publication's effort to get potential advertisers to place an ad.

For example, suppose you are contemplating a career as an information systems consultant specializing in the aerospace industry. Call the local newspaper—the market research department. Ask for any information they have on local aerospace firms. The publication will be able to supply you with dollar volume, number of employees, growth prospects, and even the type of aerospace work the company does.

If you were entering the headhunting field you could make a similar call and request information on companies and/or occupations that you hope to be dealing with in the future. It is a way to help determine the size of your potential market and the opportunity within it. The newspaper supplies this information at no cost because they hope if you are successful you will one day become an advertiser.

The Bank of America (headquartered in San Francisco) is another resource for consultants. The Bank puts together comprehensive studies of businesses and industries. It compiles data ranging from estimated sales and profits to the business's future.

The Bank publishes the information in a series of books called "The Small Business Reporter." These books, which cover a variety of industries and businesses, are available to anyone at a nominal cost (usually $2 per study). The contents are superb and will give any prospective consultants an idea as to their prospects and the future of their chosen field.

For example, suppose you wanted to enter the accounting profession. The Bank has a study on the field that gives the reader a complete rundown on the costs (of operating), how to open, the problems, and pitfalls, and the profit potential.

Or perhaps you are trying to find information on a particular type of manufacturing industry for which you want to provide consulting services.

The Bank may have a report outlining the industry's growth, its potential and problems. That kind of report can also bring to light some of the specialized consulting services an industry may need.

The Bank will supply you with a list of the publications if you call or write. The address and telephone:

Small Business Reporter

Bank of America

Department 3120

P.O. Box 37000

San Francisco, CA 94137

(415) 622-2491

Robert Morris Associates, a text found in most libraries, contains information on industry averages, business ratios, and performances. Thus, if you are thinking about entering the field and working with aerospace, you could obtain an excellent insight into the potential of the industry by checking the *Morris* book.

Most libraries also carry an *Encyclopedia of Associations.* This text contains a listing of thousands of associations throughout the country. Almost every industry has some association that represents it. These associations contain a wealth of information on the industry.

Two other reference books that will be of interest are *Standard & Poor's Corp.* and *Value Line.* S&P has financial, general, background and information on 10,000 companies. It's an excellent source if you are going to be approaching major firms. *Value Line* is similar. Both can be found in most libraries. These publications are invaluable, especially for those entering the investment advisory field.

The Department of Commerce is another resource. The department contains much more than ten-year-old census data. It updates its demographics on a regular basis. A number of ad agencies and major manufacturers purchase information from the Department in order to forecast needs.

The local chamber of commerce is an often overlooked source. The chamber executive director can usually provide you with information on companies that are moving in, moving out, buildings being planned, and the prospects for the future.

PICKING SUCCESSFUL BRAINS

There is one other resource that few utilize—the existing successful consultant. Pick out the person in your chosen field whom you admire. Call him or her and make an appointment. Sit down and pick a successful brain.

These people know every stumbling block. They have gone through it. They know the secrets to generating clients and building a firm. Why not ask them how they did it?

Will the consultant give you the time? Surprisingly, in most cases they will. Most people never ask because they do not believe the consultant will give them their time.

What does the consultant gain? What's in it for this hard-nosed businessperson? Ego. Recognition. The fact someone knows of and wants to ask about their success.

Granted, not every consultant will roll over and answer every question. Most will, however, because they are flattered. As evidence, the ten consultants featured in this book gave countless hours to the author without compensation. All the author did was ask.

Revel, whom we have alluded to previously, points out that there are thousands of experts throughout this country—existing, successful, businesspeople—who are never asked for advice. Why? Because we assume they will not give it.

One of the most important pieces of information a prospective consultant can gather is trends. For instance, society has changed greatly during the past few years. The average family is smaller than it used to be. And many families now have two breadwinners—that is, both the husband and wife work.

WOMEN IN BUSINESS

Sophisticated companies have adapted to these trends. That's why you see so many frozen dinners and cans with smaller portions in the supermarket. Remember, too, that women are becoming a force in business. Whereas previously the consultant might have dealt with a male supervisor or department head, today's consultant has to be cognizant of the role women play in corporations.

He may be just as likely to find a woman in charge of data processing, productivity, or finance as a man. Society is changing and so are companies.

None of the ten consultants in this book had any formal market research training, yet each was able to find a niche in the market and take advantage of it. The one element they all discovered, either accidentally or by design, was the importance of specialization.

The consultant who tries to be all things to an industry is in for a rough voyage. This is the age of specialization. Generalists—as is the case with general practitioners—are dinosaurs. The consultant who targets an industry and focuses on its needs can build a phenomenal practice.

For example, Larry Nickels is one of the few consultants specializing in power electronics. As a result, he has so much business he rarely has a day off. Larry Senn is a management consultant specializing in productivity and motivation, an unusual combination.

THE HEADHUNTER'S SIX-FIGURE INCOME

Fred Peters, a burly, 250-pound former football player, was unemployed and searching for a job when he stumbled into the personnel field. He observed what was going on and saw the opportunity that existed for placing software engineers.

Peters did not decide on headhunting software engineers by accident. He had worked with engineers. "The typical engineer seldom goes out and hunts for a job. He buries himself in his present position. He never looks at the want ads. If he is unhappy about something, he keeps quiet about it. He isn't like many employees who kick up a fuss and run to the supervisor," says Peters.

"The engineer only thinks about another position if something happens, a layoff or a lost contract. Only then does he think about another position." Backing his theory were five years of experience as a personnel manager. In other words, Peters knew the basics of the business.

Aside from his knowledge of engineers, Peters did some studying about the hiring habits of personnel departments. Typically, they placed ads for engineers in the Sunday paper. From Peter's standpoint, this was not only a mistake but a waste of money. "Engineers don't read classified ads. Plus, all the good engineers always have a job. Seldom would they ever look at the paper to explore an opportunity."

THE ENGINEERING GAP

By talking to personnel people and keeping his eye on the classifieds, Peters discovered that in his area (Southern California), there were 50,000 openings and only 30,000 engineers to fill them. A perfect opportunity for a headhunter.

Although personnel departments get resumés, they seldom have the time to read them. "I decided to do placements for major companies. These firms get hundreds of resumés a day. The personnel manager has little chance of going through them. He needs our help, desperately."

Headhunters operate by working with personnel departments (or the manager of the department that needs the engineer) in finding a potential candidate, screening him, and setting up an appointment with the manager and/or personnel department. In return, the headhunter earns a hefty fee—sometimes up to 30 percent of the employee's yearly salary—for a successful placement.

The candidate never pays, the company does. Peters had other reasons for wanting to place software engineers. "They are easily moved from one company to another. That is, if you take an engineer from company X and put him with company Y, he will not require retraining. He is going to be doing similar things." Two questions remained. Would personnel departments work with Peters, and how would he recruit engineers?

Peters decided to find the answers. He sat down and called ten companies and asked for the personnel departments. When he got through, he asked for the personnel director and introduced himself.

"My pitch went something like . . . 'my name is Fred Peters and I run a placement agency for software engineers. Would you be interested in working with us?' "

Of the ten companies, nine said they would, the tenth refused. Why?

"They sometimes believe we are doing their job, placing employees. In a way, they are right. But they have to work with us. They do not have the time to do anything else."

From the response, Peters knew one side of the marketplace was willing to work with him. As for the engineers, he obtained an internal telephone directory for one company and started calling engineers.

His conversation was short, to the point. "My name is Fred Peters and I run an engineering placement firm. I've got a good paying job for an engineer in your field. I thought you might know someone or, perhaps, you might be interested?"

The answers told him that although an engineer might be employed, he was curious and ready to move. "The bottom line was always money. If we had a job that paid more, there was a good chance the engineer would move."

$13,000 PER PLACEMENT

The one remaining element was price. How much could Peters earn? "The typical engineer we place makes $45,000 a year. That translates to about $13,000 a placement. Not bad. I looked at the figure, examined the calls I had made, and knew the business was viable."

Viable is a mild term. Peters's business has been just short of phenomenal. During the past six years, his income has exceeded six figures each year. In fact, within the first 30 days, he had grossed $15,000.

Obviously if a headhunter deals with a low-priced occupation, it could be difficult establishing a profitable venture. With engineers and a number of other professionals, there are big dollars involved. "Usually," says Peters, "the higher the salary, the higher the commission percentage. It's the high-priced professional who is in demand."

Peters did his research well. He could also see other things in the future for headhunters. "The computer is cutting into many fields and replacing employees. For example, senior designers will soon be a thing of the past. The same is true for draftsmen.

"If you are going into this business, take a look at what's happening and be ready to alter your plans if you have to do so."

Peters has always kept his eyes on the market. "There are a couple of other factors that make engineering placement an excellent profession. Engineers are changing. In the old days, you could get an engineer and he would work 70–80 hours a week. Friday nights, Saturdays, and holidays were standard work days.

"Today's engineer has a different outlook. He doesn't mind working but he isn't going beyond that 40-hour week. That restriction puts a bind on management. In the future, they are going to be looking for even more engineers."

The growing shortage sparked another Peters idea. Why not set up a temporary engineering placement agency. He did. "There's two things going for that approach. There are engineers who do not want to be tied to one company. They want variety. They look for the temporary jobs. This kind of engineer can pull down $60,000–$70,000 a year.

"Companies have no problem meeting their fees. They feel it is better to pay a premium wage for a temporary employee and not worry about the benefits. The temporary field, although it works differently, has proven to be an excellent divergence for us."

"THE PETERS METHOD"

The future for engineers in Southern California is excellent. Peters says he hasn't seen a slowdown for 22 years—the length of time he has been in it. And with the administration putting more emphasis on high tech and aerospace, the field will grow.

Not every area of the country is a paradise for engineers, however. Most employment and headhunting opportunities are confined to areas such as the New England states (especially Boston), several cities in Texas (Dallas, Houston), and California.

This does not mean a headhunter cannot develop a profitable consulting business elsewhere. He can and the technique is easy. Simply follow the "Peters Method." That is, start examining the Sunday classifieds. Look for the skilled professional areas that have high demand. The demand/supply relationship is the one element that will determine whether or not you are in an area that is right for headhunting.

Headhunting does not require a personnel background. Peters says it requires tenacity more than anything else, and a willingness to talk on the telephone. And there is no educational requirement for the potential headhunter.

"There's no special jargon, either," he says. "You don't have to understand engineering. All you have to do is be able to fill a need."

If you are already in the personnel business, you have an advantage because you know which professions are being sought. The next step would be to investigate the possibilities of specializing in an area. When Peters started he was willing to place any profession in order to make a living. He found that by specializing he not only upped his sales but also built a reputation.

Personnel people, when in need, will come to him. Some will even offer him an assignment to fill a particular position. In that case, he is given a third of his fee up front, another third when he comes up with a job description, and the third payment when he sends in candidates.

Even if he doesn't fill the spot, he keeps the money. It sounds sweet but Peters says he doesn't always go for the deal. "If I take it, I have to put one man on it full-time. At times, it may turn out to be more trouble than the fee is worth."

Peters has another way of generating income. Rival headhunters come to him and offer to split the fee if he will join with them on a particular search. This approach appeals to Peters. He does not have to devote a man full-time to it, nor does he have the sole responsibility of filling the position. If he comes up with the candidate, fine. If not, that's all right, too.

MONEY MANAGERS IN DEMAND

Just as needs in the employment field have generated opportunities for headhunters, changes in the economy have created a need for investment advisors, or money managers. The consultant we are referring to is not the insurance salesman or broker who wanders around giving people a business card that says, "Financial Consultant."

Typically, these "financial consultants" wind up selling the client a stock, bond, or insurance policy. Arnold Van Den Berg, however, is an investment advisor/money manager.

Money managers earn their fees from *growth* of the client's portfolio. It does not matter whether the client buys or sells—the key is growth. They do not make a commission from a sale or trade of an item in the portfolio.

This differs markedly from the typical financial consultant. Van Den Berg saw the need for this type of advisor nearly 20 years ago when he was selling insurance.

"What you would find," he explains, "was that if a client's closest advisor was in the real estate field, the client would wind up putting his money in real estate. If the advisor was in stocks, the client would end up buying something from the market. These people may call themselves financial consultants but, for the most part, they are salespeople."

Still, consumers turn to the salesperson, alias financial consultant. Why? "The economy and the pressures of investment. Consumers are confused and concerned. They've heard about the trouble with the Social Security system; they continually read about fluctuating interest rates, monetary policy, trade deficits, the federal deficit itself, and so on," says Van Den Berg.

"They are concerned about their financial future. That concern is even evident at the college level. Recent studies have shown that college students are more serious and career-oriented than ever before."

FROM SALESMAN TO CONSULTANT

The emphasis on money management has not diminished in nearly two decades. If anything, it has grown. One of the reasons for that growth is the media. Ever since the first oil embargo and the ensuing inflationary cycle, the press has made the economy front-page news.

Two decades ago Van Den Berg was selling insurance. "I wanted to structure my business without worrying about commissions. The trouble with commissions is that no matter how objective you try to be, ultimately you have to feed the family. One of the best features about being an investment advisor is you can evaluate all financial options without having 'sales' in the back of your mind. The salesperson/-broker/financial consultant has to sell if they are going to eat. The money manager does not."

As an insurance salesperson, Van Den Berg was in an ideal position to test the market. He could easily bring up the subject of investment to his policyholders. Talking to them, he could see the puzzled looks when it came to investments and how their money should be handled.

Van Den Berg also wanted to specialize. He preferred liquid invest-

Berg says, "few people would need anyone to handle a portfolio, there are great numbers of people out there now, working on regular jobs, who have substantial savings and a corresponding need for money management."

KEY TO FINANCIAL MANAGEMENT SUCCESS

The key is to stay away from being a manager who has only one concern, selling products. Van Den Berg started his business in the midst of difficult times. It has grown largely because of his commitment to steer a specialized course and to stay away from product sales.

While consultants such as Van Den Berg can see a universal need because of the emphasis on investments and financial independence today, others concentrate on specific trades and/or industries. Hugh Holbert saw the need in an industry (real estate) for a specialized attorney.

In an environment where many attorneys are barely making a living, the gregarious, always-smiling Holbert has generated a practice and income that even Jacoby & Myers would envy.

Several factors set the stage for Holbert's booming business. First, the country is "lawsuit happy." The real estate field, Holbert's chosen specialty, is not immune. In recent years developers have become cautious because of the increase in suits due to exaggerations and misstatements; thus even real estate brochures have become objects of scrutiny. Aside from consumer suits there has been a barrage of environmental litigation and real estate development laws. Regulations have become increasingly complex. All of this has combined to create a need for specialized real estate attorneys.

"Real estate law is hard to practice. There are few attorneys who come out of law school equipped to go into real estate," says Holbert. "They have to know about sales, resales, escrow, commercial property, and title insurance, plus a host of other things. Law school doesn't prepare them for specialized fields."

After five years in the real estate field as a salesperson, Holbert could see there was a lack of specialists. Every time his firm needed legal advice, "we paid through the nose. We found ourselves in the office of a general practitioner who knew nothing about real estate law.

ments. That is, stocks, bonds, and similar holdings that could be tu
into cash immediately. "Part of the reason was the economy. Years
you had a bull market and it lasted three and a half years. Today,
get up in the morning and by the afternoon the market may h
undergone a complete reversal."

Van Den Berg theorizes that there is more business—and need—
there than ever before. Anyone who deals with clients who inv
money (insurance salespeople, realtors, brokers) is in a position to
this market.

"Talk to your clients like I did," he says. "Explore their feelin
Explain money management, how it works. Most people do not und
stand the difference between a money manager and a financial cons
tant. The thing you have to explore is the client's attitude towa
someone's handling his or her portfolio."

Determining needs in the money management field is not as cut-an
dried as finding out if a firm needs a headhunter. The prospecti
money manager deals with the mass market of consumers, not a sp
cialized market consisting of engineers and personnel directors.

There are two critical things a money manager should ascertair
First, the client's portfolio should be large enough to allow diversifica
tion in investments. For a money manager to be successful, his client
should have a proper mix of stocks, bonds and other types of invest
ments. Second, money managers have to determine if their clients hav
large enough portfolios to support their practices. Remember, th
money manager works on a small percentage (1 percent–2 percent) o
a portfolio. Handling a $10,000 account is hardly enough to support a
consultant.

Some prospective money managers—such as insurance salespeople
perhaps some brokers—will already have an idea as to the size of a
client's portfolio. They will also know if clients have a money manager
or financial consultant handling their dealings.

Naturally, many clients with large portfolios will already have
someone. Surprisingly, there will be a number with large sums of
money in a portfolio who do not.

With today's emphasis on the economy, financial management is a
consulting profession that will grow rapidly during the coming years.

"Aside from the volatile economy, another factor is that many families have two breadwinners. That gives them more capital and creates
a greater need for investment advice. Whereas years ago," Van Den

"He or she would spend hours in the library learning about it and we would be paying for his or her schooling. Aside from that we would also have to pay for his or her representation."

Holbert's point is taken. There are more than 15,000 trades and industries in this country, and it is impossible for an attorney to have a grasp on each. There are, of course, specialists in many fields, but thousands of industries do not have the luxury of consulting a specialized attorney when trouble arises. Consequently there is a gap and an opportunity.

Even though he was not an attorney, the obvious need in the real estate industry intrigued Holbert. As is the case with most people in any profession, Holbert knew people throughout his industry. It was easy to surmise after casually talking to several of them that each company had the same problem—a need for a real estate attorney.

With 500 brokers and title companies in his area there was no question in Holbert's mind. Despite the time it would take, he decided to go to law school.

$20,000 FIRST MONTH

Holbert, who grossed more than $20,000 his first month in business, is an example of what a specialized attorney can do. This does not mean someone has to get into the real estate field, specifically.

"Regardless of what industry you are in," suggests Holbert, "look around. Does your industry have a need for attorneys—most do. If a company goes to a generalist, it is a sign there is a shortage of specialists."

In researching your market, Holbert says, "beware of the attorney who says he is a specialist and isn't. There are many running around. They'll tell you they specialize simply to make a buck. Throw a few of your industry's technical terms at them. That will help you decide whether they know what they are talking about."

Industry specialists are not necessarily attorneys first and industry authorities second. They often are workers who spent time in the field and saw the need—"like I did. There is an advantage for those who go to work in the industry first. You get to learn it and see its needs. Don't think you have to be an attorney to become an industry specialist."

There are numerous industries that fit into this category. They are typically trades that either are new or are in the process of going through changes.

For example, environmental laws have had significant impact on builders, disclosure legislation has affected the financial industry, and trademark/copyright/patent interpretations are critical in the high tech industries.

"Wherever there is change, there is legal opportunity. Why be an attorney who makes $100 for telling someone about divorce procedures when you can earn $500 an hour, as I do in some cases, for being a specialist?"

One of the most competitive fields is that of the management consultant. Larry Senn, who has built an exceptional consulting firm in the area, is an example of a consultant who saw the need but almost did not make the move.

Senn got his first taste of consulting while working in the aerospace industry. It was internal (at his company); he participated in a group that was charged with solving some of its department's problems.

"From the beginning, I liked what I was doing. The only problem was that as employees, we simply made suggestions. The implementation was something we never got into. That bothered me. I wanted to see more results. I wanted more freedom.

HOW TO SEE NEED

"I could see from the little experience I had that management consulting was needed. It also made me decide that I did not want to continue to be an employee in a large company. I wanted to decide my own destiny."

From Senn's viewpoint much of the need arose from the manager's inability to handle many of the conceptual problems. "In industry today," he says, "the manager has enough trouble just getting his job done and supervising employees. He does not have time to sit around and dream up ways of doing a better job.

"Finding a better way involves analysis and time. That means you need an outside consultant. I could see that when I was working in aerospace."

Like many budding entrepreneurs, Senn was young and had doubts about his ability to become a consultant. He decided more formal education would help. He went back to school and obtained an M.B.A. Then he went for his doctorate. While working towards that last degree, Senn could see additional needs.

"I wound up doing the legwork for one of my professors who was doing consulting on the side for small businesses. I had not thought much about the smaller enterprise, but the experience showed me one of the greatest needs for consulting was in the small business area."

Why? Senn could see technology was changing every business, and the small businessperson, who is usually a generalist, could not keep pace. Unlike the corporate executive who can take hours (or days) off and leave someone else to mind the store while he or she is attending a seminar, the small businessperson does not have that luxury. Usually, he or she is confined to his or her operation.

What the businessperson needed was someone who could come in, evaluate the problem, and offer a solution. Senn could see there were thousands of potential clients.

Additionally, if businesses were hiring professors for consulting, that was a sign that either companies had a difficult time finding consultants, or, perhaps, the existing consultants did a poor job of marketing their services. Either way, a prospective consulting career had potential.

Senn saw other signs that indicated a growing need. As companies increase in size, departments within the firm become more specialized and detached from one another. At times a department on one floor does not even know that another department on the same floor exists.

In this environment management has a difficult time seeing the entire picture and finding the cause of production delays, shipping problems, and even personnel turnover. The need for an outside management consultant, who can come in and objectively evaluate the operation, grows as companies expand.

THE BEGINNER'S CLIENTELE

The beginning consultant is going to be starting a practice with small business clients. "It doesn't matter where you start," says Senn, "The principles are the same. You can work for a retailer or manufacturer, and the approach would not differ. The small business is the beginning consultant's initial niche."

Larger clients drift toward the bigger consulting firms. What size is small? For Senn, they are firms in the $1 million to $30 million range. Companies grossing less than that are borderline consulting prospects. Management, in those cases, may still have a grasp (or believe it does) on the operation.

It is critical to find the right niche in which to specialize. The management consultant can get involved in any area—from marketing and sales to productivity and motivation. Incidentally, the management consultant is not restricted geographically. Today Senn has clients across the country.

With his engineering background and analytical skills, Senn selected productivity. He gave his specialty a slight twist by adding motivation to it. Every one of his jobs concentrates on increasing productivity, and properly motivating employees is a critical part of productivity.

MANAGEMENT CONSULTANT'S MARKET

In today's environment, with the number of factory workers decreasing, any consultant who specializes solely in assembly line productivity is heading down a rapidly narrowing road. Senn's productivity specialty involves both the office and factory. He is just as likely to find himself in a white-collar work environment as an assembly line.

The potential for consultants such as Senn is immense. Companies of the future will not only be more decentralized, but employees may be physically detached from offices as well. As Alvin Toffler points out in *The Third Wave,* there is no reason why many employees will not be working at home with a computer terminal.

In the future, companies may not see the need for employees to commute to the office in order to sit behind a computer terminal. Why not put the terminal at home and, with the proper training, increase each employee's output as well?

These coming changes mean that a company's operations will be more complex. And, when difficulties arise, whether they be in office productivity or marketing, the need for consultants such as Senn will become apparent.

Senn views the work of Toffler (and other management theorists) as a glimpse of the future. In his view it is another indication of the growing need for more management specialists.

Of all the consultants in this book, the most scientific in his study of the market and its potential was Joseph Izzo. Izzo had spent more than 20 years in data processing. He could see its growth and how rapidly things were changing.

Most important, he could see the impact that information systems were having on companies. This vantage point came from his position as vice president of the consulting division at Computer Science Corporation (CSC).

"Years ago," he says thoughtfully, "data processing had a confined impact. It was primarily an accounting function. If something went wrong, it had little impact on the rest of the company. After all, you could still crank out handwritten checks."

But by the seventies a change was occurring. Data processing was becoming the heartbeat of companies. If the system had problems, it was no longer "a matter of the checks not getting out. The entire company could be shut down."

DATA PROCESSING'S NEW OPPORTUNITIES

Management experienced a change of perspective as well. In the early years, when computers were initially installed, management left the operation to the data processing department. They seldom became involved, nor did they care about it.

"But the personal computer changed everything," says Izzo. "Suddenly every CEO and manager knew something about the operation of the department. It became more difficult for managers. There was interference—not malicious, but rather through management's desire to help if there were problems with the department. This interference could end in several ways, none very productive. One of the most severe was the firing of the head of the data processing department."

In the midst of this, Izzo could see the need for independent consultants who could come in, analyze the problem, work with data processing and management, and offer solutions. Izzo did not have to guess at the need, he could see the potential clients coming through his employer's doors.

"Future needs," says Izzo, "will be greater. Computers are only at the beginning of a massive growth cycle. In upcoming years we will see computers that have 'artificial intelligence,' that is, a computer system that will have 'common sense' built into its decisionmaking. It is already happening in the medical profession."

Even with his familiarity with the consulting field, Izzo decided to do additional research before he took the major step of opening his own business. A cautious, pragmatic individual, Izzo did not just rely upon his feelings of enthusiasm. There were problems in the field. Companies *were* going to outside consultants, but Izzo could see their reports gathering dust on shelves. Why?

"Two reasons," he explains. "First, some consultants found the problem was with higher management. They would not include that fact in the report. When the top executives received the document and read it, it was obvious something was missing. So they discarded it.

"Another problem was the quality of the consultants. The owner of the consulting firm may have had the expertise, but in his or her desire to make a few dollars, he or she ended up putting in neophyte consultants. This often led to a botched job."

Those two findings led Izzo to several decisions. First, if he opened his firm, he would never dodge the bullet. If it turned out top management was to blame for the problem, he would tell them so. Second, he would never scrimp on help. His office would have top, qualified personnel. Even if it meant cutting deep into the profits.

There were other questions. Would firms hire him? Izzo knew many executives in the industry, people who would be in a position to retain his services. He picked a dozen, called them and told them what he was planning to do. He asked if they could set aside some time to give him advice.

OBTAINING FREE COUNSEL

"I was surprised when I met with them. Nearly half had tried their own business. From the interviews, I was able to ascertain the main reasons they were not in business any longer—undercapitalization and a lack of marketing. Those were two additional things I underlined."

Finding the reasons for their failures gave Izzo more confidence. He knew there was a market; he could see the consulting business being generated by CSC. As for the pitfalls, he had a plan to overcome both the marketing and financial inadequacies; a plan that he knew would work for him or anyone who wanted to get into the information systems field.

And in Izzo's case the plan certainly did work. Today, eight years after his doors were opened, he has generated between $18 to $20 million worth of business and is "at the beginning of a growth cycle."

While techology created the need for Izzo's services, in other industries trends such as consumerism supplied the impetus. Jack Spahn, a land/government consultant, knows firsthand about the impact of consumerism. It has taken a once simple industry, construction, and turned it into a maze of complex decisionmaking.

For more than two decades, from 1945 until the early 1970s, builders had carte blanche. The country needed housing and most builders could get plans approved in a day or two. From conception to completion, projects could be built in six months.

With the seventies, however, came a rise in consumer issues and influence. Environmental groups were formed; people began to take issue with government decisions. Planning and zoning commission hearings, which were once empty, were playing host to standing-room-only crowds.

Public officials became cognizant of a new influence, the activist consumer. No longer were building plans rubber-stamped. Six-month projects were stretched out to two and three years. Costs soared and the builder found himself in dire need of a go-between, someone to help usher plans through a reluctant city government and an oftentimes hostile group of citizens.

DUAL MARKET FOR LAND/GOVERNMENT CONSULTANT

Spahn, who had worked both in government and private industry, saw the need. "Consumers were the stumbling block. A builder had to deal with them and negotiate. I spent many years at city hall and knew numerous builders. One thing they do not have—patience and tolerance. Whenever they met with consumers, the encounter invariably ended in a near-riot."

Builders were not the only ones who could utilize Spahn's services. Civil engineers, the professionals who worked with builders on projects, were seldom equipped to handle consumers or the problems to be faced at governmental agencies.

Yet they were often given the responsibility by the builder to get the plans through city hall. If the engineer did not have a go-between on staff who could negotiate between city hall and the consumers, he or she could be in trouble, too.

There was a third element that favored Spahn setting up a practice, his experience at city hall. He had worked in engineering and knew his way around.

Spahn's idea was reinforced by the builders. On several occasions he had been approached and asked if he would be interested in working for them.

THE KEY TO SUCCESS

"It's an important lesson for any would-be consultants. You don't have to be a technical person to work in the construction field. The key to being a success in this business is being able to find your way around city hall. If you know your way, you may be ready for this business."

Spahn saw his role as a consultant who would meet with the builder, negotiate with consumer groups and then go to city hall with a plan that had the endorsement of the consumers. He realized several other things. It might be relatively easy for a builder to find someone to negotiate with homeowners, but what about downtown? There were pitfalls in dealing with government agencies. Spahn knew them. He felt confident that he would not only be a success in the field, but he could command a premium fee for his services as well.

That's exactly what Spahn has done. His hourly consulting fee is 33 percent higher than competitors. He not only gets the fee, but he has clients waiting in line.

WHAT THE FUTURE HOLDS

The future for government consultants is immense. Politicians, because of the scrutiny of the mass media, are hesitant to make decisions when it comes to controversial issues. Environmental and consumer issues are here to stay.

Any government worker (or for that matter, any private industry employee who has experience in government) could build a similar practice. That practice need not be restricted to construction, either.

There are dozens of companies in different industries that must work through the maze that is government. Anyone who can shortcut that journey has the opportunity to become an independent consultant.

To Jack Spahn the needs were obvious. But to others who entered the consulting field, opportunities were not always so clear. Larry Nickels never did a market study. For 25 years he worked for Alice Chalmers and never thought of leaving.

As an engineer, Nickels had only one thought on his mind—doing a good job. The majority of engineers are the same. They are not preoccupied with leaving a position. They are happiest when they are working and do not look for opportunities around them.

What woke Nickels up? A friend. "He was a salesman who tried to convince me to take a year off and become an electrical engineering consultant. I thought he was crazy."

THE ELECTRICAL ENGINEER'S CLIENTS

What Nickels's friend saw were two potential clients for Nickels. First the "users." These were companies that purchased power electrical equipment from large manufacturers.

"These firms," explains Nickels, "seldom had power electrical specialists on staff. They relied on the manufacturing company to provide the maintenance. When a warrantee ran out, they turned to in-house engineers."

The trouble was the in-house engineers were capable, but not specialists. User companies did not keep power electrical engineers on staff. It was too expensive. They were not utilized 12 months a year, and, consequently, a user would be paying wages and fringe benefits for nothing.

"If a major problem developed," says Nickels, "the user relied on the manufacturer. Oftentimes this resulted in lengthy delays. Manufacturing firms do not earn substantial profits by servicing equipment. They never considered maintenance and repair a high-priority item. Thus the users had to wait."

TWO MARKETS FOR ENGINEERS

There was a second market for Nickels's services, the manufacturers. A number of these firms did not keep power electrical engineers on staff full-time, and they had one- and five-year plans as well. These plans had set schedules and goals. The design and packaging of new equipment might be part of the plan, but the scheduling of engineers was not. In order to maintain schedules the manufacturers would hire outside electrical engineering design consultants. Nickels saw this happen on numerous occasions.

There was one other factor. Computers had entered the field and had created the opportunity to create new products by "simply mixing the recipes." This meant there was more specialized equipment to service.

Both users and manufacturers would rather pay a consultant a higher fee for a shorter period of time than worry about keeping a full-time engineer on staff with his or her wages and fringe benefits.

Adding to this was the knowledge on the part of both users and manufacturers that a full-time specialist would not be kept busy by them throughout the year. They hesitated to hire a high-priced employee who would only be working a portion of the year. This was one more element that gave Nickels confidence.

Although Nickels and other engineers have the capability to specialize in a multitude of fields, does the same hold true for an accountant? Isn't accounting the same general procedure for every business? Initially, it may seem so, but there are differences.

"There are two kinds of firms," explains Hank Zdonek, "the large and the small. The large firm is usually impersonal. The client is relegated to an accountant down-the-line. He or she rarely sees the principals.

"There's another disadvantage. The large firm changes personnel often. Consequently the clients may have one accountant one year and someone else the next. They may see the benefits but never have any loyalty to the firm.

"Still, the large firm has advantages. It has more expertise and greater resources. It provides a better training program for its accountants. That's why the client is willing to suffer through the impersonal nature of the firm.

"The small firm is personal but lacks the resources and expertise of the large accountancy corporation. The minute the client feels he can afford a larger firm, he's gone. Once again, here is another case without loyalty."

Zdonek's idea was to combine the best of both. How could he grow, however, if he insisted on personalized service? And, how could a small firm (which was what Zdonek started with) convince a client of its expertise?

THE ACCOUNTANT'S DREAM

Zdonek felt the firm that combined both elements would be a magnet to clients. His reasoning was reinforced while he was at North American Aviation as a budget administrator. During that period, he generated a number of clients (on the side). Every one came to Zdonek because they had dealt with him on a personal basis at work.

They had no idea as to his ability as a CPA. Those initial accounts convinced Zdonek there was room for any accountancy corporation that did more than "number crunching." Inadvertently Zdonek had discovered one of the major ingredients needed for success in consulting (or any business)—personalization.

Modern technology has led to self-serve, impersonal businesses (gas stations, department stores, and so forth) where everyone has a category and number. Too many service businesses follow the same route. The end result is a client without loyalty.

Zdonek's idea was to combine personalization and competency. At the same time, he wanted to provide financial advice. He did not want to spend all his time adding up profit and loss statements but rather on advising the client; giving him ideas as to what he could do to achieve his goals.

"Too many accountants," he says, "fail to explain to the client what is going on. My thinking was to be an advisor. I stay in touch with each client. The actual accounting is done by CPAs who work with us but I get involved with each account in helping them reach their financial goals.

"Accountants should be consultants. Clients need to talk to someone. They want that personalization. Give it to them and you would be amazed at how successful you can be."

Aside from the personalization, Zdonek had to answer the client's need for resources and expertise. He did so by developing (along with his partner) a computer hardware/software system that he can customize for any account. It has enabled him to project and develop forecasts rapidly. And it has given clients confidence in his firm's ability.

Ed Pearson is another who built an enormously successful firm because of his ability to not only provide service but to see where his industry, civil engineering, was going and how the needs of his clients would be changing.

When Pearson entered the civil engineering field more than 20 years ago, business was booming. Land was being developed everywhere. Still, Pearson was cautious. Before he opened his offices, he looked at census figures, population trends, and building activity.

"Present demand, in the civil engineering field," he says, "is no way to judge future requirements. When we entered the field, I studied both long-term and short-term growth figures. Anyone could have done the same. Not many people took the time. Back in those days—the late fifties—you could open an office and be successful almost anywhere."

Today, however, things have changed. "There is just as much if not more opportunity," he says, "but the needs have changed."

TWO MAJOR CHANGES IN CIVIL ENGINEERING

The two major changes are the economy and consumers. A volatile economy has changed the client's needs. "Years ago," says Pearson, "the only thing a builder cared about was how much are you going to charge. Today, that isn't even a consideration. He or she is more interested in how long it will take and are you competent enough for this project."

The builder is anxious about time because of high interest rates and what he finds himself paying to develop land. A second issue is the consumer. Much as Spahn has to deal with consumerism, so does Pearson. Through the years, he has seen it coming and has developed the expertise.

Pearson recommends several steps in researching the market. "Your clients will be the developers, but talk to others as well. Traditionally developers are optimistic. To balance their opinions, talk to local bankers.

"What are their feelings about building? Does it look promising? How does the bank feel about developmental loans?

"Building will continue to be a major industry for years to come but different areas of the country will show varied activity. Twenty years ago the West was the leading growth area; today it is the South and Southwest.

THE TRENDS TO EXAMINE

"Will those trends continue? A good indicator is the population shifts —which show a steady move to the South/Southwest—and where new businesses are emerging. These are all indicators that the prospective civil engineering consultant should examine before deciding where to open a business."

Whereas location is an important market consideration in the civil engineering field, it has little significance when it comes to sales consulting.

Sales consultants are needed by companies throughout the country and, as is the case with Tom Hopkins, their job site is more on-the-road than anywhere else. Hopkins travels nearly 50 weeks a year. For that grueling schedule, he is rewarded with a minimum fee of $17,500 a day. Or, you can have him at a bargain rate—$10,000 for an hour lecture.

It wasn't always that lucrative for Hopkins. He did not become the most successful trainer in the country by accident, either. In fact,

Hopkins's realization that there was a tremendous market for a good trainer was primarily the result of his own failure.

It started in the early sixties, when Hopkins was a neophyte salesperson. After six months of pounding the bricks, he had earned a total of $40. Needless to say, Hopkins was more than a little discouraged. As a last-gasp effort, he attended a sales training seminar and, for the first time, he could see the techniques he was lacking.

That session inspired Hopkins and opened his eyes. He went from flop to success almost overnight. Within a few months, he had become one of the most successful real estate salespeople in California. What struck Hopkins, however, was not only his success but the tremendous lack of expertise in the sales profession. By dealing with salespeople on a daily basis, he could see why some were able to sell and others were not.

Hopkins became so proficient as a salesman that he began to give seminars in his office for other company personnel. That soon expanded and before he knew it he was spending nights and weekends conducting training sessions.

What Hopkins was doing—only he did not realize it—was test-marketing a product, his seminar. That test went on for more than three years and it convinced him of several things.

"First, not only did salespeople lack training, but they realized this fact as well." Hopkins was struck by another thought. There was no reason for sales training to be confined to the real estate field. Every industry needed help.

Hopkins, of course, could see the need through the attendance at his sessions. What had started out as a favor to his company and other brokers was rapidly developing into a full-time business.

"The principles of selling are universal," Hopkins says. If you can sell real estate, you can sell cars; if you can sell blankets, you can sell furniture. The lack of trained sales personnel is universal, too."

Hopkins discovered that most companies survive because 20 percent (or less) of their salespeople account for 80 percent of the company's sales. But what if a trainer could come in and not only improve the performance of that 20 percent, but also get a portion of the 80 percent moving? That is what Hopkins does.

Hopkins proved the need for his services through an internship. He spent more than a year training real estate salespeople and worked for nothing in order to hone his skills.

Today, there is no need for internship. "Companies," he says, "realize the need. They have gone through several difficult periods during the past decade and they know the importance of a well-trained sales force.

"Still, there are many companies that do not have an active training program. They have not been approached. That's one of the reasons for the opportunity in this field."

WHY THE SALES TRAINER IS NEEDED

With industry becoming more specialized and marketing more sophisticated, there is a "growing need for the good trainer." The salesperson no longer faces an "unsophisticated buyer. Telephone sales is no longer a novelty; sweepstakes, gimmicks and games that flood the direct-mail channels are brushed aside. The customer is more aware and the salesperson has to be as well."

The untrained salesperson is not the only one at a disadvantage. His or her company cannot survive the intense competition without competent personnel. Companies realize this and they are open to the idea of professional training. As long as there are products to sell, there will be a need for competent sales training consultants.

Growth. That's the prospect for every one of the consulting professions discussed in this chapter. Some determined their potential through scientific studies. Others, through experience and stumbling.

Regardless of the different methods these consultants utilized, there was one thing they had in common—a gut feel.

THE CRITICAL ELEMENT

Starting a business is not all scientific study. Certainly, you have to establish a need and a market. But most important is the belief and faith that you can be successful.

No one guaranteed any of these consultants success. Yet they built companies and businesses. Some, as we shall see, overcame enormous obstacles and developed building techniques that virtually any potential consultant can follow.

Beneath it all, however, was a belief that they could do it. That was the key to their success.

And it is the key to yours.

CHAPTER 2

HOW TO START PART-TIME

It was 1976. America was in the midst of its bicentennial year; Jimmy Carter was elected president and in a small California town a 22-year-old college junior was about to start a part-time venture that would soon turn into a multimillion dollar operation.

The student's name was Bill Guthy, an ambitious young business student who was working for Ambassador College's tape duplicating department. The college only used its duplicating equipment during the day and confined its operation to producing tapes for those on campus.

That gave Guthy an idea. Suppose he approached the college and offered to rent the duplicating equipment on a part-time basis. He would use it in the evenings, after normal working hours.

The department agreed and Guthy went to work. He started approaching companies and selling them on his duplicating services. Before long, the business began to grow. Guthy's evenings expanded into weekends.

By the time he graduated, he was so busy that he had to buy his own tape duplicating equipment. His office was an apartment during the evening hours and a manufacturing facility in the daytime.

That was eight years ago. For Guthy, it was the beginning. Today, that part-time operation has grown into a $2 million a year business. It has become one of the fastest-growing tape duplicating facilities in the country.

PART-TIME—THE WAY MANY START

Part-time. It's an opportunity that many prospective consultants ignore. Yet it is one of the best ways to start a business. In fact, in many cases it is not only conceivable but advisable.

Four of the consultants in this book started part-time. A fifth was ready, but his clientele was so large that he changed plans and went full-time. Two others recommend part-time. The remaining three started full-time but have suggestions for those looking at a part-time venture.

Whether you start part-time or full-time, there are requirements. First, attitude. Every consultant—and for that matter, businessperson —who is successful is a positive thinker. That does not mean Norman Vincent Peale and Zig Ziglar are required reading.

What it does infer is that consultants must have a consistently bright outlook on life. Certainly, there are disappointments in every business, but successful consultants, at least the 10 who are in this book, share one distinct characteristic—they never feel down for long.

Attitude may seem insignificant but it can be everything. Working part-time you are generally alone. There isn't anyone around to cheer you up or pat you on the back. But if you go in with the right attitude, you won't need those cheers.

Whether you work two hours a day or four hours a week, it takes commitment and dedication. That's the unanimous opinion of the consultants in this book. Arnold Van Den Berg has even put together a tape called "The Power of Commitment," reflecting his philosophy. It gives listeners an excellent idea of what it takes to become a success in business.

MORE THAN FINANCIAL REWARDS

Although each has a different background and industry, the one thing they have in common is the amount of hours and work they had put into their practices before they became successful. Fifty- and 60-hour weeks are commonplace. Working forty hours is a rarity.

There are rewards. Aside from the obvious financial benefits, consultants call their own shots; they have tremendous tax benefits and, in many cases, prestige. Not one would trade what he or she is doing for a corporate position.

Building a consulting business is like playing baseball. Nobody expects you to bat 1000, but if you nail one out of three you'll make the all-star team.

In consulting, if you hit one out of ten, you win the World Series. The only way you hit one out of ten is to keep swinging. In other words, if you talk to one potential client and he or she says no (for now), keep going.

Fred Peters says, "This business is a law of averages. If you never try to sell anyone, you won't ever hit. But if you keep plugging away, you would be amazed at how many clients start coming through the door."

Hank Zdonek puts it this way: "The harder I work, the luckier I get."

Each occupation entails different qualifications. Hugh Holbert went to law school, Zdonek is a CPA, Senn has a doctorate, and Peters has a bachelor's degree. That does not mean higher education is a prerequisite for success. There are consultants in this book without any college education.

An important trait is to understand what business is about. "I can't stress enough," says Van Den Berg, "the importance of being able to run a business. Many people ignore the business aspect when they open their doors.

"That is, they forget the importance of good record keeping and watching your overhead and how much cash you spend.

"Those areas are just as important as generating business."

Holbert says, "Do not underestimate the value of your time. That is the most important thing a consultant sells. Be sure you price it right."

One mistake the neophyte businessperson makes is to spend too much. That isn't a good habit, especially in a volatile economy. In consulting, famines can strike. The consultant should be prepared; thus the need for a regulated cash flow.

SUBTLETIES OF PART-TIME

The consultants with business acumen have learned how to handle those ups and downs. They know how to keep their business on an even keel. Ups and downs are not of great concern to a part-timer, but he should still be aware of the phenomenon, know how to handle it or avoid it if possible.

Consultants should keep business subtleties in mind. Consultants must follow through; never leave anything dangling. As a part-timer, you would not have a full-time staff. Corporate employees have the advantage of delegating. In consulting, especially in the early, part-time phase, delegating is not possible.

Regardless of how many hours a week a part-timer puts in, there must be extraordinary effort put in as well. Successful consultants think, live, breathe, and eat their professions. Van Den Berg carries a tape recorder to bed. Sometimes, in the middle of the night, an idea will hit him and he immediately puts it on tape.

"You would be surprised," he laughingly says, "how many inspirations occur to you when you are in bed, relaxed, with your mind flowing."

Consultants are continually thinking of new and better ideas that will help clients and build business. Zdonek's firm developed its own accounting software package. They opened the door to more business by offering training seminars in accounting software. At the same time they also put together hardware/software systems for clients and others in business.

THINKING SESSIONS

These 10 consultants do not waste time. Good part-timers may only spend 10–12 hours a week at their profession, but they should be thinking about it 24 hours a day. Those thinking sessions germinate the seeds for new ways of doing things.

There are issues that should be resolved before a consultant hangs his part-time shingle. What about your present employer? What will they say? Should you tell them? What happens if you do not and they find out?

As a rule if there is not a conflict of interest, there is nothing wrong with building a part-time practice. In many consulting occupations, the issue of conflict never arises.

Hugh Holbert entered the legal profession part-time and built a practice. He told his employer in advance he would be practicing law, but not by taking away from company time. As a result there was no conflict.

Electrical engineers and accountants can do the same thing. The financial, sales, management, attorney, headhunter, and data processing/information systems consultants are all in a position to start part-time. (There is, incidentally, a difference between moonlighting and part-time. Moonlighters are in it for kicks and a few bucks. Part-timers are serious. They are on their way to full-time.) Although part-time is possible for civil engineers and government/land consultants, there are obstacles.

Ed Pearson (civil) and Jack Spahn (government/land) both agree on the difficulties of starting part-time in their fields. "The drawback," explains Spahn, "is you have to spend time downtown or at city hall. Government agencies are usually not open at night or on weekends. You have to arrange something with your employer. You need a couple of hours a day to make it viable."

Spahn says he would make a deal with any employee who wanted to try and start a business on the side. "I would give them the time off; however, I would not expect to pay them for the missed hours."

Whether you are trying to arrange for time off or you have the opportunity to start your practice at night or on weekends, part-time is an exciting proposition. The advantages are numerous.

NO JOB RISK

You do not have to risk your job. Most important, you do not have to take any client who comes along. If you are a full-timer with office, secretary, other overhead, and so on, you must bring in money to pay the bills. With that pressure you may take on a client you would prefer not to. That leads to strained relationships. It's a pitfall the part-timer can easily avoid.

In other words part-timers can be selective. If they turn down a consulting job, no big deal. They still have their regular job.

Part-timers have capital at their disposal, too. Their capital is in the form of a full-time job. The obvious advantage is one can pay the bills at home. But there is more to it. There's an axiom in business: every businessperson makes mistakes, not only when he or she starts but throughout his or her career. And mistakes cost money. Part-timers have capital. They can afford to make those mistakes while learning. That capital gives them an added sense of freedom.

Part-timers have another advantage. They can enter the business slowly and determine whether they like it or not. Part-timers can fold up their tent; there isn't a problem. Full-timers may face obstacles if they decide they do not like the profession. Their investment is greater and they may be faced with contracts such as leases.

Accounting is near the top of the list when it comes to consulting fields that can be started part-time. Although Zdonek says he prefers that his employees "do not work on the side," he readily admits he did. Accountants spend time interning with CPA firms before they go out on their own. It is during this stage of their careers that opportunities initially surface.

It can start with friends or relatives asking for tax advice or help. If the accountant is thinking of building a practice, he or she will not limit it to his or her family or friends. Zdonek joined service clubs and civic groups. "It enables you to meet people. Every person you meet is a potential client."

Zdonek found part-time clientele while working for North American Aviation as a budget administrator. Prior to that he had worked for Arthur Young & Company, a large CPA firm.

"Young had taught me a lot of things. At North American I had the chance to translate many of those ideas and numbers into something that was concrete. North American also gave me a new perspective.

"Prior to that, I had always been with accounting firms. This was different. As budget administrator, I traveled and worked with people outside the accounting department. They would often ask me questions relating to tax and finance. I could see their needs and how answering those needs could be translated into an excellent accounting practice of my own."

Zdonek's ability attracted fellow employees. They asked him to do tax returns and sought his advice on financial matters. Zdonek never felt there was conflict. He wasn't taking work or time from his employer.

NO OVERHEAD, HIGH PROFITS

The beauty of the part-time venture is the overhead (almost nonexistent), the profit, the knowledge that your client knows you work for someone else and yet he accepts it.

An accountant can go on indefinitely with this type of practice. Sooner or later he should make the decision as to whether he wants to expand. If he does there are other elements that must be added.

For the accountant, a computer is a must. With it the part-timer becomes more efficient. He can handle more clients. "All you needed when I started was a pad, pencil and adding machine," says Zdonek. "Things are moving much faster today. A computer is a necessity."

Letterhead is another consideration. If you intend to turn part-time into full-time, do not hesitate to get the letterhead designed and printed. Designers may charge anywhere from $750 to $3,000 for a logo and letterhead package.

Visit the art department of a local college. Tell the office staff you are looking for a junior or senior art student who wants to make some money on the side. You will get the letterhead for a fraction of the cost.

IMPORTANCE OF IMAGE

Plain white paper may work for friends who are clients, but when you add other clients this looks amateurish. The client is going to wonder —even though he or she knows you are part-time—if you are professional enough to handle his or her business. Letterhead does not sell a client, but it connotes a definite image of what you and your company are all about.

When seeking clients, you will find consulting is more of a surface than a substance business. Before a client knows anything about your expertise, he will have an opinion based upon your letterhead, brochure, and appearance. The first impression is often the one that sticks.

It's more than the letterhead that makes an impression. Brochures portray an image. They do not close the sale but they can open the door. Initially, Zdonek did not worry about having a brochure. He was dealing with friends and acquaintances. But when he opened full-time, that became one of his concerns. Today he has a six-color brochure that is sent to potential clients.

Correspondence is important to the part-timer. Watch out for letters with typos. Use an IBM or similar-quality typewriter for letters to clients. There's nothing wrong with computers, but make sure you have a letter-quality printer. There is nothing worse than a computerized letter with the dot matrix appearance.

Do you get an office? No. That's a step that applies only when you go from part-time to full-time. A more practical consideration is an answerphone or answering service. Ideally, from the standpoint of image, a "live" secretary cannot be topped.

As a part-timer, that's a commitment you will not be able to afford. The next best thing is an answering service. Granted, there are few good ones, but they are a necessity. Check with other business acquaintances for recommendations of local answering services. Answering machines are an alternative.

Some accountants bypass the part-time stage and go full-time as soon as their internship is complete. There are pros and cons to this approach. The negative is that unless the accountant has sufficient funds, he or she will be operating out of a shoe box and will be using an answering machine instead of a secretary.

Zdonek says the full-timer is "not aware of the amount of capital and revenue he needs in order to support an office. I have seen numerous CPAs open and find they were short of capital. Consequently, they became desperate for work. They underbid jobs and wound up overworked."

DEVELOPING CLIENTELE

Part-timers do not have to rely only on friends or relatives for business. They have an opportunity to develop clientele during tax time. It isn't any secret that accountants put in seven months of work during the first four months of the year. By April 15 they have generated 50 percent of their yearly income.

The advantage of doing tax returns for friends, relatives, and fellow employees is that they may turn into clients. Zdonek developed several that way.

"Nobody knows you're in business," says Zdonek, "unless you get out and meet people in your community. There are many accountants who do well; others poorly. I believe the difference is the amount of time they spend meeting potential clients."

That's not the case with electrical engineers. "Engineers would rather spend time with other engineers discussing new innovations and their projects," says Larry Nickels. "That's probably why you do not see many starting their own businesses—even though there is a phenomenal opportunity."

Electrical engineering is a profession that offers part-time opportunities galore. It is easier to build an electrical engineering consulting practice than one in accounting.

"Engineers," says Nickels, "deal with potential clients every day; clients who desperately need their services and would hire them if they knew they were available."

Nickels's field is power electronics. "Our industry," he explains, "is split into two parts. There are users and manufacturers. The manufacturers produce equipment that the users purchase. If you are working for a manufacturer, there is no conflict doing part-time work for a user. And vice versa."

When Nickels opened his office, he was astounded at the amount of business. "I had been in the field for 25 years and never realized the opportunities. Initially I was going to try a small, part-time venture but there was so much business, I went full-time immediately."

Nickels worked for a manufacturer so his market would be user companies. "Let them know you are available for weekend or evening assignments. Specialized engineers are in demand."

THE ENGINEERING OPPORTUNITY

Why aren't more engineers out there? "Many are like I was," explains Nickels. "They are only concerned about their jobs. They seldom think about expanding their services because they think it will take a sales effort. It doesn't."

Nickels proved that. He built a business without ever selling his services to a client. Others in the field can do the same. How? By picking up the telephone and contacting salespeople in your industry who make a living by selling to either users and/or manufacturers.

It is this salesperson who is frequently around when problems develop. They are in a perfect position to offer the name of an engineer to a company. All you have to do is supply the salesperson with business cards.

That's what Nickels did. In fact, a salesperson he knew for several years finally convinced Nickels of the opportunity. He had been badgering Nickels for years, trying to convince him there was business to be had. Nickels always politely declined. One day he finally agreed. He let the salesperson represent him and he has been busy since.

The same opportunity is available to other engineers. Find the salesperson. What about the one who makes calls on your company? Make contact, find out what other clientele he or she calls upon, and let him or her know what you have in mind.

Salespeople are in business to make money. They know how to sell. They make anywhere from 3 percent to 20 percent on sales. Twenty percent, however, is a rarity. Why not offer the salesperson a 15 percent commission on any door he or she opens that turns into a sale. Use another 5 percent for incentive.

Nickels spent 25 years at his company before he decided to take the plunge. Initially he was going to take a leave of absence—in case things did not work out. But there was so much business that he forgot the "leave" and gave his company notice.

With a technical profession such as power electronics, "there isn't any need for a brochure when you go part-time," he says. "An 8½ × 11-inch sheet detailing your capabilities, the equipment you have experience with, and what you are prepared to do is sufficient. Supply the salesperson with a quantity."

For engineers, working for another company can be a selling point.

If you work for a manufacturer who has sold and installed the client's machinery, the client has one more reason to believe you know how to service it. The sales rep opens doors. To close the sale, it will take a call or visit from you to the client.

Because of the shortage of specialized engineers, there is business in every area of the country. Look through the Yellow Pages and add up the number of companies that are purchasers of equipment. Even the smallest cities present opportunities.

Nickels worked for years in Milwaukee without ever running shy of clients. He is still there and recently opened a second office in Phoenix, Arizona. Servicing can be done on weekends or off-hours. The repair equipment is supplied by the client or can be rented as part of the job.

The key is for the engineer to make contact with the outside salesperson. He or she will be the catalyst for any part-time venture. For the electrical engineer who follows this approach, the move from part-time to full-time does not take long.

SHORTAGE OF ENGINEERING CONSULTANTS

In contrast to the shortage of engineering consultants, there has been a proliferation of investment/money, sales, and management consultants. For the past decade, this country has gone through a tremendous surge in the numbers of professionals in those fields.

Despite the abundance of consultants, there still is enormous opportunity: "more today than ever before and it will continue to grow," says Arnold Van Den Berg (investment) and Larry Senn (management).

One reason for the opportunity is that most consultants are generalists. They try to be all things to all companies. This is the age of specialization. We go to doctors who are specialists. There are specialists in printing, insurance, banking, and virtually any profession you can name.

Senn, Van Den Berg, and Hopkins found specialties within their fields. Senn specializes in productivity and motivation; Hopkins sales training; Van Den Berg money management with an emphasis entirely on liquid investments.

THE GROWTH FIELD

There are keys to building an investment practice and part-time is possible, especially if you are working in a field where you sell stocks, insurance, real estate, or similar investments. If you are, you are already dealing with a client's financial position and money matters; a client's long-range goals and his or her portfolio can easily be discussed.

If your clients have utilized your services to purchase products, they have already demonstrated faith in your expertise. They may be willing listeners when you start describing the investment advisory service you are establishing.

Remember, the money manager is not interested in selling, only managing and advising. The consultant in this area must be someone who is an economist and forecaster as well as an astute financial advisor. It is only a small step from product sales to consulting.

From Van Den Berg's standpoint, the ideal way to break into the field is with "a brokerage house. Anyone with a broker could build a business. If you are with a broker, you have clients. These people have portfolios that need management."

Van Den Berg explains there are some brokerage houses that will allow salespeople to manage a client's portfolio for which a fee is charged and stay on in their sales/account executive position as well.

These firms will ask you to sign a discretionary management form, which is actually a limited power of attorney. It gives the broker the authority to buy/sell products for and from the client's portfolio. If there is a need for transactions, they are put through the brokerage house.

If you work out an arrangement of this type, the key is to be objective. "You may be earning a living from the brokerage house, but do not let that prejudice your opinion as to where the client's money should go. If you do, you will find yourself back in the product sales business."

Van Den Berg recalls his early days in the business with a smile. "The most important thing I had going for me was I wanted to be a good investment advisor. Sure, I wanted to make money, but I knew the most important thing was to make money for the clients. If I did, my earnings would certainly grow as well. In this business you have to be realistic and be able to perform. Every quarter the client evaluates you through his or her statement."

Whether you start part-time out of your apartment or with a brokerage house, research is the backbone of the successful investment advisor's practice. Van Den Berg spends countless hours talking to brokers and research analysts at various brokerage houses.

Through the years, the successful money manager has built up an information network. He or she has learned which brokers are reliable and which shade the truth. He or she has learned the value of the research analyst. By sifting and culling through the information these people supply, the money manager is able to make intelligent—and profitable—decisions for his or her clients. Van Den Berg's know-how is illustrative of this point: he was buying gold for clients when it was $42 an ounce.

OPPORTUNITIES IN MONEY MANAGEMENT

There is little risk to money management, especially if you are already working in a financially-related sales field. "Don't just think of money management as stocks, bonds, or commodities," Van Den Berg points out. "Realtors are in an excellent position to enter the field as well. It is a profession that deals with a person's investment portfolio."

For those who are not presently in a financially-related business but want to get into money management, the obvious start is with friends and relatives. They need help as much as anyone. As trite as that may sound, it works. Van Den Berg, who handles in excess of $20 million in portfolios, started by giving free advice to a couple of friends. Eventually, they asked him to manage some of their funds. He did not even charge a fee to start. His idea was to prove himself. That does not mean that you should decline a fee. Remember, people tend to put a high value on a service when they pay for it and a low value when it is free.

The growth of Van Den Berg's practice is evidence of another phenomena in consulting. "Advertising," he says (and every consultant agrees with him), "does not pay off in the personal service business, especially when you are opening your doors. Once you have a track record, then you can advertise.

"Initially, you need credibility; satisfied clients who will provide that important word-of-mouth that leads to business."

Management consulting is a profession that offers a chance to start part-time. One way to find part-time work is to scour the colleges and universities in the area. Talk to the management professors. They frequently are consulting on the side and they utilize students or out-siders to help.

Typically they work with small businesses. Senn, who had all the technical expertise, needed practical experience. By working with the college professor he got it. In fact, he spent nearly five years working with small-business clients that had been generated by a professor.

Working with a professor has advantages. You are not out on the street trying to sell your services. Usually the clients come directly to the professor. You get involved with a client and learn, firsthand, what client relationships are like, what the client complains about, the diffi-culties.

You have no overhead to carry and most important, no risk. The professor's clients are usually small businesses—the same kind of clien-tele you would be after when you open your doors full-time.

Senn worked with laundries, and dry cleaners and specialized in the linen business. The part-time experience put him in an ideal position to learn the practical aspects of the profession before going full-time.

By the time he opened his practice, he not only knew the psychology of the clients but the importance of specialization, too.

HEADHUNTING IDEAL PART-TIME

An excellent occupation for part-time start-up is headhunting. Peters has part-timers working for him today. He even trained several engi-neers who worked for him part-time and eventually opened their own firms. Part-time fits this field because it is not the typical, 9 to 5 person-nel agency business. Headhunting—or "executive recruiting or search" as it is oftentimes called—differs markedly from a personnel agency's method of operation. The headhunter is not filling everything from clerical to professionals. He or she is searching for a particular individual—usually a high-priced employee—to fill a slot.

The part-time headhunter has two markets. He or she must first sell the company and its personnel director on using his or her services. Then the headhunter has to go out, find potential employees and sell them on the service as well.

The contact work is done on the telephone. There isn't any need for a large office. You can "start headhunting out of a spare bedroom at home," says Peters, "but remember to have a separate line installed. As a rule, clients will never come to your office, so there isn't any need for one."

The part-time headhunter should select a field in which he or she wants to work. Fred Peters took engineering placement because there were more want ads for engineers than anything else. That shows there is a demand on the part of employers. That's what you want: a profession that is in demand.

As an example, there may be one column of ads for chemists and three pages for programmers. Take the programmers, they are the better target. There's more demand and, obviously, more opportunity for placement.

Stay away from placing all categories. That dilutes your efforts. You want to become known as a specialist for two reasons: first, personnel people know when you call it is about one occupation; and most important, word gets around to the professionals that your company is the one to see because you deal exclusively with their occupation.

If you are working part-time as a headhunter, Sunday will be spent scouring the classifieds and making a list of companies that are in need of help. On Monday you get on the telephone and pin down some of those companies. Then find out exact requirements for positions you will fill.

At the same time, you recruit candidates for those jobs by making calls. Peters, for example, spends several hours a day on the telephone with engineers, telling them about positions that are open and exploring their interest.

A full-time headhunter will spend about four hours daily on the telephone. "Any longer," explains Peters, "and you'll burn out."

FLEXIBLE HOURS

If you are in a job with flexible hours, there is no problem. You can easily set aside an hour or two in the morning or afternoon. If your job has no flexibility and you only have weekends, visit a headhunter and ask for part-time work. Peters has several people who work for him on weekends. There isn't any calling done, but you will work with resumes and learn the business.

Part-time entry into the civil engineering and/or government/land consulting field presents one problem—both require dealings with government, and government operates during the day.

Ed Pearson says part-time entry into the civil engineering field usually happens with government employees. "You'll find," he says, "a number who want to design street plans working on the side."

It isn't difficult for them to find work, either. The city hall worker has builders coming in all day long. He or she sees there is a need and is in a perfect position to offer his or her services.

If you aren't a government employee but you want to get into government consulting or civil engineering, city hall is an excellent place to start.

Make the rounds of various engineering and planning departments. Pass out business cards and let them know you are available for part-time work.

City hall is where the builder in need can be found. Many would be interested in retaining a part-timer to handle his project.

One of the fastest growing fields—and another that beckons to the part-timer—is information systems or data processing. With the rapid expansion of the computer industry and the growing dependence of companies on systems, information specialists are in demand.

Joseph Izzo bypassed part-time to enter the field on a full-time basis. He had more than 25 years experience in the profession and was a consultant for a large data processing company when he launched his practice.

THE METHOD FOR SYSTEMS CONSULTANTS

Izzo has definite opinions as to skills and procedures that the information systems' specialist should follow. "You need," he says, "management skills, knowledge of how companies and corporations function, and, of course, general knowledge about data processing."

Izzo, who heads one of the most successful information system consulting firms in the country, believes the most important qualification for entering the business—whether we are talking full- or part-time—is management skills.

"A consultant has to be able to weave his or her way through the

corporate maze," says Izzo. "He or she has to understand how companies function, and has to realize that information systems affect the
entire operation of a firm, not just accounting as it did years ago."
There are two places the part-timer can start. If you are working for
an existing consulting firm, you have the analytical skills needed to
examine a company's system and determine where problems may be.

Don't target the same customers as your company; that's a conflict
of interest and there is no reason for it. There is so much business, you
should be looking at other industries.

If your company specializes in aerospace, go for building. It takes
more than a day or two to analyze an information systems' problem.
For the part-timer, the best route is to start with small businesses
where the time frame may be shorter and the jobs less complex.

Small businesses have smaller budgets and less capability to hire a
major information systems firm. They would be interested in an individual who had the expertise. The small businessperson needs as much
help as anyone in making his or her computer system more efficient.
He or she cannot afford the high-priced consultant.

The small businessperson also understands you have other obliga-
tions. There is a better chance of setting hours so there is no conflict.

The part-timer should get acquainted with the local SBA (Small
Business Administration). A great many businesses come to the SBA
when they cannot afford outside, premium-priced help. The organization promotes seminars as well. In attendance are small business people—the part-time consultant's potential market. Those seminars, incidentally, are frequently given by outside consultants.

The part-timer can generate business in other areas. Why not approach computer stores and make a deal with the sales manager similar to the one Nickels made with sales reps. Any referrals that end up
in business for you will earn the manager a commission.

Take it a step further. Contact some of the computer salespeople in
the area. They can sell but they do not have analyzation skills. They
run into clients who need system revisions. We're not talking about
giant clients but small businesses, the place where the part-timer
should be starting.

There is another option. Go to work (part-time) for an information
systems firm. Izzo employs nearly 40 people. Many firms will hire you
on a part-time basis. They prefer the part-timer because they are not

faced with having to provide fringe benefits. Start knocking on doors. You will be amazed at the need. This industry is growing rapidly.

THE PART-TIME LAWYER

Part-time was the way Holbert entered the real estate law field. He did it with the knowledge and blessings of his employer. He worked for a title company in a responsible executive position. Now how did he go about developing a legal practice after hours?

Holbert approached his employer and told him he wanted to practice law. He agreed to confine legal activities to the weekend and evenings. He pledged to give his company the 40 hours a week they expected.

Holbert's employer agreed. They were satsified when he said he would not represent anyone they had dealings with. Thus, no conflict of interest.

What would he have done if they had said no? "I was prepared to leave and go on my own full-time. After five years in the field, I knew there was business. I preferred, however, to start part-time. I saw no reason why I shouldn't be straightforward and ask my employer."

He was the only real estate attorney within miles. He knew more than 200 brokers and realtors in the area and there was a need. Whether he went part-time or full-time, he was ready.

Obviously, attorneys spend time in court and court time is always on a weekday. How does a part-timer get around that obstacle? By simply not taking cases that involve the court. In the real estate field —as in every profession—legal work does not necessarily mean court time.

Once his company agreed, Holbert began to pursue business. He let every one of the brokers and realtors know he would be available in the evenings or on weekends for consultation. He made telephone calls and sent out announcements. Within two weeks, he had more business than he could handle. And within a year he had opened his office full-time and was grossing $20,000 a month.

Holbert's case brings up an interesting point. If he were an attorney working for a law firm, would part-time work? Would a law firm be willing to let one of its staff handle clients outside the office?

For the most part, any client attorneys handle outside office hours is a potential client for their firm. They are taking business from their employer, an unacceptable situation. Few attorneys can launch a practice part-time . . . unless they find themselves in the same employment environment as Holbert.

DON'T WORK FOR LAW FIRM

Holbert says the attorney who wants to specialize should not be working for a law firm. "He should pick an industry and spend a few years in it. That's where you learn. I spent five years in real estate. I knew every phase of it. By the time I went to law school, I knew exactly what I was going to do when I graduated.

"Don't work for the big firm. Your chances of specializing and getting out on your own—even part-time—are minimal." Tom Hopkins was more than willing to start part-time because it made the most sense. Hopkins was trying to establish himself as a sales training consultant, a lucrative field but one that takes time to get into.

Hopkins object was to reach companies that would hire him as a trainer for their salespeople. He needed credibility and experience before he could start pounding on any industry's doors. Hopkins started with his own industry, real estate. He was a top salesperson and his boss was thrilled when Hopkins proposed giving free training seminars for the office personnel.

The training enabled him to formalize his training procedures and hone them. As it turned out, Hopkins was so good, other offices began to ask him to train.

Once a month for three years he gave training sessions. "I wanted the exposure. Every time you talk you learn something. The key is to get as many audiences as possible to talk to. About every six months I also had myself critiqued by the audience. They'll give you an objective opinion."

The impact of positive word-of-mouth is evident in Hopkins's case. From one real estate office, he found himself in demand throughout Southern California. He would speak and train people anywhere within the area. His name also appeared in publications such as the *Program Exchange,* a book that most service clubs utilize in order to find speakers.

"It doesn't matter what industry you enter. Sales training principles are the same. Consequently, I could talk to any group."

After nearly five years of part-time, he became a full-time trainer. It took more than a year before Hopkins was ever paid for a training session. His first one earned him $50, but he stuck to it.

"The nice thing about starting part-time in the business is that your sessions seldom interfere with your job. Most are given on a weekend or in the evening. It's an ideal situation."

Hopkins has been an inspiration to other budding trainers. Through his sessions, he has trained and put at least a half-dozen other successful consultants into the field. His efforts epitomize what Van Den Berg calls the "necessity to dedicate yourself to a goal."

THE REQUIRED LICENSES

In almost every consulting field, there is some kind of licensing required. A business license and DBA (Doing Business As) are standard in most states. Neither takes long to file and you can determine the requirements with a call to any local city (or county) office in your area.

A DBA is required when doing business under an assumed name. If your name is John Johnson and you want to open a firm and call it "The Management Consulting Team," you have to file the DBA in most states.

It is an easy process. Most DBAs are filed at local newspapers and cost between $40 and $80. The newspaper has the forms. The entire process will not take more than 15 minutes. When opening a business account, many banks will ask for a copy of the DBA paperwork.

The cost of a business license varies from city to city. It ranges anywhere from $50 to around $300. Civil engineers and investment advisors have additional licensing requirements. The engineers may require one in the land development field. The investment advisor may require one from the SEC (Securities and Exchange Commission).

If you are entering one of these fields call the local county (or city) offices to determine requirements. The investment advisor should contact the local SEC branch. Investment advisors come under scrutiny because they are handling funds. (Actually, Van Den Berg never has any client's money in hand. All transactions are done through bank transfers.)

Headhunters may have added licensing requirements. In the state of California, agencies that place workers in the lower- to middle-income brackets (the state has set dollar figures) have to be licensed. The firm that places the higher-bracket employee does not have licensing requirements. (Peters would fall into this latter category.)

The reason for the licensing provision is that lower- and middle-bracket employees usually pay placement fees themselves. The state is concerned about unscrupulous operators fleecing workers and not providing jobs.

During the sixties and seventies a number of scam operators surfaced. They would tell the job seeker they had a job for them and all they needed was a deposit. Once the operator had the funds, he either took off or found an excuse for the job never coming through. Thus, licensing provisions were adopted. Although Peters has one, he never uses it because in the headhunter's case, fees are paid by the employer and there is no financial risk on the part of the prospective employee.

FORMS OF BUSINESS

Aside from licensing, there are other considerations when entering business. One is the form of business your practice will take—i.e., partnership, sole proprietorship, corporation. Each has its advantages and disadvantages.

Many people incorporate because of the legal liability advantage. That is, if something goes wrong, the plaintiff winds up suing the corporation and not the individual. This type of protection is not foolproof. In recent years, courts have ruled individual directors and officers can be sued under certain circumstances.

The corporation's best advantage is in regards to income. As an employee of the corporation, you can take a salary and have the corporation pay for a variety of your expenses ranging from automobile and life insurance to entertainment.

Seldom does the IRS question the corporate deductions in this area (unless they are flagrant). If an individual operates a business as a sole proprietor and takes those deductions, he or she may be audited or questioned because they are individuals.

Corporations have less chance of the audit. Consultants forming a corporation should seek the advice of an attorney and/or accountant.

A sole proprietor means what it says—you are the sole owner and operator. It is oftentimes the method by which most consultants enter business. It is also the least complicated way to open.

When part-time goes full-time, the sole proprietorship can be changed to a corporation for the benefits and protection. Tax laws are constantly changing, however, recent changes have given sole proprietors virtually the same pension plan benefits as the corporation.

Partnerships imply there is more than one owner. Nickels did not have a partner when he started. Later, his salesperson friend was given an interest in the firm. Electrical engineers may seek a (sales) partner before opening. Or, they could give an option to salespeople—if they bring in business they would be able to own a piece of the firm.

Senn started his firm with a partner. Each had different skills. That's the advantage of partnerships. You can bring people with a variety of skills together, each holding a financial interest in the company.

PARTNERSHIP PITFALLS

Izzo has partners, too. His approach differs from Senn's and Nickels's. "I believe anyone who is interested in the company should be willing to invest hard dollars before they receive any equity. To me, that shows real commitment."

Partnerships are more complex than they appear. If there are two, and each has a 50 percent interest, who wins if there is a disagreement? Partnerships are like marriage and they can be as difficult.

The mistake consultants make when launching a partnership is not looking to the future. For example, in the beginning there may not be much business or income to worry about. But what happens when income starts to flow? Some partners want to increase their take-home pay. Others prefer to put the money back in the business.

These items should be decided before the business is launched. Once the doors are open and money begins to flow, it is too late. Money does strange things to people. Do not leave partnership rules to chance. Even the best of friends have wound up enemies through a partnership.

Consultants who are heading for a partnership should see an attorney. Have a partnership agreement drawn up. Put all the rules in it, including such key elements as the right of survivorship and a buyout clause.

Talk to people you know who are in business before you decide upon one of these forms of operation. They will give you additional insight into the pros and cons of each. Deciding a business form of operation may not be important today but it could be critical tomorrow.

Another thing to consider before entering the consulting business are skills. Obviously, if you are going to be an electrical or civil engineering consultant, you have a degree. (Interestingly, half the consultants in this book have engineering backgrounds.)

But there is more to success in business than degrees. Nickels, once again, had a degree but did not believe he had sales ability. Thus, he sought out sales help to balance his firm. Van Den Berg had an ability to visualize and project things into the future. In money management that's an excellent trait. At the same time, his business is sophisticated. In his office are thousands of files and reams of data on stocks, bonds, the market, industries, trends, and myriad other financial items.

To make this information available, it has been computerized. Van Den Berg does not operate the computer. Instead, he brought in Joe Gold, a computer specialist who not only knows how to operate the equipment but also how to find things fast.

HOW TO BLEND WINNING SKILLS

There's a blending of skills in other firms. Hopkins is the trainer but he cannot sell himself (and he knows it). To compensate, he has brought in a full-time sales manager who does nothing but sell Hopkins to companies.

Zdonek is a creative accountant who saw the need for computerization. Today, he has a partner, Tom Lieb, who has developed software systems for the firm's clientele. Through Lieb's efforts, the company has been able to become more efficient and expand more rapidly.

Knowledge of a profession is only one part of success. There are other ingredients needed. These 10 consultants have not hesitated to add those components.

Of those ingredients, sales is the most important. Nickels shied away from it yet, today, he generates a good portion of the business himself. Why? What has changed? Nothing, only Nickels has discovered that a good salesperson does not have to twist arms or apply pressure.

When Nickels makes a call he sits down and chats with the client. He finds out what the client needs and evaluates it. If he can, he informs clients as to how they might solve the problem themselves. Nickels has found there is no reason to fear sales. A good salesperson is a communicator. If consultants know their fields, they become excellent communicators.

To Van Den Berg, who was a salesperson before he got into money management, the most important thing "in business is to conduct your practice like a business. That means regular hours, attention to details, follow-up. Budget. Watch your income and outflow. When business is booming watch your spending. Look at the long run."

Consultants should be aware of the need to "form a banking relationship, too," says Van Den Berg. "Find someone in the banking business that understands what you are doing. Look for a bank that caters to people who are in similar-size businesses."

What is often forgotten is that bankers are businesspeople. They are not just guarding a fort. If they do not make loans they will not be able to show a return on the funds invested by depositors.

"Don't go to the banker with hat-in-hand," says Van Den Berg. "They need your business, too." Van Den Berg suggests that consultants form banking relationships before they need money.

DEALING WITH BANKERS

"The mistake businesspeople make is they never get acquainted with the banker until they need a loan. One of the first things a consultant should do is find a bank and meet the manager. It doesn't matter if you are starting part-time, either. In fact, you will have an advantage at that point. You will have two incomes—one from your regular job, one from the consulting practice."

It is unlikely the part-timer will need a loan. "But the time to establish credit is when you are in a healthy financial position," suggests Van Den Berg. "Don't wait until you need funds. Get the ratings and credit lines established when you are financially well-off. If you wait until you hit a crunch, you may not be able to qualify."

Start-up capital is insignificant for the part-timer. Even with full-timers, the cost of going into business is small compared to that of retail or manufacturing. Nickels started with a telephone and worked out of his home. Spahn still works out of his home. Van Den Berg had a room as small as a "closet" donated to him by a business acquaintance.

The major cost variable is office and labor. Zdonek invested in a secretary immediately. "If you use an answerphone or answering service it says 'you're small' to the potential accounting client. That means you may not have the resources of the mid- or large-size firm."

Overheads grow as the firm does. Zdonek has his own building and occupies 10,000 square feet of space; Izzo's firm takes up nearly an entire floor; Senn provides word processors for every employee; and Holbert has a lunchroom as well as an open refrigerator that he stocks with supplies for employees.

There is no necessity for an expensive office. This choice is up to the consultant, since for the most part, clients do not make a habit of visiting consulting firms. They would prefer the consultant to come to them. It saves them time.

What is often more important than office appearance is good credit. Firms that pay bills on time get better service. When vendors have to hound you for payment, they are not anxious to rush your orders.

Appearance and credit are things that all consultants should keep in mind. Another aspect of consulting that determines how successful you can become is your ability "to read the client."

That means more than understanding what a client is saying. "It means that consultants should have an idea of what the client's environment is like," says Izzo. "Understand how the company functions. Realize that politics are not confined to Washington, D.C. Politics are part of business. The consultant often finds himself in the middle.

"That's why it is of major importance for consultants to master the art of listening. Regardless of whether you enter this profession full- or part-time, remember one thing—don't just hear what people are saying, listen to those underlying meanings."

CHAPTER 3

HOW TO SELL CLIENTS AND BUILD BUSINESS

For more than 20 years, the engineer faithfully went to work every day and never complained. His record was in his job. He was able to plan and build things, to watch new products take shape.

Then one day he heard the rumor. They were going to move him to a city more than a thousand miles from his home. The thought of that move angered Larry Nickels. He was perfectly content to work where he was, to be passed over for promotions, but he was not going to move.

That evening he went home and did a great deal of thinking. He could quit, go elsewhere, maybe even take a leave of absence. His friend, a salesperson who sold products to many of the companies in his field, had been urging him to open a business of his own.

Larry had a great desire to open his own business, but he knew there would be problems. Even if he was able to master the bookkeeping and running of a business, there was one thing that scared him—sales. How could he ever sell? He wasn't an arm-twisting, high-pressure type of individual.

Opening a business would be ideal, but he could never sell. And he certainly did not have enough money to hire an outside salesperson to do the selling for him.

Nickels felt he might as well forget the dream and get back to his electrical engineering. If the company told him he would have to move, he would make a decision at that point. For now, however, Larry Nickels wasn't ready.

Larry Nickels, of course, went on to become one of the most successful electrical engineering consultants in the country. He was forced to make the decision when his company informed him he was going to be transferred.

So, Nickels not only opened his own business but discovered that he enjoyed selling as well. He still regards himself as "introverted and certainly not the sales type." In fact, most of the consultants in this book regard themselves as "nonsales" types. How, then, did Nickels—and the others—become successful?

They simply discovered that selling was not what they imagined. Sales is not backing someone into a corner and pressuring them. If that were the case, none of the consultants in this book would have become successful.

Selling is answering needs. That's why each of the consultants in this book was successful; they all had the ability to answer the needs of their customers. That's the key to building a business.

To build their businesses, our 10 used a variety of techniques, all easily duplicated. They ranged from a unique telephone solicitation program to direct mail, speeches, news releases, and community involvement. (None used any advertising.)

Arnold Van Den Berg gave seminars and taught classes; Joseph Izzo and Larry Senn wrote articles for magazines in their industries; Jack Spahn served as a volunteer on countless builder committees; Hugh Holbert lectured on wills and estates to senior citizens. These were only some of their methods.

Their techniques were in sharp contrast to most businesses. Typically, the new business budgets a percentage of its (anticipated) gross sales for promotion and advertising. For a new business, that percentage can be as high as 20 percent, sometimes higher.

AVERAGE AD EXPENDITURE

Once a business gets rolling, the expenditure drops. The average expenditure for an established business runs somewhere between 1 percent and 5 percent.

Several of our consultants did not advertise because they did not have the funds. Others because they could not see the point. One of the points brought out by the consultants was that credibility was what was needed to gain customers and advertising does not give it to a consultant unless his or her business is already established.

The public has changed greatly during the past decade. A recent *AdAge* survey of adults showed that commercials were being perceived by most readers/viewers as being just "slightly above unbelievable."

Even more indicative of the value of ads today—and especially tomorrow—is another survey that was taken of high-school students. In it, 26 percent of the kids surveyed said they "did not believe the ads they saw on TV, read in the newspapers, or heard on radio." Just imagine what happens when that group reaches adulthood and becomes pessimistic.

In this climate it is not surprising that the 10 consultants did not advertise. Ads do not often work for consultants. And it is understandable. Consulting is a personal service. It isn't a business that has quick turnover. Customers do not come in and pull a widget off the shelf.

HOW THEY GENERATE BUSINESS

Consulting firms generate business through referrals from satisfied customers. Which brings up the question: When you're opening, where do the referrals come from? How do you initially generate clients?

Some consultants take clients with them when they leave an employer. Zdonek had a small base, enough to enable him to open his accounting doors. He did not rely on that for long, however.

Zdonek discovered a way to expand his business without spending money—that discovery was almost entirely by accident. It started when an insurance salesperson came by Zdonek's first office. The insurance salesperson was trying to sell a policy. Before he walked out, Zdonek had taught him a lesson in tax. He showed him how a salesperson could use tax laws to sell clients on insurance.

The salesperson was impressed. He told his boss about the experience. His boss called Zdonek and asked if he would mind coming in and explaining the technique to the rest of his people. Zdonek agreed. He was a struggling young accountant and anything that might help his practice was worth a try.

By the time that first "speech" was over, Zdonek was convinced that one way to generate business was to give talks to groups and organizations. He also realized something else.

If he had talked to those insurance people about tax, they would have been bored. Instead, he gave them an overview of tax and tied it into their business. He showed how it applied to insurance. Most important, he showed them a way to use tax as a vehicle to help them sell policies.

Zdonek gave additional sessions for the agency, and interesting things began to happen. Several of the attendees began to refer their insurance clients to him. By working with the agency Zdonek had not only built a rapport, but also the agents developed confidence in his ability as a CPA; enough confidence to encourage their clients to visit him.

Then a thought struck Zdonek—if it worked with this industry, it would probably work with others.

He began examining other industries that could use tax expertise to help in sales. He called trade groups and volunteered his services. Before he knew it, he was involved in several of the leading civic organizations within his city. The local university asked him to serve as a part-time lecturer.

SEMINAR SECRETS

That experience taught Zdonek two valuable lessons. Meeting people in the community on a personal level was a potent way to market services.

More important, he discovered why so many so-called seminars fell flat. The speakers were only interested in selling themselves and their services. They failed to recognize the audience's need. If a consultant concentrated on those in the audience and tried to help them, the potential for generating clients was significant.

In other words, do not just talk about your profession. Explain to those in the audience how your business ties in with theirs and how your business can help theirs.

Zdonek spent 20 percent to 25 percent of those early days selling himself to others. Aside from meeting life underwriters, he had dinner with bankers, attended civic functions, and became a volunteer worker.

Word-of-mouth and referrals made his firm one of the fastest-growing accountancy corporations in the country. Those referrals came, of course, from satisfied clients. Referrals, however, are not automatic. Although clients do refer, oftentimes they have other things on their mind and don't think about a referral unless someone specifically asks them—"who does your bookkeeping?" or "who did your management consulting program?" For the most part you have to ask the client for the referral.

If you are doing a job for someone, it isn't a problem—just ask. Bring up the subject at your next meeting. Ask if there is someone they know who might benefit from the same service.

Do not just leave them hanging once you pose the question. Lead them along; is there someone they work with or otherwise know—a dentist, doctor, relative? Do not hesitate to suggest these or other occupations. The suggestions are intended to jar their memory.

While Zdonek built his business through grass-roots trial-and-error, Joseph Izzo utilized a sophisticated approach. Although Izzo says, "I am not a salesman," his techniques would be admired by most in the sales field.

Izzo used his memory and persistence to find clients. Weeks before he opened, he says, "I sat down and made a list of all the people I knew. These were people in the data processing field. I confined the list to decisionmakers, people who were in, or would one day be in, a position to give me business.

"Putting together lists should be part of every consultant's initial marketing thrust. You would be amazed at the number of people you know and how many are in positions of influence," he says.

HOW TO USE LISTS

Izzo's list came to 160. He sent each an opening announcement. It was part of a long-range campaign to keep his name in front of potential clients. Three months later he followed-up with his first brochure. And three months after that with a letter. Every quarter, for the past eight years, Izzo has mailed something to the list. That list has grown to 1,500.

Initially, he followed the mailing with a telephone call ("give it about a week to arrive"). The call was not high-pressure. It was in the form of a chat. "I would call, say hello, and tell them about the service we had just opened. I would make sure to ask them about their company: what was happening, how they were doing."

None of the chats lasted long. A few minutes at most. "If they wanted to go on longer, it was their prerogative. Don't make the mistake of calling busy executives and keeping them on the line when they have other things to do. That's one sure way to kill a sale."

During the telephone calls, Izzo answered numerous questions. "On several occasions I was able to solve a problem. Naturally, we did not get paid but the call and the problem-solving were building goodwill. I felt with that approach we would be called in when they had major problems."

Izzo cautions other consultants not to just send an opening announcement with a business card. "It doesn't do any good unless you follow up; contact the prospect after the mailing has arrived.

"Too many new consultants send out one mailing piece and then hope the potential client will remember them a year later. That does not happen. Keep your name in front of the prospect. Mailings are reminders to him or her. They should arrive regularly."

Izzo maintains that no mailing in itself will sell clients until they perceive a need. That need "may not exist when they get your first mailer, but it could three months later."

He's also quick to point out that the follow-up telephone call is not a sales call. "It's casual. Just to let them know you are around and care about their company."

HOW MAILINGS BUILD SALES

Mailings do more than keep a consultant's name in front of a prospect. The piece itself projects an image of you and your service. Izzo was dealing in the high-tech/high-expense field. Potential clients expect quality, proficiency, and thoroughness. His quarterly mailings are the epitome of those characteristics.

His first brochure, which went out three months after the opening announcement, was a quality, two-color piece that cost $4,000. That's not too expensive, but it is not cheap, either. When it was mailed it carried Izzo's logo and was an accurate reflection of the image he wanted to portray.

In eight years Izzo has produced some classic mailers. They are unquestionably among the finest brochures produced. One, which was a minibook, cost in excess of $20,000. Expensive mailing pieces are not a prerequisite to success. In fact, there are few consultants that can afford a $4,000 mailing piece, let alone a $20,000 minibook.

Larry Nickels was one. When he opened he had little capital so he went in the other direction. He printed an $8\frac{1}{2} \times 11$-inch sheet that explained his services, expertise, and the equipment he could handle. A second sheet covered Nickels's electrical engineering background.

Nickels utilized a printer who had design experience. Thus, he escaped artist fees. By using colored stock, a pamphlet begins to look like a four-color brochure. Nickels used two-color.

Both Nickels and Izzo projected an image of neatness and efficiency. You can spend a great deal on a brochure or a small amount. But small does not have to mean cheap.

The client examines a brochure and gets an immediate impression. If it is professionally designed and well put together, you score points. If it looks as if it were drawn on the kitchen table and printed at an instant printer, you lose. Image is critical in the consulting business.

BEST CONTENT FOR THE BROCHURE

Brochures should be informative and educational. They should explain your service, background, expertise. Try to find a "hook" for your brochure. That is, play up a part of your service that is important to the client but is not often talked about. Or focus on a portion of your service that others do not provide. The hook sets you apart from the rest of the field.

Izzo picked turnaround management. (To this day, he is the only information systems consultant who offers it.) It gives the brochure's copy a focal point. Whatever you pick, cautions Nickels, "be sure the brochure explains, in easy-to-understand terms, what you do. Keep it simple."

Typeface is a consideration, too. Make it easy to read. Avoid using italics throughout the mailing piece. Try to put an intriguing message on the cover, something that will get the recipient to open it. A question on the cover sparks interest.

Another element in a consultant's sales effort is follow-through. If you send an announcement or brochure, do not drop the ball at that point. Every piece of literature that goes out should have a personalized letter with it.

Avoid lengthy letters. Letters with brochures should be short. They should close with a statement that reads something like the following: "I'll give you a call to see if we can be of any service." Do not expect potential clients to call you. It seldom happens. Put the burden of the call on yourself.

Give the announcement/brochure about a week to arrive. Then call. Once again, this is not a high-pressure call. This call is to simply outline your new business and ask the prospect how things are going. Be casual, easy-going.

Mailings are not the only way to build business. For those in data processing/information systems, a good place to start is computer stores. These retail outlets sell equipment. Many of the companies that buy through them need help. All they get from the store is installation and a few training sessions.

A consultant could approach stores and make a deal with the managers. Give them a commission or finder's fee for any clients they lead you to. These outlets can help the data processing consultant reach potential clients.

Zdonek does something similar with the software system he has developed. His firm is referred (with no commission involved) by more than 50 retail computer stores that carry the software. Zdonek's firm is the only one that offers training for the software package. The computer store tells customers about the training—it makes the software selling job easier. Each store carries a quantity of brochures.

CONTENT OF A GOOD SALES LETTER

Sales letters are another business-building vehicle. "Make them educational and informative," advises Arnold Van Den Berg. "People like to learn. If you can write a one- or two-page letter with important information in it, that's a sales letter. Good salespeople sell through education, not arm twisting."

The thought of having to make sales calls bothered Izzo. "My hands still get cold when I make a call. But," he says, "you are not going to grow unless you make calls. Sales is a business that relates to a law of averages. The more people you talk to, the better the chance of success.

"Remember, do not base your future on a presentation you make to one potential client. Keep as many prospects on the line at the same time as possible. I usually have 10–15 going at all times."

Izzo found the calls he made after his first mailing paid off. Within three months he had his first contract. He still recalls the conversation. "They asked if I could get started immediately. I was ready to jump for joy and tell them we could start that very minute. But I held back. You have to maintain an image. If you come across as too hungry, you can lose the prospect."

Izzo told them he was just finishing an assignment and could get to theirs the following week. Despite the steady growth of his business, he has never forgotten the importance of sales. His mailing list has grown and he no longer has the time to make the follow-up calls. But he continues with the mailings. "Out of every mailing we get at least one client. Now, fortunately, they call us." That one client is significant when you are talking about contracts that often exceed $1 million.

HOW TO GET YOUR NAME IN PRINT

Izzo does not stop with brochures. He pursues trade magazines and writes articles for them. Izzo is not a writer, yet he has managed to get dozens of articles published. He makes up for his writing inability by studying trade magazines and copying the style they use.

"Between myself and some of the other people in the office we have been able to put together dozens of articles, although none of us are professional writers. Other consultants can do the same if they study the approaches and themes that are used."

Larry Senn is another who has written articles. "I'm not a professional writer but the average consultant would be amazed at his own writing ability. We already spend time writing proposals. Articles are not that different."

There is a tremendous benefit in getting articles published. The article indicates to the reader, "hey, this publication thinks so much of Izzo, that they are willing to let him write a piece. If they regard him that highly, maybe I should. Perhaps I should talk to him about the consulting help we need."

Articles have a life span greater than the shelf life of the magazine. What Izzo and Senn do is cut, paste, and reprint articles. Then they send them to present and potential clients.

They do this because there is no guarantee that every prospect will pick up the magazine the month you have an article published. By reprinting and mailing it, you guarantee they will be exposed to it.

Izzo's new client package contains his brochures, booklets, and about a dozen reprints of articles he has written for various trade papers. The reprint gives Izzo an edge.

"Put yourself in the potential client's place," explains Izzo. "Suppose you had two packets from two different consultants. One had a reprint, the other only a brochure. The reprint gives you credibility, an edge. That's what you want."

THE PROVEN GIMMICKS

There are tricks to writing articles for magazines. You want to make sure the magazine is going to reach your potential market. If you are after clients who are in the insurance field, write for magazines that are sent to insurance executives.

There's a reference book in most libraries called *Bacon's Publicity Checker*. There are two volumes, one for newspapers and the other for magazines. The magazine directory lists every trade publication in the country by category.

Let's say you are trying to generate clients in the information systems field, as Izzo does. Look in *Bacon's* under Data Processing. You will find a number of publications. The code under the publication's name tells you if the magazine utilizes freelance features. If it does, give them a call. Ask for the advertising department and request a sample issue. Study it. Then call back and explain your idea to the editor. Usually, they will want to see an outline. In some cases they will tell you to write and submit it.

Magazines are not interested in self-serving articles. These seldom get published. They want articles that will benefit readers. In data processing, ones that could be of interest might revolve around the theme "the changing data processing workspace" or "how to solve the conflict between data processing departments and business units." (Elsewhere in this book you will find copies of some of Izzo's articles. Study the themes he wrote about and notice how they relate to all readers of the publication.)

These are themes that affect companies with information systems. The magazine, should it accept the article, will give the author a byline and sometimes a photograph, and occasionally they may even list your firm's telephone number.

FREE PROMOTIONAL VEHICLES

Another free promotional vehicle that several of the consultants utilized was a "news release." When you open, send a news release to the business editor of the local newspaper. Send it to the chamber of commerce (they have newsletters and publications). The media prints these at no cost. Send it to trade papers.

News releases contain five basic elements—who, what, when, where and why. A release seldom has adjectives or quotes. If Joe Jones were opening his firm in San Francisco, it would be worded in this manner:

Joe Jones Data Processing Consultants has opened offices in the Richmond Towers at 33 Pleasant Street, San Francisco.

Jones's firm will specialize in the analysis of information systems for companies in the aerospace industry.

Jones has been a data processing analyst for the past 15 years. Prior to opening his firm, he was with The Farraday Company in Oakland for 10 years as vice president of its consulting division.

A graduate of the University of California (Berkeley) in engineering, Mr. Jones makes his home in Sausalito.

The release is similar to an announcement. There is no editorializing in it. The release, like a mailing piece, keeps your name in front of potential clients. If you are offering a special program for an industry, send a release to the trade publications (listed in *Bacon's*) that service that industry.

Some firms use releases to forecast trends in their field. Fred Peters could send one about next year's increased demand for engineers to business editors. He could base it upon conversations with personnel directors (whom he talks to daily). If the media uses the release your firm, its business (placing engineers) is usually mentioned.

These trend-type releases can often result in a feature. The editor sees it, gets interested, and assigns a reporter to talk to you in order to do a more in-depth piece.

News releases are used extensively by Fortune 500 companies. General Motors, for example, is constantly sending out news about their new products to auto editors of newspapers and magazines. Other companies do similar things.

Releases are not restricted to forecasts and openings. If a consultant is giving a seminar (e.g., Zdonek), he can send one. The media is discerning. If your seminar is self-serving and lacks information, they will not print it.

Topics the media will grasp are the same as those that audiences will go for—that is, how to improve yourself (or your business) and trends that will affect your business or life-style.

INEXPENSIVE HELP

There's an inexpensive way to get help with a release. Go to the local college or university and ask the public relations or journalism professor for the name of a junior or senior student who wants to earn a few extra dollars. A student may write one for $25 or less. You can get article help, too.

Obviously, lecturing takes time. You have to call organizations and prepare the talk. Aside from the potential client contact, there is another benefit to lecturing. Consultants who are on stage sets themselves up as an authority. Just as positive media exposure gives a businessperson credibility, so does the lecture circuit.

Scheduling a speech is only one-half of the job. The other is to make sure you have material that applies to the group and to give a good seminar. Many seminars give attendees information but fall flat. Why? Because they are dull and the lecturer was poorly prepared.

There is a way to make sure you give a good speech—practice. Do not ever "wing" a talk. It seldom works. Well-prepared talks give the impression of being off-the-cuff. Organizations generate speakers through word-of-mouth from other groups. If someone is good, he or she will soon find his or her speaking calendar filled.

Some cities have a booklet that lists speakers, topics, and availabilities. Program chairpeople at local organizations usually subscribe to this publication. They can supply you with its name and address. They will not charge to list your name and topic(s). Hopkins used the booklet to generate numerous engagements.

Although speaking was critical in the rise of Hopkins, he utilized another written form to build his business—thank-you notes.

"Don't underestimate the importance of a thank-you note," he says. "No one sends them anymore. Consultants should be sending them all the time. You'd be amazed at the number of occasions that arise that call for a thank-you or a congratulatory note."

HOW NOTES WORK

If Hopkins sees a prospect, a thank-you note is in the mail the next day. If he makes a presentation to a group, a thank-you note goes to the program chairperson and the group. If he makes a presentation and is turned down, a thank-you note goes to the prospect for his or her time and consideration.

"Anytime I make a presentation to a prospect, I send a note. Even if the client hires someone else, send the note. Remember, the client's relationship with the person he or she has hired may change.

"Clients know other businesspeople, too. They give references and referrals. Even if they did not hire you, they will be indebted to you for the thank-you note. If someone asks their opinion, there is a good chance your name will be mentioned." Hopkins scours the newspaper, too. If he sees a story about someone being promoted, he sends a congratulatory note. He looks through the DBAs (Doing Business As) that carry information about new businesses and sends congratulatory notes. (Other consultants compile DBAs and add them to their prospect list. DBAs are newly opened businesses. They have a need for a variety of services, many in the consulting area. This type of approach would be particularly effective for the accountant, attorney, financial manager, and perhaps the information systems consultant, depending upon the size of the new firm.)

"It is a sales message without pressure," he explains. "Thank you are the two most appreciated words in our language. No one says them enough."

Hopkins's mastery of the thank-you note is equalled by his ability in front of the microphone. He was a trainer and his work was always done in front of an audience. Giving a talk is similar to putting on a performance.

When Hopkins is on stage he is selling. What he says, and how he says it, are important in determining whether that company or others will hire him. There are always people in the audience who can help or hinder your career.

Hopkins studied public-speaking techniques. "Humor and stories have their place in a talk, but do not think you have to be Will Rogers to be successful on stage," he says.

"People are there to gain knowledge and perform better, not to learn jokes." For Hopkins, a good training session is as important as a sales call.

Hopkins was at home in front of a microphone but had doubts about his other skills. He felt uneasy about selling himself as a trainer. "So, I hired someone to sell my services. It has worked well."

BUILDING CLIENTS WITH OUTSIDE SALESPEOPLE

Larry Nickels had doubts as to his selling ability, too. He made a deal with a sales rep who called on users and manufacturers. The route that the pair chose is not unusual. Many consultants make arrangements with others to sell their services.

Outside salespeople work on a commission basis. The fee varies with profit potential. Fortunately, consulting practices are not like manufacturing firms. There is an enormous profit margin and a generous commission is not out of line.

When hiring outside salespeople, try to avoid putting all your dollars on the table at the same time. Offer a salesperson between 10 and 15 percent. If he or she generates business, throw in a bonus (another 5 percent).

Reps are like everyone else. If you give 20 percent to start, they get used to it. There is nothing special about it—or you. But if they have incentives, they try harder.

Even if a consultant hires a rep, that does not remove all the selling chores. Consultants are always selling, whether they know it or not. Even if an outside sales rep has opened the door for you, when you meet the prospective client he or she still has to be sold on you.

The clients' first impression of you will come through your brochures, letters, and letterhead. Their second will be when they meet you. Confidence in your ability is important. If you feel uneasy about the job and your competence, that will come through.

Izzo emphasizes the importance of that first client meeting with a quote he picked up from the CEO of Litton Industries. "If you believe in yourself strongly enough, you will drive your energies and the odds of becoming successful are high. If you do not believe and you have doubt, you will fail."

Few believed in themselves more than Izzo. "I hocked my house and everything else. I left my job and felt certain I could compete. There wasn't anything that could discourage me."

To do your own selling, you do not have to be a "Sammy Glick." Good consultants are self-assured but soft-spoken. They find out what the client needs and explain how they can answer those needs. In other words, they educate and inform the potential clients. They do not press to get a signature on the bottom line.

With the exceptions of Hopkins, Holbert, and Van Den Berg, none of the consultants in this book had any sales background. Several even maintain they are introverted. Yet they have all been successful at selling their services. Why? Perhaps Nickels has the best explanation.

"I was always afraid to sell. I consider myself an introvert. But the first time I sat in front of a client all I did was ask him about his problems, his needs. Then I explained what we did and how we might solve his problems. That's all it took. There was no pressure involved. The client's main concern is your ability to do the job."

Today Nickels sells and enjoys it. At first, however, he found sales help. "Find a salesperson in your industry who calls on prospective clientele for his or her employer. They may sell machinery or parts. Or they could be a copy or computer salesperson. Match the salesperson with your profession.

"Good salespeople generally know what is going on in a company. If there is a problem, a consulting need, they may hear about it before it even gets outside the company. They are in a perfect position to open the doors for you."

Nickels offers a word of caution. "The salesperson cannot close. He or she does not know the details of your service. All you want are the doors opened. Then you either close through a personal visit or on the telephone."

Once a client is sold, consultants have to be cognizant of the effect they will have on the company's employees. "The consultant is an outsider," says Izzo. "He has been called because there is a problem that cannot be solved internally. This can cause anxiety among the department's supervisors. In turn, they pass that unrest on to the employees."

A consultant "has to gain the confidence of all those people," adds Senn. "To accomplish this they must be good listeners and hold what people say in confidence. If a supervisor gets wind of your telling management what he told you in confidence, the job becomes an impossibility."

PSYCHOLOGY AND CLIENTS

Consultants are amateur psychologists. They have to continually sell employees on the fact they will not destroy their jobs. "A good consultant should have empathy. Put yourself in the supervisor's place," says Senn.

Honesty is critical, adds Senn. "Do not be aloof. Talk to supervisors and explain the issues. Impress upon them that you need their help."

Being honest does not mean being blunt and coarse. Consulting should have the effect of a thin, fine razor, not a dull axe. "When you enter a company and find the cause of a problem, do not try to change the firm completely. You will lose the client. If there are radical changes required, take it a step at a time," advises Senn.

Communication with top management is critical. When a job is taken "arrange for regular meetings with the people who brought you in," advises Izzo.

How far should communication with top management go? Is socializing a sales requirement? In general, no. What consultants should keep in mind is that their private and business lives are separate. There is no reason to mix the two if you feel uncomfortable about having clients home for dinner or playing with them on the golf course.

All the consultants in this book agree on that point. Although some do have an occasional lunch or dinner meeting with a client, for the most part they keep business and private lives separate.

If you hit it off with a client, there is no reason you cannot become friends. The bottom line is your services will be judged on how well you perform. Few managers can afford to keep you if your firm blows the job—irregardless of friendship.

Instead of brochures and letters, some consultants find they can communicate with present and potential clients through a newsletter. The effectiveness of a newsletter depends not only upon how it looks but upon what it says. There are companies that sell newsletters to professionals. All the consultant has to do is have his or her name and photo imprinted on it. Many of the newsletter companies provide this service as well as mailing.

How effective is this approach? Because of the proliferation of these newsletters, there is little impact. Clients are sophisticated. They recognize the mass-produced newsletter with its generalized stories.

Newsletters, however, can be effective. They can be an excellent communication and sales tool if handled correctly. Stay away from generalized stories. Be specific. If you are in the sales training business, stories should be oriented toward new sales training techniques; effectiveness of sales training in increasing sales; surveys; success stories.

Give it a different look as well. Most mass-produced newsletters are subdued, on grim, gray, washed-out stock. They are uninteresting. Put it on glossy stock. Use photos. Get a designer to lay it out for you. If you have problems writing, seek the services of a professional writer.

That may involve more of an expenditure than you want to make. For a typical four-page, 8½ × 11-inch, self-mailer newsletter, it could cost anywhere from $1,000 to $2,500 to have the stories written. Photography (black-and-white) may run another $500. Printing—no more than two-color—will be the cheapest part of the job. Your printing bill should be around $1,000 for as many as 5,000 copies.

There are ways to save on newsletter writing and production. Go to a local college and hire a junior or senior journalism student to do the writing. You can cut your editorial costs in half or less. The student should also be able to design it.

Van Den Berg has found written correspondence can be an excellent communication tool. As a financial consultant he does extensive research. He may spend weeks researching a particular industry to determine what its future may be and how good an investment it is for his clients.

When he comes up with something, he may send a letter to his clients. It shows them that Van Den Berg is on top of that industry. Similar letters could go to prospects.

GENERATING CLIENTS, DOLLARS THROUGH RESEARCH

Research reports can be money-makers as well as business-building vehicles. They can be repackaged and sold to others interested in investing. "We recently made a study of the banking industry," explains Van Den Berg. "We spent weeks digging out trends and talking to people. We did it for our clients, but it is the kind of report that could be sold to an investment house or even bankers themselves. It was authoritative and objective."

Spreading well-done reports can pay off for the consultant. "They can be selling tools. Take the banking report. Suppose a banker obtained a copy and liked the thoroughness of what he read. He conceivably could recommend us to some of his bank clientele. That's true for any industry."

Consultants have to "pay their dues" in order to build a practice. For some, dues paying included volunteering for civic activities, working with the local chamber of commerce, YMCA, or other charitable groups.

Zdonek donated hours of time to the local chamber of commerce. As a result he was elected as one of its directors. Every director and chamber member is a businessperson—ideal clients for Zdonek.

These activities take time but they pay dividends. You become known throughout your community. You meet other businesspeople and find your sphere expanding. Consultants generate business "through other people," says Zdonek. "If you never meet anyone, your office is going to be vacant."

Most of the 10 consultants credit the growth of their practice to (1) the people they have met through community work and (2) referrals from other clients.

That does not mean you spend 40 hours a week working for the local United Way. It does indicate you should be willing to put in several hours a week for nonpaying volunteer activities.

The mistake some businesspeople make is they believe all they have to do is join an organization and business will come to them. That does not happen. Like Zdonek, you have to go beyond the joining stage. You have to put in time.

Remember, too, you have expertise in a specific area. You might be a prime candidate to teach an extension course at a local university or college. The teaching enables you to meet additional potential clients, plus it builds your credibility. Both Van Den Berg and Zdonek taught courses. (Van Den Berg still teaches one at the local college.)

HOW IMPORTANT IS THE OFFICE?

Consultants' offices are a mixed bag. That is, some consultants need an office that projects affluence and success, while others can work out of a telephone booth. It depends upon the practice, the clientele, and the methods of operation. It is important that your office reflects your service.

Izzo has clients visiting frequently. They want to know who they are hiring to handle a contract that may be worth hundreds of thousands of dollars. As a consequence, he has always had impressive offices, even when he first opened.

Zdonek's offices fall into the same category. Zdonek found intimacy was important. "The prospective client does not like to sit across the room while you are behind a desk. It is more effective to have a small conference table where you can sit across from each other."

Zdonek's first office was small. Still, he made room for a mini–conference table. Senn's offices are elaborate. "We don't get many clients in here. We decorated the offices primarily for ourselves."

Spahn works out of his house. "No one ever visits. I'm either at the client's office or downtown at city hall. There's no need for the expenditure."

Ed Pearson has clients visit frequently. He has shied away from a fancy office. "If clients visit and find themselves in palatial surroundings, they may get the idea that they are paying for the extras. We deal with developers. Their interest is in saving money. We don't want to give them reason to believe we're spending it."

Nickels, Hopkins, Peters, and Van Den Berg are in positions where clients seldom come to their offices. Nickels always goes to the client, as does Hopkins. Van Den Berg's offices are modest. They are plain, austere, functional. He has no problem with clients who visit. They accept the offices' appearance as a reflection of the way he handles their money. It gives them a feeling of security.

Secretaries are a psychological selling point. If you yourself answer the telephone, the voice on the other end wonders how big of an operation you have. "That was one investment I made from the beginning," says Zdonek. "Aside from image, there are many things a secretary can do to facilitate a CPA's practice."

As to the consultant who cannot afford one, there is a possible solution. There are offices throughout the country that rent "executive suites." That is, along with your office there is a common meeting room that is shared by those on the floor. There is also a receptionist who answers the telephone.

You have a private number, but it rings through to a central switchboard. The receptionist answers with your firm's name. She has an intercom that goes directly into your office.

Regardless of decor and image, the bottom line in every practice is sales. Consultants generate leads through direct mail, personal contact, community involvement, and telephone.

HEADHUNTER'S PRIME SALES TOOL

Fred Peters has built his business with one tool—the telephone. Peters's potential clients are the personnel department and the engineer. When he opened his practice, he began by looking in the Sunday classifieds. From those ads, he plucked the names of 10 companies that were looking for software engineers.

"That Monday I got on the telephone and called the personnel departments in each of those companies. I told them I had an agency that specialized in placing software engineers. Would they be interested in working with me, in interviewing our applicants." Peters did not always get an enthusiastic response. "Some of them felt as if we were taking their jobs away. They needed us, though." Still, despite the need, some turned him down. "From one in ten, the answer was no, they did not want help from a headhunter." The other nine said yes.

Once Peters had his personnel people lined up, he was ready to go after software engineers. Some might construe his method for finding engineers as vengeful. "I would start calling all the software engineers within those companies that said they did not want to work with me."

His pitch, when he got an engineer on the telephone, was straight to the point. He would tell them his name, that he was an engineering recruiter, and that he was looking for a particular kind of engineer. He would describe the type, the approximate skills, and the compensation. He would ask engineers if they knew anyone who was interested.

"If the engineer was interested, he or she would ask about the job. If not, he or she might recommend someone. If the engineer is interested, I then ask about his or her background, skills, and current earnings.

"You have 30 seconds to get their interest," explains Peters. "If you can't do it in that amount of time, forget it." To make sure he utilizes those 30 seconds effectively, Peters uses a prepared script.

"I've used one for 20 years. I know it by heart, of course, but I still use a script. I've trained everyone in my office to do the same. Before you get on the telephone to either a personnel director or engineer, write down what you are going to say. It helps you avoid pitfalls and you use the time effectively."

Most of the time, the engineer's attitude is "why are you bothering me. That's the reason to say it all in 30 seconds. You can determine his or her interest immediately."

If the engineer begins to look like a candidate, Peters asks for a resume. "One thing I've come to recognize is that not all resumes are accurate, nor are they written well. When I get a resume, I usually rewrite it. Everyone should. Write it with the emphasis on the job description. Resumes should not go more than a page or page and a half. No one reads beyond that."

FEE FOR ENGINEERS

Peters also offers a referral fee to engineers. If a company suddenly lays off a group of engineers, Peters will be the first headhunter in town to know about it.

Chances are there is an engineer within the company that he placed. The engineer calls Peters and tells him what is happening. Peters immediately goes after the engineers who have been given notice. He pays the insider a referral fee.

As Peters builds a relationship with a company, he tries to move past the personnel department to deal directly with the department manager or whoever is going to do the hiring.

"They know what they want. It can save a lot of time if you can talk to them directly." Peters says you can—"after you have placed a few engineers for them and they have confidence in your ability."

At that point, Peters will talk to managers and present candidates to them. He will tell the personnel department first. "It's courtesy. I let them inform the manager that I am going to be calling. Personnel may be a hindrance at times, but you want to keep them involved. Alienate them and they could destroy your relationship with the manager."

Peters gets clients with 200–300 openings. He says if he could fill 1 percent of the open job orders, he would make $1 million. "The toughest thing is to find the applicants. Any idiot can get the job order. The major task in this business is recruiting engineers. That's why companies pay $10,000 on up. It's tough. But I've never seen a business with more opportunity."

Some of Peters's business is generated by engineers he has previously placed. They may get tired, bored, or dissatisfied and they call him looking for another position.

"I make it a rule never to recruit an engineer from a company where we place them. If they call and ask to be moved, I call the personnel or industrial relations department. I tell them 'Joe X' is upset. He wants to leave. What should we do? Personnel keeps these things confidential. They might talk to the employee. Only if he tells them he definitely wants to leave, will I work with him."

$15,000 FIRST TWO MONTHS

Peters has no need for brochures or a plush office. His most important tool is the telephone. With it he generated $15,000 his first two months in business.

That's almost the same as what Holbert generated his first month in business. All of it came from real estate clients. He knew hundreds of realtors in town. Still he was not content to trust the building of his firm to past relationships.

Holbert emphasized speaking engagements. As an attorney with specialized skills, "I found dozens of realtor organizations that wanted me to address their group. I would always talk to them about something that related directly to their sales. The important thing was to speak in ordinary English. I never used legal terms. If attorneys do, they lose their audience."

Holbert built a reputation through his talks. New clients were added as well. He even went to several retirement villages and spoke on wills and trusts. ("Afterwards, I realized that an attorney could generate an excellent clientele by speaking at retirement villages. I was mobbed by people asking questions.")

SEMINAR SECRETS

Holbert's talks were a success for the same reason that Zdonek scored. He did not try and sell anyone anything. While his talks to seniors were primarily for image building, he spoke to realtor groups in order to make himself know and build his business—and he did because he was the only one who spoke their language.

Language, incidentally, is important to any consultant when giving a seminar. The thing to remember is that the audience may not understand industry terms. Break it down, keep it simple. Let everyone follow what you are saying.

"Consultants have expertise, clients do not," Holbert explains. That distinction is important when speaking at a seminar or to a client across the desk.

Jack Spahn volunteered many hours of service. He joined trade committees and organizations. He served countless hours as a volunteer. He not only met future clients but he saw the problems builders were having. It gave him an insight into the consulting business and how to approach builders.

Spahn wore out more than one pair of shoes walking the halls of government agencies. He would pop in on old acquaintances, keeping himself visible. There were two selling reasons.

First, his practice was dependent upon the decisions that those at city hall made. He wanted to know them on a personal level. "Most of the time they see someone, he or she has a problem. Or, he or she wants a favor.

"I made it a practice to stop by when I did not want anything— simply to say hello. There's an advantage to that approach. People begin to believe that you are not just there for a favor. You get to know them. Psychologically, that will mean something later."

The second reason was that "I wanted people to think of me when they thought of a land consultant. In this business, builders come into city hall, throw up their hands, and ask people for help; someone they would recommend. If you've been around, you are on their mind. And you may get the recommendation."

Spahn's visits, incidentally, were not long. "I would stick my head in some commissioner's office and just say hello. They weren't long, involved visits. Or I would go to the planning commission office and do the same. Keep it short. There's no need to sit down and drag out a conversation for an hour. Time is valuable."

Senn took the direct-mail route to launch his practice. "I mailed 1,000 letters to small businesses in the area. I got six returns—four were wrong addresses and two others had inadequate postage."

That doesn't mean direct mail is ineffective. It can be effective, but it takes follow-up. Just mailing a letter or brochure and waiting for a response is a long shot. The typical businessperson is busy. He or she gets your letter, scans it, and throws it in the round file. The only exception is if your letter happens to hit exactly on the day—and the hour—the businessperson has a specific problem. Then he or she might call.

With any direct mail, use telephone follow-up. Although Senn's mailer was a disaster, it taught him something else. "Consulting is a personal, one-on-one business," he says. "You have to meet the person before he or she becomes a client."

CENTERS OF INFLUENCE

From that theory, Senn developed his "centers of influence" concept. Such "centers" are meeting places (clubs, organizations) where influential people gather.

"Even though you may believe you do not know people who are influential, you probably do. For example, your banker and CPA are two people who are key centers of influence. In other words, they are people who are in a position to let you know who might need your services."

Senn got involved in organizations where centers existed. He targeted local civic groups. "They all have bankers, accountants, attorneys, and insurance people as members. Those are the people who deal with my potential clientele. Most know what is happening in those potential client companies as well."

Another potential center for consultants is the SBA (Small Business Administration). The SBA provides counseling to small businesses. Most of its clients cannot afford a high-priced consulting firm, hence they go to the SBA. The SBA utilizes independent consultants to talk to these businesspeople and even give seminars. For the beginning practitioner, these sessions are an ideal way to meet clients.

Ultimately, it was through a center that Senn got his first client. It was a referral. That first client is important. "He or she is in a position to praise you or not say anything. We worked round the clock on ours.

Looking back, we undoubtedly lost money on the deal, but it was worth it."

That client was pleased. He gave Senn referrals and, today, 16 years later, he still calls on Senn for consulting services.

HOW TO USE TRADE SHOWS

Senn took advantage of trade shows and conventions. He attended whenever possible. He would either set up a booth or have a hospitality suite. The trade show was a door opener. It gave Senn the chance to meet decisionmakers within an industry.

"Don't try to corner potential clients at one of these shows and sell them on the spot. These people have many booths to visit and calls to make. The best method is to acquaint them with your services and follow with a letter and telephone call."

There are more than 15,000 different industries in this country. That's one of the reasons for specialization. Without specializing, it would be impossible to get to know the decisionmakers. A consultant could attend trade shows 365 days a year and gain nothing but a pocketful of business cards. Stay in one industry. That way, you see many of the same faces and you get to know them.

If Senn made a proposal to a client and was turned down, he always made it a practice to find out why. "I would approach the client and ask him or her to be honest and tell me why we did not get the job. You can learn a great deal from someone else. They may help you change your entire sales approach.

"Once," Senn recalls, "we had spent a considerable amount of time making a proposal to a client and showing him how he could save hundreds of thousands of dollars. He turned us down.

"I could not figure it. So I called him. He told me that our ideas were good, but what he really wanted was to become the biggest company in the city. He wanted his name known throughout the community and his picture on every billboard in town.

"His focus was on growth, ours was on how he could become more profitable. That taught me an important lesson—listen to what the client is saying. Sometimes consultants talk too much. They do not really listen to what the client is telling them. Don't think you have all the answers until you are sure what the problems are."

Listening has been an important part of Ed Pearson's growth. Few industries have changed as much in the past two decades. A short time ago, "how much money do you want" for your services was the most important thing on the client's mind. Now, it is how fast can you get it done.

Pearson has built quite a track record. Today his business comes from referrals, but yesterday it was a different story.

Pearson started his business much like the Fuller Brush man—he knocked on the doors of builders. In those days the deciding factor was price. In other words, which civil engineer can do it cheaper. Today, the decisionmaker is service, which engineer can get it done first.

HOW TO MAKE COLD CALLS

Cold calls are certainly a sales outlet. If you make them, do not just knock on a door, leave a card and hope the prospect will call. Pearson followed up. He kept in touch.

One way to make regular follow-up calls is through a filing system of 3×5 cards. Write down the names, addresses, telephone numbers, and any personal information you obtain on the potential clients.

Periodically, drop them a note. If prospects have a certain way of doing things and there is a new and better way of accomplishing the same task, let them know about it. Do not tell prospects they are doing it wrong. Use the note or letter as an educational/informational piece. Let them decide whether they are doing something wrong. Business people do not like to hear it from someone else.

NO PRESSURE NEEDED

These notes should be a service. No high-pressure selling. If you exhibit knowledge about your profession and give the prospect information that he or she can use, eventually he or she will come to believe in what you say and, perhaps, retain your firm.

Do not get anxious and press. Remember, it takes time for companies to make decisions and even more time for them to implement them.

When you're talking about limited clientele (such as builders), tele-phoning, setting up appointments, and knocking on doors are sales tools that cannot be ignored. Pearson had a brochure that went along with his pitch as well.

When making cold calls, remember that a casual, uninvited visit should be short. The businessperson you are talking to is busy and did not count on you interrupting his or her day. Don't take more than five minutes, unless you're invited to sit down and chat. After the call, make sure you send a thank-you note for taking his or her time.

The other technique is to call ahead for an appointment. When you set one, don't make it a hard-sell occasion. Introduce your service and find out what potential clients are doing. If you get them to talk and describe their activities, a thought may suddenly occur to them about a project where you may be of help.

ENGINEERING PROMOTIONAL EVENTS

Pearson also developed a series of promotional events. He sponsored a golf tournament for both lenders and builders. Through the lenders (i.e., banks and savings and loans), he met influential people. They were in a position to tell him about the activities of particular builders. He found out where the next project was and what engineering needs might develop.

He also held fishing trips, Christmas parties, and other events where both builders, community leaders—and people from his company—would get together. At some of his Christmas gatherings he had as many as 700 guests and many potential clients. Pearson's events became an "in thing."

Building clientele is a formidable task but no consultant handled it better than financial specialist Van Den Berg. The obstacles he overcame should be an inspiration to many. They show that anyone, if they apply themselves, has the ability to build a successful practice. Van Den Berg went from insurance sales to money management. He had no formal background in the field and minimal capital. His office was given to him by a business acquaintance, and today they have turned it back into what it was originally intended to be—a closet.

In Van Den Berg's estimation, the most important attribute a consultant should have is love for his or her business. And the most important thing for any consultant to determine is that there is a need for his or her service.

Armed with those two things, Van Den Berg went out to convince clients to let him guide their financial future. At first, he gave free advice to anyone. He was even willing to handle investments without a fee.

Van Den Berg worked 12–14 hours a day studying the investment field. At night, or during lunch, he gave lectures on the economy and investments to anyone who would listen. He spoke to church groups and civic organizations. He never pushed investments; he only tried to educate the audience. That was the key. His topics were of interest to anyone who had some excess capital. He spoke about the history of money and inflation and anything that would have an impact on a person's portfolio.

While other consultants built their business through myriad techniques, Van Den Berg developed his through the incredible knowledge he garnered by studying the market and talking to research analysts. What sold clients? "I knew what I was talking about and I was sold on the validity of my service. I knew it was needed. Any consultant who feels the same way I did will eventually sell people."

Van Den Berg did not do any direct mail or advertising. He did not even have a brochure. (Even today he does not have one.) His initial clients came from the ranks of friends or of those he met while selling insurance.

PRACTICE BUILT IN LESS THAN A YEAR

It took him five years to build a practice; five years to finally enter black ink in the ledger. On the other hand, it took Izzo less than a year. Van Den Berg looks back on the period as a learning experience, a time that strengthened his will.

It could have, Van Den Berg says, been much quicker "if I had a background in the market and money management. I did not."

Aside from the education, he believes others could become established much quicker if they used the telephone. "Brokers work on the telephone, so why not investment advisors?

"You could set up appointments and use the telephone as a door opener. Remember, more people need the service today." Every consultant in this book maintains that building a business takes sales and marketing. But sales and marketing do not involved high pressure or back slapping.

Sales means you have to talk to people, communicate with them. The consultant has only to find out what the client needs and to explain how he or she can answer those needs. Then it is up to the client to say yes or no. A sales call is no more than a friendly conversation. There is, of course, some psychology involved.

But, most of all, the successful salesperson is the one who perseveres. Sales is nothing more than a law of averages. If you only talk to one potential client, there is not a great chance you are going to get him or her. If you talk to 10, the odds in your favor increase dramatically. The important thing is not to stop at one.

Talk to the ten . . . and you can build the kind of practice these consultants did.

CHAPTER 4

HOW TO
SET FEES

After four years of law school, months of studying for the bar exam, and countless weeks of waiting for the results, Hugh Holbert was anxious to open his law office.

Thanks to an understanding employer, Holbert would be able to keep his full-time job and take legal cases in the evening and on weekends. One of the first things he had to do was decide how much he should charge clients; what should his hourly fee be?

Fortunately, Holbert had dealt with attorneys who provided service to the real estate industry. He made a few calls and found out what other attorneys in the area were charging. Some billed as much as $80–$100 an hour. The lowest fee was $60, a figure Holbert decided he would charge because it seemed reasonable and it was a dollar amount that could easily be divided into 60 minutes ($1 a minute).

What happened in the next few months surprised Holbert and taught him an important lesson about fees. At $60 an hour, he found himself working 17 hours a day on weekends and late into the night on weekdays.

Why the high demand? Holbert was a specialist and a bargain. He was one of the few attorneys who specialized in real estate law. He understood the profession and the technical terms. It was difficult to find real estate specialists. If you did, they charged at least twice what Holbert asked.

In his desire to be fair, Holbert underpriced his services and joined the long list of other consultants who have a difficult time choosing the right price when they open their doors.

FEES CAN BE DECEPTIVE

Fees can be tricky and deceptive. Consulting can be a mine field when it comes to setting them. Consulting is an intangible. In contrast, customers go into a hardware store and they get a hammer for their dollars, in the grocery they get a box of soap, at an auto dealer a new car.

Those products can all be felt and seen. Consulting may end up with concrete results but, initially, it is invisible. The customer is buying a "bag of air." He has only the belief that the consultant will do the job.

Because of the intangibility factor, there is much psychology involved when it comes to setting and collecting fees. The psychology issue comes to the fore when the client and consultant have their initial meeting.

There are two things that should be accomplished at this session. "First, the consultant should get a clear idea of what the client needs," emphasizes Larry Nickels, a consultant who has gone through numerous initial meetings in the electrical engineering field. "Second, the client should come out of the meeting completely familiar with the consultant's services and abilities."

To determine needs, the consultant has to be an interviewer. He has to ask questions and get the client to respond and explain, in detail, his business and what the problem may be.

Consultants want the client to talk, to dominate the conversation. Everyone likes to hear themselves talk. It is similar to a social situation. Suppose you go to a party and meet another person. If the person spends an hour asking you questions, you respond, express your feelings, and come away with the thought that you had a good time.

People feel good when they are able to talk about themselves and their business. It does not matter whether it is a social gathering or a consultant in an initial meeting with a prospective client. You want the prospect to feel good about the meeting. If he or she does, there's a good chance he or she will have a positive impression of your services.

A game? Perhaps. Remember, people buy for emotional reasons. Later they defend that purchase with logic. Buying relates not only to a can of soup but to services as well. The first order of business is to come loaded with questions. Probe the client about his or her firm.

There is another reason to get the client talking. He knows the problem and possible causes. If you spend the interview telling him about your services, you will never get any insight into what needs the client has and how you might solve them.

Once you have heard what the client has to say, you can relate your services to his or her problem. Fred Peters, for example, knows personnel departments have openings for engineers. He never sends a resumé out until he receives a job specification sheet from personnel.

Peters looks at the sheet for areas of emphasis. That shows the need the company has. He sits down and rewrites the applicant's resumé to lead with the areas that the personnel department is emphasizing. It's his way of showing that his applicant fills their needs.

Hank Zdonek may spend hours in an exploratory accounting session with a client. He may find the thing bothering the prospective client is his or her firm's inability to get its IRS reporting in on time. That gives Zdonek an opportunity to discuss the computerized system his firm has designed that assures such reports will be filed promptly.

Larry Nickels might listen to a client express concern over the inability of his or her company to accurately forecast the servicing requirements needed for certain types of power electronic equipment.

Nickels can jump in on the opportunity and outline the regular maintenance/inspection program his company offers. He can explain the emergency service that guarantees on-site repairs within 24 hours.

In each case, the consultant relates his expertise to the client's problem. The problem would not surface if the client did not talk. The consultant who walks in the door and begins to tell the client about his company's capabilities misses an opportunity.

WHEN DO YOU GET PAID?

Consultants may spend hours, sometimes days, in preliminary meetings with clients. At what point does compensation start? How many
"freebee" sessions must you have? Suppose you go through a facility,
spend hours with employees and supervisors, and write a proposal. Is
there a charge for the proposal?

Most consultants do not charge for initial client interviews. Interviews are sales calls. A consultant may spend an hour or two on these
calls. Sometimes a half-day. Still, no charge.

During these sessions, consultants may find another interview is
needed. Or, the initial meeting may lead management to ask you to
come back and meet some of its employees and/or department heads
to obtain a better insight into the problem. That happens. It did to
Joseph Izzo on more than one occasion.

"I came back to three different meetings with one company. I sat in
three, one-hour management sessions and heard department heads
kick around a problem. There was no compensation involved," says
Izzo, "but there was the chance for a substantial contract."

But, free time cannot go on forever. Some prospective clients
will brain pick until you have solved every problem. Holbert trusts
"my instincts to determine which clients are serious. If they call,
I'll spend 10 to 15 minutes talking. I'll do it at no cost or obligation."

If the case is promising, he invites them to come to his office. When
they arrive, they are given a fee schedule. "They understand the
charges up front."

Jack Spahn has to determine if a client's project has a chance before
he commits and starts to bill. Spahn cannot afford to take a project that
has little chance of approval. Each building case must be presented to
governmental agencies.

"If I am not sold on the validity, I cannot sell anyone else," he says.
"If I took the case anyway, I would soon find myself an unwelcome
visitor at city hall."

Spahn must be convinced the case is reasonable and has a chance for
approval. If he comes in with losers, his credibility takes a beating at
city hall. "It's like the boy who cried wolf. They'll begin to question my
judgment."

Spahn may spend several hours (free) with the client analyzing the project. Then he may spend several additional hours (no charge) roaming city hall, talking to department heads and getting their feel for the project.

If there is a chance, he returns to the developer and explains some of the things that will have to be changed. Will the developer go along? If so, Spahn takes the case. If not, he declines and loses time in the process.

Spahn has an interesting caveat. If he takes the case, he bills for the time he has put in as well as for future hours. Thus his initial interview with the client requires keen judgment. Without it he would be traveling to and from city hall for empty pay envelopes.

Initial meetings enable consultants to determine if the problem is significant. Does it warrant the company hiring an outsider? On several occasions, Izzo has found himself in a position where the problem does not require his services. He lets management know.

"They respect your honesty and integrity," he explains. "You are turning down a fee but, at the same time, you are opening the door for more business and referrals."

Declining a contract can be traumatic. Consultants should do so whenever they feel a situation cannot be resolved or it does not warrant their expertise. Holbert recalls many cases where clients come in for an expert's opinion, pay for several hours of advice, and then go out and do exactly what they want.

"It's human nature," explains Holbert. "Everyone has an opinion of how things should be done, even in the legal field. They confuse fairness with the law. If they want me to handle the case but won't take my advice, I always suggest to them that we part company before hard feelings arise."

Tom Hopkins faces similar decisions in the sales training field. He has perfected sales training techniques over a period of years. He may be called into a company to train. At the same time, the sales manager may have ideas about training that are the opposite of those of Hopkins. They may be ineffective, outworn ideas—concepts that will not improve sales performance.

If Hopkins goes ahead and uses them, the end result may be a sales force that is no better off than before. Hopkins will wind up with an unhappy client and poor word-of-mouth.

Successful consultants do more than generate fees. They keep their eye on the future. They know tomorrow's business comes from today's satisfied customer. They avoid situations where there is no solution.

HOW LONG IS THE PROPOSAL?

Those initial meetings lead to phase two for some consultants—the proposal. Proposals can run anywhere from 1 page to 50 (or more). Senn's proposals run 15–20; Izzo's as little as 2 pages. The proposal should contain an analysis of the situation, a statement or generalization of the problem, ways of resolving it, and a brief background of your company.

While most proposals are not paid for, Senn has developed a system whereby the potential client does compensate his firm for the work. During his first meeting, Senn explains his services and determines the client's overriding needs.

HOW THE SURVEY GENERATES BUSINESS

If the need is something that Senn believes his company can handle, he attempts to persuade the client to let his management people spend a few days at the facility. The purpose of the two or three days is to conduct a survey and file a report, which is actually a proposal.

If management goes for the survey, there is a cost. "We do not attempt to make money with the survey," explains Senn. "In fact, we usually only charge half the daily billing rate."

Senn wants to sell an entire consulting program, not a two-day survey. The survey is the basis for his report, a 15–20 page document that analyzes the problem and poses possible solutions. This is the program that he will sell to management. It would not be possible without the first two interviews.

"If they let us go ahead with the survey, three out of four companies wind up buying the proposal and full program," Senn says.

TWO SALES AREAS FOR INFORMATION SYSTEMS

Izzo operates similarly to Senn. He visits clients and may spend from an hour to several days learning about the operation and problems. He returns to his office and prepares a short proposal, usually only two pages. It outlines the problem—which he has already discussed with management—and the action to be taken.

There is a fee and time schedule on page two and a place for management to sign if they go for it.

Izzo offers two services. The first is turnaround management. That is, he will take over the information systems department with his own personnel and supervise it. His people will work with existing employees and supervisors, but they will remain until the systems are completely revised. This is a long-term program, lasting up to a year or more.

His second service is strategic planning. Once again, his people come into the firm but this time they do not supervise. They enlist the aid of supervisors, employees, and management.

Typically, this is the way most firms work. Turnaround management is rare. Seldom will consulting firms tackle it. Regardless of which program Izzo is selling, his proposal approach is the same.

Senn's is lengthier and more detailed. Still, it does not give the entire solution. The proposal is a "document that shows the client you understand the problem," Senn says. "It also demonstrates your firm's ability to think creatively."

The proposal may have one or two ideas or it can compare a current problem to a similar situation that was solved for another company. A proposal has sizzle; it does not sell the steak.

In other words, while a consulting firm may outline solutions, it does not give them all away. If it does, there is always the chance the firm may hire another consultant—and give him your ideas and solutions.

For example, there may be a frustrated builder seeking Spahn's services. He has been stonewalled at city hall. In his initial interviews, Spahn examines the builder's plans. He notices there is a shortage of greenbelt or parking, or a wall around the project is wood instead of brick.

Spahn may have seen similar plans run into difficulty. He may have even represented builders on these cases. Without visiting city hall, he knows the problem. There is no guarantee the plan will fly, but Spahn has a feeling it would if changes were made.

If he made a proposal to the builder and pinpointed the problems, there is always the chance the builder would go to city hall and try to make the changes without Spahn. Or he could hire another, cheaper consultant and give him or her Spahn's thoughts. Therefore, the way Spahn approaches the project is to tell the builder he has worked "on similar cases" and has carried projects through with similar problems.

He can take it a step further and explain there are problems with "his or her greenspace, parking design, and perimeter wall. But they can be resolved."

SIZZLE AND PROPOSALS

That's sizzle. A consultant never gives a step-by-step solution. He drops bait. That gives the client a reason to retain your services. Consultants have only two things to sell: time and expertise. It is important to put some mystique around those skills. Make them wonder.

Nickels may spend an afternoon answering questions for potential clients. He may travel to a customer's plant and spend half a day giving free advice before writing his proposal. When the proposal is completed, Nickels takes it back and explains it to the prospect. It contains everything from costs to procedure.

Not every consultant makes a formal proposal. Zdonek spends an hour or two with a prospect. He tries to determine the client's financial goals.

"Accounting is more than a profession of adding up the bottom line," he says. "You have to show clients you can think creatively in these meetings. Show them you have the ability to transfer numbers to ideas."

To do that, Zdonek makes a study of the client's company (he obtains the firm's latest financial report) and of the industry. When the client visits (or if Zdonek calls on the prospect), he can display a knowledge of the industry and its future. None of this is in written form. It comes verbally from Zdonek.

Proposal writing is not difficult. There is commonalty in each client case. The symptoms are similar. What differs is the cost estimate of the project and the way consultants bill and arrive at fees.

Most consultants have a minimum-fee policy. Holbert has many clients call and pose questions on the telephone. He may answer the query in a few minutes, but it takes him another ten minutes to log the call and its purpose. His policy is "to charge a $30 minimum for any call. The fee escalates as the time mounts. I'll give them as much as 10 to 15 minutes for that $30."

His purpose is not to discourage calls but to encourage economy on the part of the client. "If they think they can call anytime at no cost, I would be on the telephone all day answering inane questions. When people have to pay, they think first."

Zdonek's philosophy differs. "I'll take calls and answer questions at no cost—within reason. In the long run it helps us. It may enable the client to put his books in order before we arrive."

Holbert's billing policy is spelled out in his letter of agreement. Other consultants do the same or, if they prepare a proposal, the fees are included. How fees are presented to the client is important, especially in a proposal. A letter of agreement may contain the consultant's hourly rate as well as a proposed budget of total costs.

PROPOSALS AND HOURLY FEES

Proposals, however, should go beyond hourly fees. They should not just state a budget without backup. For example, if a client is presented with a proposal that contains a budget cost of $10,000, it should also explain what the client gets for the fee. Consulting is intangible. Numbers without rationale make clients nervous. Let them know what they will receive.

Some consultants break the fee down. They may show seven hours of interviews with employees, four hours with supervisors, six hours of analyzation after reading past-department reports, and so on. If each step is explained, and cost per hour outlined, the bottom line becomes more acceptable.

ARRIVING AT FEES

There are methods for arriving at fees. "You can," suggests Holbert, "call competitors in the area. Tell them you would like to have an idea of their hourly charges. Before I opened, I called attorneys in the area. I also asked about their rates for specialized assignments."

Holbert billed $60 an hour when he opened. He had two reasons.

"Sixty dollars was the lowest rate attorneys charged. It was also an easy billing rate. One dollar a minute."

His business built quickly. He found himself working "17 hours a day, seven days a week. I couldn't say no." To ease the load he upped his rate to $100. As a result he found himself working less and making more.

"Being the cheapest consultant in town," he cautions, "does not always guarantee you the clientele you are after. If you find yourself working endless hours, it may be time to reevaluate your fees."

Today, he has split fees into two categories, specialty and nonspecialty items. For nonspecialty, that is, work relating to the industry that does not require added research, his fee is $150.

"Much of it is boiler-plate. An attorney who did not know the field would have a difficult time, but for us it isn't complex."

TWO-LEVEL FEE STRUCTURE

His second-level fee is $500 per hour. This relates to situations where he knows the problem but realizes it will take research to find a solution. The fee may seem high, but Holbert is involved in cases that relate to land use or the environment. The stakes are millions of dollars being risked in each case.

He still maintains his $30 minimum for telephone calls. If the call goes beyond 15 minutes, the client is switched to the hourly rate ($150) divided by 60 minutes.

Holbert established his fees by watching competitors. Other consultants arrived at their rates by deciding what they wanted to take home.

"When I opened," recalls Zdonek, "I knew what the overhead (office expense and secretarial) was and I was aware of how much money I needed to take home in order to exist. I figured there were 160 hours (four working weeks) in a month. I took 40 hours and set them aside for marketing (these are hours that would not generate direct income). That left me with 120." He divided the 120 into the total funds required (office plus home), and that was his hourly rate.

"You would be amazed at the number of consultants that do the same thing." Even today, Zdonek uses the same method. His overhead has grown but so has his take-home pay. "The technique works."

Zdonek updates his billing structure every six months. He is in a field that is constantly changing. Computer software is an expense. He also has a growing labor cost with the increasing number of accountants he hires.

THE 160 FORMULA FOR CPAs

"I put all employees into one hat with the rest of the overhead and the projected profit." He uses the same 160 formula to determine their average hourly rate.

Zdonek has often been asked to work for a contingency. That is, he works on a case and if it turns out, he gets a percentage. In fact, the courts recognize him as an expert witness due to his experience in evaluating property and businesses. Still, he says, "I've always stayed away from contingencies. I think it is wise for other accountants to do the same."

Nickels deals with companies that have government contracts. When he bills, they want overhead, expenses, and profit margin documented.

"I add the overhead and expense categories. Everything related to our business is entered, from insurance and health costs to maintenance and employee salaries. I then tack on 10 percent to the figure— for a corporate profit. I also include my yearly salary. This gives me total yearly costs."

Nickels converts the yearly to daily costs. He subtracts weekends (52), vacations, holidays, sick days (5), and about 20 additional days for project development (marketing). He ends up with approximately 200 working days and divides that into the yearly figure.

When he determines the rate, he divides it by the number of employees he has. For example, if he had 10, each employee would have 10 percent of the daily rate. He then multiplies that rate by 1.5 when he bills them out.

HOW TO SET RATES

Izzo examined firms he wanted to compete with and set his rates accordingly. He wanted to build a company that could go head-to-head with the Big Eight accounting firms, the companies that dominated the information systems field.

He also considered several other things. "I wanted to bring in top consultants to work with the firm. That meant we would be paying higher salaries." His fees were set accordingly. They broke down to $400 a day, or $50 an hour.

Izzo has a formula for billing his employee's time. He takes an employee's base pay, multiplies it by 3.6, and divides by 2,080, the number of working hours in a year.

"If an employee earned $20,000 a year, that figure would be converted to $34 per hour, the employee's billing rate." The figure is within 10 percent of what other information systems consulting firms are billing.

LONG-TERM ASSIGNMENTS

Izzo has never been interested in one- or two-day assignments. His thrust has been geared toward the long-term contract. He is willing to give one or two days of free time, if the job has the possibilities of leading to a $50,000–$100,000 contract. That philosophy has paid off. His contracts now range from five to seven figures.

Izzo's success makes an interesting case for giving a potential client nonchargable free time. Many consultants would be eyeing the $1,000 for working a day or two. Izzo believes that looking for the quick, one-time, one-day fee, may be shortsighted, especially when you have the opportunity to work with larger clients.

In the years he worked with the college professor, Senn could see fees were set by the "seat of the professor's pants. There was nothing scientific about it." That has changed. Today, Senn has a daily billing rate.

"It's a multiple," he explains, "of the person's salary, overhead, and profit. Typically, one-third of the rate is the person's salary; one-third overhead; one-third profit.

"That's not accurate because few firms make a 33 percent profit. To simplify things, what we do is establish a multiple per employee. If a person earns $150 a day, we multiply by three ($450). Our rates run anywhere from $450 to $1400 per day. That billing rate allows for our profit. I think most companies would come out equally as well if they used the same multiplier."

Senn does not charge traveling time within the city. "In other words, if a consultant can drive to the location, there is no charge." His business takes him throughout the country and his policy is "wherever we travel we charge traveling time as well as expenses to the client."

Peters's fees are based upon a percentage of an engineer's annual salary. He gets 1 percent of each thousand dollars (of salary) up to a maximum of 30 percent. When he places an engineer who earns $40,000, his commission is $12,000. The fee is paid by the company.

There are two kinds of fees in the field, contingency and search. "I prefer contingency," he says. Contingency is where a company pays only if Peters finds and places the candidate. With a search, the firm pays Peters, regardless.

"They may come to us and say they are looking for a specific kind of software engineer. Do we want to go out and find one. We might be talking about an engineer who will earn $80,000." Peters's fee would be $24,000.

$24,000 FEE

The company pays $8,000 when he agrees to conduct the search. When he writes a job description and starts the search, he gets another $8,000. He guarantees he will bring in five qualified applicants. He gets the third $8,000 after he presents the five candidates. Even if none of the five are hired, he gets his final $8,000.

Even though there is no guarantee, Peters prefers contingency. "I have to assign one, full-time employee to the search. I would rather have them working on a variety of placements. They will earn more and so will I."

Peters points out that a search for a specialized engineer could take considerable time. Although he has participated in searches ("and always filled the position"), he prefers to stick to the traditional contingency methods.

There is a third way he generates income. It happens when a personnel department retains another headhunting firm for a search. The headhunter may have to approach 40 companies to find five candidates.

To save time, the rival headhunter goes to Peters and makes a deal. He offers to split the search fee if Peters will hit half the companies. On numerous occasions, Peters has agreed because of the "limited

liability." Finding the candidate and answering to the company remains the responsibility of the headhunter who was hired.

Peters offers a straight commission to his headhunter assistants.
The range is from 30 percent to 50 percent of the fee paid by the
company. He doesn't give them an advance. One sale can bring them
$5,000—or more. The employees know they are only getting half (or
less). "It becomes a temptation for them to leave and set up their own
operation," he says.

Peters discourages those thoughts by reminding employees they
have freedom he does not enjoy. They can leave anytime they want.
They do not have to worry about rent, overhead, or taxes. "It works,"
he says, "some of the time. But others just take off."

Spahn has two billing tiers. He gets $150 an hour "if I have to travel
and visit a governmental agency. That includes meeting as well as
travel time." That's about 30 percent to 50 percent more than competitors. "I've got the track record." And Spahn certainly does. About 98
percent of his cases end up approved.

"That's another reason to only take on the cases you firmly believe
you are going to win," he adds. His second billing rate is $74 per hour.
That applies to office time. During office hours he prepares sheets,
plans, and calculations for presentation. He does not leave the office
during this period.

Spahn's fee and batting average are interesting points for prospective consultants to ponder. The more successful you are, the more
clients flock to you.

"Once you've exceeded your overhead and are making a profit, you
should become more selective. Take only those clients you believe in
and are sure you can satisfy. Do not be afraid to raise rates when your
schedule gets crowded," he advises.

CONSULTING TRUISM

There is an interesting truism in consulting. It is better to deal with
a client who can afford your rates, rather than one who is barely getting
by. Those who are struggling are often desperate. They put pressure on
the consultant. They are less flexible and present problems.

In Spahn's field a builder who can barely afford Spahn's rates may not have much leeway when it comes to changing plans. He may have spent the funds he has allocated for architectual design and changes. He is stuck with what he presents for approval.

On the other hand, a well-capitalized builder can afford the changes. He will make them and his project will have a greater chance for approval. Spahn's batting average increases with the well-to-do client while his average declines with the client who is just barely making ends meet.

Tom Hopkins's fees are based upon demand, too. "When I started sales training 15 years ago, I asked $50 a session." As demand increased, his rates climbed. Today, he has become one of the highest-paid sales trainers in the country. He earns as much as $17,500 for a full-day session or $10,000 for an hour-long talk to salespeople.

There was nothing scientific about the way Hopkins raised fees. He moved slowly, raising where he could. As demand increased, he felt more comfortable, his confidence increased. Today, he spends 50 weeks a year on the road.

"I guess I could cut the road time by raising fees," he says. As yet, he has not tired of the grind—or the $17,500 a day.

There are two possible fee structures for the money manager—profit sharing or percentage. "Profit sharing means if the client's portfolio value increases, your share increases, too," explains Van Den Berg. He opposes this approach because it "can cause the money manager to be more aggressive and gamble."

In some ways, profit sharing is similar to the "commission incentive. One of the underlying reasons managers want to trade and sell assets in a portfolio is because of the commission."

Van Den Berg sets fees solely on a percentage of the portfolio's value. He gets no commissions or extra fees. His income is based upon growth of the portfolio.

MANAGING A MILLION DOLLAR PORTFOLIO

"Most investment advisory firms get around 2 percent of a small portfolio and 1 percent of a medium to large one," he explains. "The definition of small has changed significantly through the years, particularly since inflation entered the picture."

Van Den Berg cited a specific case. In 1974 he started managing a portfolio worth $75,000. His compensation (2 percent) was $1,500. Today, 10 years later, the portfolio is worth $500,000. His compensation is $6,750, or 2 percent of the first $150,000; 1½ percent of the next $50,000; and 1 percent of the remaining $300,000.

To manage a $500,000 or $1 million portfolio takes "no more effort or time yet the consultant can earn twice as much, even though the percentage (1 percent) is smaller."

The consultant still has to be cognizant of the economy, where it is going and what industries look good (and bad), whether he manages a small-, medium-, or large-size holding.

"The consultant who operates on a percentage is basing his business on long-term growth of the client's portfolio. The quick-commission salesperson is looking for the buck today, and there is little thought given to next year.

"This set percentage can be an excellent selling point when it comes to pointing out the differences between how a broker operates as opposed to an investment advisor."

Unlike Van Den Berg, Ed Pearson faces the same problem other civil engineers encounter when providing services for an account. He has to hire people ranging from draftspeople to surveyors.

"The rate structure has been dictated by the surveyors' union. Everyone falls in line behind them. What I usually do is double the rate an employee makes when I bill his or her services."

ONE COMMON BILLING PRESSURE

Consultants share one common billing pressure—to reduce rates, or work cheaper, when business falls. The advice from the 10 consultants is "once you set your rates, do not change them."

Fee reductions cause problems. There is a danger of revolt if your present clientele finds out you "worked a deal." If you give one client a reduced rate, there is a good chance he will tell others. You find yourself strapped into the lower rate.

If you set rates and know they are competitive, stick to them. "Price in the service business," says Pearson, "is seldom the determinant."

"If a client cannot afford your services," explains Holbert, "giving him a reduced fee may not mean anything. He still may not be able to pay. Rather than a reduced fee, I prefer to give a client advice gratis. If it is someone I know and he needs help, I'll give it to him. It is better to give it away then reduce it and look cheap."

There is one situation where rate reductions are legitimate. If the client is out-of-town or his business is on hiatus. "The wise consultant," says Izzo, "will recognize this event in advance and voluntarily approach the client with either a reduced fee or a suggestion that services be put in abeyance for a short time.

"The client appreciates honesty. Remember, you deal with clients more than once. They are in a position to give you repeat business. Don't milk it dry."

COMMON SENSE AND BILLINGS

Common sense comes into play when billing time comes around. Every consultant has his or her own technique but it is important to remember that consultants—like doctors—are often the last people to be paid.

Zdonek discovered that the hard way. In his first year in business, he worked hard and built up an enormous accounts receivable. Approximately 50 percent of the funds owed to him were never paid. It taught him a lesson.

"Be more selective in choosing the clients you do work for, and make sure the client understands what you are doing and approximately how much it will cost."

Even today, Zdonek is careful about his billing. One thing he has discovered is that clients may inadvertently take advantage of his firm.

"I might send an accountant out to a firm for a specific job. We have agreed—the client and I—as to the cost. When the accountant gets there he discovers the bank statements have not been reconciled. The bookkeeper asks him or her for a hand in doing several other things. Before you know it, the accountant is doing twice as many things as we sent them to do."

Those extras cost money "and can lead to misunderstandings. If the client gets a bill that is twice what he expected, he is going to question it. Or at the least, wonder if he is being ripped off. The client has no way of knowing that the consultant was asked to do additional work when he arrived."

AVOIDING MISUNDERSTANDINGS

To avoid misunderstandings, Zdonek has a firm policy. If the extra work is significant, the employee is told to return to the main office and the job is redefined. The client is contacted and brought up-to-date.

"Consultants should remember that clients are sophisticated," Zdonek cautions. "When they get a bill they examine it. They make a judgment as to its fairness. They may not say anything if they feel it is unfair, but if they get a couple of others they question, they may just take their business elsewhere.

"If you have any question as to the bill and how the client will accept it, I recommend talking to him and explaining it. Do not just send it and hope for the best."

Holbert estimates 10 percent of his fees, which are billed on a monthly basis, will not be paid. Much of the work he does is law-related and clients do not understand the steps involved.

To help them comprehend what goes into his hourly billing, he keeps a log of all calls and work he does for a client. The reasons for the activity are listed. When the client gets the bill every item is listed and explained. It answers questions in advance and thus avoids problems.

Loss of accounts receivables is not new to any business. Retailers build theft (both internal and external) into the cost of goods. If a consultant runs into a high loss ratio, he should re-examine his billing procedure as well as the credit procedure he utilizes when checking on clients.

Consultants should not ask the client directly for references. A good idea is to discreetly talk to businesspeople and bankers in your area. Find out what kind of reputation the firm has insofar as paying vendors is concerned.

Pearson maintains that consultants who do not keep on top of their billing are not long for business. In his field, he deals with builders who are slow to pay. They tend to hold money as long as possible. In many cases they do not have the capital to pay an engineering bill until the project is finished.

Pearson understands and as a result he is not surprised when some of his receivables are nine months to a year old. But the bill's being old does not mean you will not be paid. "I've been in the business a long time and know who will pay and who will not."

He has learned from owning a business. "School does not prepare you for the pitfalls of business. Many engineers are not financially oriented. They should get some training."

If not financially oriented, he recommends hiring a bookkeeper or accounting firm that keeps on top of the receivables. "Ultimately it comes down to your gut feeling about clients. Will they pay or won't they?"

The building industry is more volatile than most. When working with developers, it is strongly recommended you obtain references. Ask what engineering firm they worked with previously. Call and check their credit. Call their banks. Civil engineering can be financially rewarding but the clientele should be checked.

Nickels bills monthly. He keeps time sheets on employees. He justifies the billing with copies of the time sheets. This eliminates questions and builds credibility. He never sends a bill without backup. In his industry, there are two kinds of clients, fast and slow payers. "The fast ones usually pay within 20 days; slow within 60."

NO COLLECTION HAZARDS

Senn's theory, based upon past experience, is that there are no collection hazards when dealing with companies that are sound financially. If your client is struggling, there may be problems.

Senn bills monthly for the days his people have spent on the job. He includes expenses and is paid within 30 to 45 days. Seldom does he have an uncollectible debt because his clientele fall into the "established" category.

Beginning consultants may be dealing with smaller, less-capitalized firms. There could be payment delays. That's one reason why Pearson stresses the importance of "cash flow."

Spahn says many people "hate to pay their bills." He gets a deposit on his fee up front. It comes to one-third of what Spahn estimates the consulting job will cost. The rest is divided into payments that run the length of the job. Amounts are spelled out in his contract. He keeps track of his hours and bills monthly. He is paid within 30 to 90 days. His clientele are in the building and construction industries. "People in those industries are slow. They like to work with someone else's money," he says. Spahn, however, has an edge.

GETTING QUICK RESULTS

Some consultants may do the entire job and then wait for payment. Spahn does a job in stages. If the payment is not in his hands in a timely fashion, he stops work. That gets results—quickly. Spahn also has a service charge of 2 percent a month on the unpaid balance.

Van Den Berg bills clients on a quarterly basis and seldom has collection problems. His business is one in which the client needs his services on a continuing basis. Should they fail to pay, he drops the management of their portfolios. Only once did that happen "and that individual was one of those whose profession it is to uphold the law— an attorney."

Izzo bills monthly. His rates are spelled out in a schedule that he gives to each client. When the bill arrives (monthly), it reflects the hours that each consultant has spent on the project. His payments are due in 15 days. Most arrive in 30.

CONSULTANT'S MOST VALUABLE COMMODITY

There isn't a consultant who enjoys going to court. Several prefer writing off the debt rather than going through the time and hassle of arguing a court case. Unlike a company that delivers a tangible product (which oftentimes can be repossessed), consultants deliver something intangible—time.

Time is a consultant's most valuable commodity. To spend it in court is a loss. Despite the reluctance to go to court, agreements are important. Agreements are documents designed to prevent court action. They are not complex. They spell out the duties of the consulting firm and the obligation of the company that is retaining the consultant. All are short and to the point.

Senn's agreement is not formal. It is a letter that explains the functions his firm will perform. It says he will report monthly to the client. In return the client agrees to pay the specified fees.

The fee structure is outlined and payment due dates are listed. There is no room for misunderstanding. The client and Senn both sign. The client retains a copy.

Izzo's agreement is a letter/proposal that lists the hourly rates, payment schedule, estimated costs, and the work that will be done. This document has space for both Izzo's and the client's signature.

"Lawyers," says Izzo, "can kill more relationships than anyone else." (Even Holbert agrees with that. His agreements avoid legalese. They spell out the fee schedule.) In eight years, Izzo's firm has generated nearly $20 million worth of consulting business and has failed to collect $4,500.

The important part of an agreement is that it lets the client know, in formal terms, when his or her fees are due and what he or she will receive. This can be done in a one-page or, at most, two-page document. A long legal document scares clients. It is no more effective in court than a one-page letter.

HOW MUCH PROFIT?

Once the consultant builds his clientele, what can he or she look for in terms of profit? Each consultant has generated a different sales volume but one thing they share—businesses that are extremely profitable, more so than any other type of service business.

Their investments range from a few hundred dollars to thousands. Arnold Van Den Berg operated out of a "donated" shoebox. He had telephone and subscription overhead. His total investment was under $1,000. Van Den Berg does not recommend others follow the same path. He suggests an office ("not fancy but clean and nice") and a secretary ("if you can afford one").

Spahn and Peters say you can start their types of businesses out of your home. Peters has an office, but Spahn operates out of his house. The biggest expenditure for Peters is labor (he has four full-timers and two part-timers) and telephone. Nearly every call is local.

Hopkins sees no need for any significant overhead, either. He has a full-time marketing/sales person who generates training engagements. But when he started he did everything. Hopkins major expenditure is for travel (usually included in the training price) and his marketing labor.

Nickels is another who maintains you can "start with virtually no overhead. Work out of your home. All you need is the telephone."

LOW COST START-UPS

Those five consulting businesses would all qualify as low-cost start-ups. Not one needs brochures. Letterhead could be printed for a couple of hundred dollars. Telephone installation would be required as well.

Moving into the higher investment bracket is Holbert, Zdonek, Pearson, Senn, and Izzo. In their fields, offices are required. All five need secretaries, letterhead, and telephone services. Pearson and Holbert got away with not having a brochure as did Zdonek.

How much does it cost to start one of these businesses? "Much depends," explains Izzo, "on how you are going to start." Izzo had a year's worth of capital set aside. Van Den Berg had about 20 cents.

There are many cost variables in each of these businesses. The prospective consultant should determine how he or she wants to start. If he or she is going part-time, the cost will be cut further. Full-timers may be able to cut costs by sharing office space (check some of the local business publication ads in your area).

Unquestionably, Izzo's was the most expensive start-up. In his first year, he grossed more than $250,000 and "lost $25,000." (It should be pointed out that Izzo's loss was on paper. In business, there are many write-offs. A negative figure on the bottom line does not mean you did not take money home.) Izzo did, however, spend considerable funds on marketing and labor support.

Contrast this with Van Den Berg. He spent several hundred dollars to launch his investment practice. The payoff did not come for five years. (Much of that delay can be traced, he says, to his lack of education and lack of knowledge of his field.) On the other hand, Holbert and Peters looked at five-figure incomes within 60 days.

The bare minimum recommended is an office, secretary (part-time), and telephone. Budget your practice around those three elements.

Izzo's idea of having a year's capital put aside is good—it relieves the pressure.

Consulting is not a labor-intensive business. A consultant can generate more than $500,000 in sales and do it with the aid of one employee, a secretary.

MINIMAL CAPITAL REQUIRED

At the same time, consultants do not require capital for machinery or other expensive equipment. In some fields a computer is helpful, but aside from hardware/software about the only other expenditure would be for furniture and telephones.

A consultant has a unique choice. He can keep his business small with a minimal overhead or he can expand, increase his overhead, and build a substantial firm. Not many businesspeople have that option. In most businesses, if you do not grow, you die.

The bottom line is that each of these businesses can be started with an investment of $5,000 or less. And they show a gross profit of anywhere from 10 percent to 50 percent.

Holbert was grossing more than $250,000 a year as a sole practitioner. His overhead was one secretary, a modest office, and some telephones. His overhead was 20 percent of gross sales, an incredibly low figure when compared to manufacturing or retail businesses.

He decided he wanted his firm to grow. There are a variety of reasons, such as ambition and the need to take time off and let someone else mind the store. Since he made the expansion decision, his gross has soared.

Holbert allows 5 percent for clients who go broke; 5 percent for clients who will not pay; rent runs from 8 to 10 percent; hired help 10 to 20 percent; fringe benefits (buying employees lunch, Christmas parties, etc.) another 5 to 10 percent.

His 80 percent gross income dropped to 50 percent, still substantial, especially with a business that will easily generate sales volume in the mid-six-figure range.

Izzo chose to expand his firm as well. He has a staff of more than 30. He spends more on marketing than any consultant in this book. His firm is nationally known and its sales volume is slightly under the Big Eight firms.

GROSS PROFIT OF $2 MILLION

Despite his overhead, Izzo maintains a gross profit (after salaries and before taxes) of 16 to 24 percent. His firm generates consulting contracts in the $1–$2 million range. In eight years, his gross sales are between $18 and $20 million for a gross profit of approximately $2 million.

Nickels has kept his firm small. He will gross around $250,000 with a profit of 10 percent (before taxes, after salaries). To him his independence is more important than size. He could expand and "perhaps turn this into another Bechtel," but he prefers working jobs himself with a small staff.

To maintain his independence, he has shied away from long-term projects. He avoids letting any one client occupy more than 25 percent of his time. Nickels has a point. Consultants can find themselves employees if they let one company dominate their services. Nickels has built his firm slowly and intends to continue doing so.

Senn's firm looks at a 20 percent profit (before taxes). When he started, his clientele were in the $1–$30 million a year range. Today, he deals with clients ranging from $30 million to $3 billion. His staff has expanded, of course, but so has the gross income. For a consultant who deals with firms of this caliber, contracts of $50,000 are not uncommon.

Hopkins sales training firm is highly profitable, but he pays a price. He spends 50 weeks a year on the road, generates anywhere from $10,000–$17,500 per day in fees (in addition to sales of books and tapes), and has a low overhead. His major expense is labor (he has a secretary and sales manager who approaches companies to sell Hopkins's services).

Spahn runs a small, tight practice. He will usually handle one or two cases a week, each taking anywhere from 4 to 8 hours. Those 8 hours do not reflect the amount of hours he bills for office work. When you combine the office work and case work, he puts in 10–12 hours daily.

For 8 of those hours, his earnings will be $150 per hour. For the rest, $74.

His overhead is a telephone and answering machine. His biggest cost is "insurance, for my automobile."

Another operation that can be run with one office and one man is headhunting. Peters says the successful headhunter should make $25,000–$35,000 the first year; $35,000–$40,000 the second; and $45,000–$70,000 by the third.

SALARIES DECEPTIVE

Peters's income has been six figures for the past four years. Salaries are deceptive. If a consultant forms a corporation, he or she can have the company pick up many expenses. It can pay his or her life and health insurance (and the family's as well) and for a car and entertainment. The idea is to try and get the company to pick up as much as is (legally) possible. Peters does.

Van Den Berg has added to his financial-consulting business without taking on significant overhead. His major expense is labor (he has a full-time computer operator who inputs materials and cranks out client reports) and secretarial help.

In the beginning, he was handling one or two accounts with a portfolio value of around $10,000–$20,000. Today, he is up to $20 million and his "operation is more efficient than ever thanks to the computer and the help I have."

Van Den Berg, like Izzo, is a believer in reinvesting in his company. He has a research library and will subscribe to any publication that enables him to gather more investment data. He spends upwards of $10,000 a year on publications such as *Value Line* and on a European publication, *The Economist*.

"Money management is not just a domestic matter. Today it involves the world; that is one of the reasons we subscribe to *The Economist*." He does not subscribe to any stock services because "too many exist to hype an issue. We prefer to gather our own data from independent sources."

The key is his relationship with brokers and research analysts. He draws regularly from these sources and their value is "incalculable."

The most important books in the field according to Van Den Berg are those by Benjamin Graham. In particular he recommends *The Intelligent Investor, Security Analysis,* and *Financial Ratios.*

Izzo and Senn must keep abreast of management developments and trends. Aside from books by Peter Drucker, they read everything from *The One-Minute Manager* to *Megatrends.*

Senn recommends spending funds to join professional management groups and subscribing to industry trade publications. "If you select an industry," he explains, "you want to know what's going on in it. A good way is to subscribe to several trade journals."

Hopkins is the author of a best-seller on sales training *(How to Master the Art of Selling Anything),* but he does not hesitate to purchase anything that may improve his skills. He recommends Varude's *Complete Speakers and Toastmaster's Library,* published by Prentice-Hall.

Pearson subscribes to the *green sheet* to keep abreast of new construction jobs, but he says the best business builder "is still personal contact."

Peters subscribes to the *Fordice Letter* and attends employment seminars and trade shows that cover the personnel industry. He also belongs to the Professional Industrial Relations Association (PIRA) to keep abreast of "what's happening."

Zdonek used local libraries for CPA material when he first opened. Today, he recommends the *Commerce Clearing House* (CCH) handbook and the one by Prentice-Hall as "necessities."

IMPORTANCE OF CCH

CCH, he says, has a series with 11 or 12 volumes that highlights interpretations of the tax code. That 12-volume set is "a minimal library every CPA should have." There's also the Small Research Institute of America series, which is updated monthly.

The beginner, he says, should plan to spend about $40 a month on various journals and books, including the CCH series. The alternative is the library; however, "your time will be much more efficiently spent if you subscribe to the series."

There are two ways for an attorney to handle his or her library, according to Holbert. He or she can look for a lawyer who is leaving the field ("check the legal journals") and purchase books second-hand. Or "locate your office close to a county courthouse. Generally, the judges use the county law library and it is a good one."

Holbert has invested more than $7,000 in his library, including a number of specialty books on real estate law. Holbert's and Zdonek's libraries are the most expensive. Still, the amounts expended were minimal in comparison to their gross sales.

It's another example of the low investment and high return that consulting offers to the prospective practitioner.

CHAPTER 5

PITFALLS
AND CRITICAL
TURNING POINT

Every consultant has found pitfalls but none is more illustrative of the problems a neophyte consultant can run into than the experience Larry Senn had when he opened his doors.

As a start-up management consultant, Senn knew most of his clientele would come from the small-business area. So he targeted his initial mailing to 1,000 businesses—and waited.

With his education and experience, Senn was certain that first mailing would generate at least enough response to keep him busy for several months. To his surprise, he had six returns—four were wrong addresses and the other two had inadequate postage.

Senn had only been in business a few weeks but he quickly discovered that although direct mail can be enormously effective for many businesses, consulting is a personal service and it takes follow-up in order to generate clients. Don't, cautions Senn, depend upon clients to just answer your mailing when you first open your doors.

"When you are the new kid on the block, you have to follow up; make the calls yourself, stimulate the client. Don't do what I did."

For Senn, the mailing was important because it taught him first-hand about one of the pitfalls in business, and it also made him redirect his marketing effort. That redirection was what ultimately led to his success.

Every business has pitfalls, including consulting. Several consulting fields are sensitive to economic cycles. Senn's business is one. When times are tough, companies are likely to cut back on outside management help. They are primarily interested in surviving. Senn came up with an idea that would enable his firm to prosper in both good and bad times.

AVOIDING ECONOMIC PITFALLS

"We came up with a plan," Senn recalls, "which would enable us to sell long-term 'productivity improvement' when times were good. These programs take time to implement. They take even longer before management sees the results on the bottom line. If companies are doing well, there is no problem. They will wait. But, if there is a crunch, they want something that will produce fast results."

So Senn designed a short-term program that could be sold in tight economic times. "That's when management wants to see immediate bottom-line results. Our short-term program accomplishes that goal." Senn's short-term program enabled his firm to not only weather hard times, but grow during them as well. "It's a lesson for every consultant . . . be aware of outside influences on your clientele and the impact it has on them—and could have on you."

Larry Nickels has seen the economy impact his business in a different way. Interestingly, Nickels does well during good or bad times. When the economy tightens, companies lay off employees and engineers. They turn to outsiders—such as Nickels—for cost savings.

They would rather retain a specialist for a short time period than carry a full-timer with the required taxes and fringe benefits. The tendency to go for the outside consultant, says Nickels, is stronger during rough times. A tight economy also means more service business for Nickels. "They would rather service old equipment than buy new."

Where tough times do have a negative impact on Nickels is in the design of new power electronic equipment. Firms are not as anxious to ask Nickels to develop new products when cash is tight and business slow. Still, he more than makes up for it in the service sector.

As you might surmise, Ed Pearson's civil-engineering firm is sensitive to the economy. Pearson deals with builders and when interest rates rise, sales slow and builders back off. Interestingly, that does not have an immediate impact.

"Projects take anywhere from a year to three years to complete. If the economy slows, we still keep working. By the time we are finished, hopefully the economy will have turned and we will get additional business," he explains.

If anything, the economy has had a positive effect on Arnold Van Den Berg's practice. Whenever things get unstable, consumers become concerned. They become more cognizant of investment consultants and their importance. They want his specialized knowledge.

Van Den Berg says that it is during these times that the need for constant study on the part of investment advisors becomes more obvious. "There are many economic pitfalls that the investment advisor can fall into unless he has the background and has made a careful study of the market. Volatility is the rule today."

Whether the economy is good or bad, there is one inescapable fact: "Don't count on a bank to finance your business. Consulting has few physical assets. Banks will not loan money to that kind of enterprise," advises Van Den Berg and others in the field.

In 22 years the economy has never been a problem for headhunter Fred Peters, but he has other worries. "We deal with resumés that are not always accurate. Applicants tend to list things that may be exaggerations," he says. "My concern is to make sure the resumé is accurate."

That burden often falls on his shoulders because personnel departments don't have the time, explains Peters. A firm finds out that an applicant doesn't measure up after he or she has the job. Usually the supervisor complains, berates personnel, and, if the candidate comes from Peters's firm, personnel turns around and yells at him.

Peters knows this and he makes every effort to check resumés before he sends in a candidate. He may even call a previous employer himself.

He questions the applicant. "Seldom do I accept a resumé on face value."

Peters faces other pitfalls. He has to wrestle with the job description. The description originates with the department head, that is, the person who will do the hiring, then goes through personnel to Peters.

"Typically," he explains, "those specs are a half-page. The manager has crammed in every qualification he can list. Personnel gets the specs and it tries to ensure the applicant fits it completely. That's almost impossible. Most of the time the spec sheets are exaggerated. Personnel does not understand engineering. The chances of them recognizing the exaggerations are slim."

Through the years, Peters has been able to alleviate the problem. He has been able to establish communication with the supervisors who will do the hiring. "In 70 percent of the cases I talk directly to them. In many cases supervisors will call and tell us about the opening before they even talk to personnel. It takes time—years—to gain that confidence."

Peters does not shut personnel out. "It isn't a good policy." If he gets a call from a department head, he lets personnel know. "You don't want to get any vendettas going. It's wiser to keep personnel in the 'loop.'" He may bypass personnel, but he does not alienate them.

RECOGNIZING COMPANY PERSONALITIES

In Peters's field it is important to recognize a company's "personality." Some firms are noted for high turnover. "If an engineer is aware of it, he may not want to work for the company. We have to alleviate his fears. What I do is call the manager who is going to hire him and explain that the engineer has reservations.

"'Why are they saying these things about your company? If you want this guy, you better talk to him and ease his worries.'"

Peters's major pitfall is having his own employees take off and set up their own shop. "This is not a difficult business to master. After someone works for me for a short time, they understand the ins and outs. I have them sign agreements but it isn't worth the court time."

Joseph Izzo has the same worry in the information systems field. He has employees sign nondisclosure agreements the day they are hired.

They also sign one that says they will not take clients if they leave. Izzo is concerned about these areas but his primary worry is employees walking off with the sophisticated systems he has designed.

LOW CAPITALIZATION REQUIREMENT

Senn explains the ease with which employees can take off is due to the "low capitalization required to start this business. It's a temptation." Senn and his partner maintain client contact for that reason. They make sure they visit the client at his place of business on a regular basis. There's one other reason for the contact—"It's important for us, and every consultant, to make sure the client is happy. You don't know that unless you keep contact."

Izzo, Senn, and Nickels have one common, delicate area: dealing with supervisors and employees within client companies. Unlike other consultants, they enter client companies and try to remedy problems that existing employees have been unable to handle.

In some cases (Izzo's turnaround management) they even become supervisors and run the department. That can lead to hard feelings and stumbling blocks.

The key to overcoming objections is "to make the supervisor and employees feel like partners," says Senn. "Let them know you realize they have valuable ideas and you want to hear them." "In my field," says Nickels, "I think it is more of a potential problem than an actual one. I thought I might run into it; however, when I started working in client firms I discovered there was no difficulty once the engineers understood we were just there on a short-term basis to solve a problem."

THE INFORMATION SYSTEMS CONFLICT

Izzo's conflicts are more complex. He must first assure departments within the client company he is there to help, not to replace anyone. Then he has a second problem. Some of the data processing departments he enters are not only afraid of losing their jobs, but they also want to maintain control over the information system.

"In extreme cases," he explains, "you will find an adversary relationship has developed between DP and the business units within the company that need the information. The units are upset because they cannot get timely data. DP tells them to hang on, they will get it. In some situations, the business unit will go out and get its own computers and forget DP."

While data processing may be at fault, Izzo cautions consultants about jumping to conclusions. The problem can oftentimes be outside of DP. "It may even be the president."

Izzo has found himself in those situations as well. Regardless of the problem, not everyone "is going to be happy. The trap some consultants fall into is trying to make everyone happy," Izzo says. "That cannot be done."

The great temptation is to give management what it wants to hear. "Don't," emphasizes Izzo. "If you do, everyone ends up smiling and your report finds a place on the shelf. Management may not like what you say, but they will respect you if there is honesty."

Being honest does not mean trying to change a company completely. "Change works slowly," says Izzo. "Introduce one step at a time. Let the managers come up with the solutions. Lead them to it but let them say it; let it be their idea. Management has an easy time accepting what it has proposed."

THEORY OF FLEXIBILITY

Senn follows a "theory of flexibility." If there are two solutions to a problem and the consultant prefers one, management the other, "go with management's. It is ridiculous to argue for a principle if it makes no difference."

Both Senn and Izzo caution about the need to avoid politics. "You can and should understand them," says Izzo, "but do not play the game. People within the client company will perceive you as being unethical."

Attorneys have pitfalls. The major one, according to Hugh Holbert, is "their ego. Put your ego in your pocket. Because you have a license to practice law does not mean you are better than someone. We are all human. Too many attorneys take the approach that this is a 'big problem' when it isn't. They make it more complex than it should be.

"That can create a strain between you and the client. The client may use your services, but he will dislike you. And, if he dislikes you there is not much chance he will refer your services to someone else. Attorneys should not look up or down at people, but horizontally."

Hopkins warns against the same vice. "Trainers have a tendency to start talking down to their audience. That's a terrible trait. It alienates the audience and you defeat your purpose."

Seeing all sides is critical in Jack Spahn's position as a land/government consultant. Spahn has several audiences he deals with daily who can be adamant. There is the builder, usually an entrepreneurial type who "doesn't give a damn . . . 'I'll never change my plans.' "

Then he has to deal with city/county agencies. They will make suggestions and want plans changed. Last, and sometimes most difficult, is the consumer he finds opposed to a project.

Spahn makes it a practice to know the faces at the city/county agencies. Before he ever submits a plan, he will "sound" them out as to their attitude, possible objections, and what they would like to see happen.

"I have to come into each situation and listen closely. I have to be careful to play my cards right. In negotiations your starting position is crucial. I start high so there is always something to give.

"You always have to negotiate. In the old days, we could be forthright and honest. That does not mean you lie today; you never do. What I'm saying is you don't always tell the 'entire' truth. You have to hold some cards."

Interestingly, with builders he does not negotiate. He tells them what is possible and what they may have to give up. "Builders must understand they cannot have everything they want. The laws and attitudes of officials have changed."

WHY BUSINESS HAS CHANGED

Spahn's business has changed because of "pressures that politicians have from consumer groups. In the old days, you would only have to answer the requirements of the staff. They were the ones who made the decisions. Now, with the activity of consumer groups, the staff—and politicians—have added pressure."

Spahn says you also need the ability to "outguess the opponents, particularly the consumer groups. They will come out of left field with an oddball request. Nothing surprises me when it comes to dealing with them."

In his position he finds himself in front of commissions and various agencies. His job is to explain the plan and answer questions. "I come prepared to answer but I never come with a canned speech. It will never work. There is no rhyme or reason to the questions you will get, especially when it comes to those who are sitting in the audience."

He insists his clients "stay home" and not attend meetings. "If I represent them and a question is posed, I can always say 'I'll have to consult my client, sir.' But if the client makes a mistake and shows up, he or she gets hit directly. Chances are he or she will answer incorrectly and be sorry later."

Spahn makes it a point to never deal with consumer groups until he has filed a plan. "If you approached them beforehand, the demands would be out of the question. When they see a plan, they have a tendency to be more realistic. They are usually willing to make suggestions based on the plan."

Van Den Berg cautions start-up consultants to maintain "good business practices. That can be your greatest problem." He remembers his first experience with a lease and the costly ending it had. Similar traps await businesspeople in the areas of insurance, accounting, and, of course, hiring personnel.

AVOIDING THE MARKETING TRAP

Marketing is another potential trap for consultants. The tendency is to get two or three good accounts and then coast. "That's when you get the peaks and valleys in this business," says Izzo. He tries to balance his by always having "10 or 15 prospects."

He also maintains a tight schedule on speeches and articles. His firm publishes at least a dozen or more per year in various industry publications and Izzo, or one of his associates, will give close to two-dozen speeches before groups. Most of those speeches will end with media coverage and another reprint for Izzo's prospect package.

Senn maintains that one way to avoid the ups and downs is by having a firm with balanced management abilities. "If you are good at engineering, find someone who is good at sales. One person in the firm should be a sales specialist."

Izzo agrees. "It may be difficult working with a partner (or partners) but there is greater input. The job becomes easier. Building a firm takes on a new dimension."

Pearson runs into unusual marketing problems. He has two possible clients, builders or cities. The latter award contracts on a bid basis. They are nice contracts to have if the economy turns downward and building in the private sector slacks off.

But Pearson has not been able to land these projects. He traces it to his dealings with developers. "It might be that the cities look upon us handling one of their projects as a possible conflict. They may be saying 'if we [consultants] work for developers, how can we work for them [cities]?' It isn't a conflict, but that's the only answer I can come up with as to why we are unable to get into the field."

Although he doesn't miss the business, Pearson cautions that new civil engineers should keep these markets in mind when soliciting business. It may even make sense to specialize in one area or the other. "There are, in fact, companies that do confine work to either municipal or private work."

Capital can be a problem, especially in Pearson's field. "We may go six months to a year before we are paid."

Pearson believes the best way to avoid the pitfalls and learn the ins and outs of the field is to work for a civil engineering firm for a short time. "That's how I learned the field." Unlike other consulting businesses, the client loyalty develops between the developer and the engineer, not the principals of the company.

"It's the engineer who works constantly with the builder. Unless the owners step in and personally deal with the client, it will be the engineer who is in a position to set up shop—and take the client with him or her."

But in 28 years Pearson has not run into the problem of employees running off with business. "What happens is people in this business sell out to the younger engineers. Seldom do you see the engineer taking off with the client, although it is a possibility." Capital haunts the CPA, too. Hank Zdonek laughs about it. "You would think of all people CPAs would be aware of profit, loss, and how to run a business. They do a great job for others but forget themselves. As a consequence, they underbid and overwork."

Nickels uses expensive instrumentation, and capital could be a consideration, but he has found a way around it. "There are too many types of equipment, plus technology is constantly changing," says Nickels. "We rent the equipment and the client pays for it. That's an understanding we have up front and it has never created a difficulty."

More than capital, the thing that stymied Holbert was his personal life, his marriage. He found himself working so many hours, it broke up. Nickels cautions about the hours and the impact it can have on family life. The average time put in by the 10 consultants was 63 hours per week when they started.

Workaholics? Some psychologists may give them that tag but, in reality, it takes long hours to build a successful business. There is no short cut.

Competition is intense in consulting. None of the 10, however, show any particular concern, because of the specialized services they offer. Zdonek, for example, has numerous competitors. Yet his CPA practice has grown rapidly because of his personalization.

Zdonek also credits his willingness to "give free advice" as an important growth step. "I did not think about it at the time, but it was important. By doing something for others at no cost, it establishes your credibility. It doesn't mean someone owes you something but they do appreciate it. And they tell others about it. That played an important part in our growth. I don't think there were many competitors doing the same thing."

ABUNDANCE OF BUSINESS

Peters shows little concern about competition. "There is plenty of business out there. Anyone can make it in this business—or any other—if they are willing to put in the time and effort. Competition is the last thing that should scare someone away from the consulting field."

What concerns Peters more than competitors are industry trends. He constantly monitors the needs of companies. He watches if an occupation's demand declines. He also keeps track of new technology and how it will affect software engineers and related occupations.

"If you are in this field, keep close tabs on what's happening. You don't want to be hustling an obsolete profession."

Another trend to watch, according to Peters, is the swing to equal opportunity and how it affects headhunters and personnel departments. "Anyone getting into the business should be aware that it pays to have a minority-owned firm. My wife owns 51 percent of the business. This helps in getting contracts called 'set asides.' That is, companies set aside a certain amount of business for minority-owned firms."

Senn decided to skirt competitors by giving his firm a slightly different direction. With an engineering background, specializing in productivity was a natural. But Senn combined productivity with motivation. He is one of the few who specializes in both.

Spahn and Nickels seldom encounter competitors. Spahn has experience in both government and private industry. He knows his way around city hall. That's one of the reasons he commands a premium fee. On a national level, there are only a handful of electrical engineering consultants who have set up business and can rival Nickels's credentials.

KEY TO PROFITABLE BUSINESS

Specialization—and a willingness to provide service—has enabled each of these consultants to build a profitable business that few competitors can even approach.

Nearly every consultant went through a period they look upon as "that critical turning point." For some, it was psychological; for others personal; and for still others a business decision.

For Nickels it was psychological. For 25 years he worked for the same company in power electronics. He watched as the firm brought in others and promoted them. The event that provoked Nickels's turning point happened when his company informed him he was going to have to move from his home (Milwaukee) to New Orleans.

Nickels realized that after all the years of service, he had no say in his future. Was he going to stay with the firm or change jobs? "Do you leave a secure job for the insecurity of your own business? I thought about that a great deal before I made the decision," he recalls. "I know other engineers have thought about the same thing.

"I was concerned about my skills. Could I run a business? Could I sell? It seemed impossible." Nickels did leave. Much of the credit goes to a friend who convinced him there was business for a talented electrical engineer. The turning point? "I guess the day I gave notice. It was a big step after 25 years."

Peters faced a psychological crisis. "I was a boozer. It took me a long time but four years ago I straightened out my life." Since that time, he has generated an income in excess of six figures every year. What made him stop drinking? "Nothing special," he says. "It was gradual. I realized if I was ever going to do anything, I had to get serious."

THE TURNING POINT

Peters was at the bottom when he faced a turning point; Izzo at the top. He was vice president in charge of Computer Science Corporation's consulting division. But, he wasn't satisfied. "From the time I was a kid, I always wanted to be in business. I just never did it.

"I also had an idea as to the kind of firm I wanted. I wanted to build a major consulting company, one of the largest in the world." Today, his firm is on its way toward that goal. He has nearly 40 employees and does work for several Fortune 500 companies.

None of it would have happened were it not for that day eight years ago. "I just sat down and said to myself, either go out on your own or stop talking about it. If you don't have the courage, forget it. If you do, go out there and make your dream a reality."

Izzo quit the secure, high-paying job to sublet a $250-a-month office. Today, he occupies nearly an entire floor of a posh, high-rise office building. "At one point in your life, you have to sit down and evaluate where you are and where you want to be."

An entrepreneurial flair came natural to Senn. When he was a youngster, he ran a carnival in his hometown. In college, he started a business selling flowers on street corners. He expanded the business and introduced the product to supermarkets that, up to that time, never sold flowers. Senn was able to convince them with a device he invented that held water without getting the floor wet.

But the turning point came several years after he opened his practice. "The principals were spending too much time on the projects. We would go out and sell the client and do the work as well. I know that's the way you start, but it is not the way to grow. We needed help."

Senn and his partner made a decision. They would hire capable people who could do the work and free Senn and his partner to prospect. "The people we decided to hire would be the kind who could one day be partners. We wanted capable, competent professionals." That took capital. It meant that Senn and his partner would be giving up a chunk of their take-home pay. Consulting is lucrative. Sole practitioners can find themselves with an astonishing net income. To give part of it up is difficult. Senn made the decision to reinvest in the company. From that point, his firm started on a growth curve that has never ended.

REINVESTING CAPITAL

Reinvestment is often hard for consultants to comprehend. Many confuse it with buying new machinery or building a new structure. In consulting, it usually means investing in labor.

That decision was not the only one that paid dividends for Senn's company. A second was made when they decided to refine their product and specialize in the productivity/motivation area. Although the firm had been profitable, there had not been rapid growth. It was the second decision that enabled the company to reach its present level.

Hopkins faced a critical decision nearly 10 years ago. He was lecturing and training in Southern California. His practice had grown. He was known throughout the real estate industry as the field's top sales trainer. He gave it all up to move to Phoenix and join a training school.

"Looking back," he says, "someone might ask why in the world would you do that? Especially since it was less money. But I looked upon it as an opportunity to concentrate on training full-time. The school was my chance."

OVERCOMING RISK

Hopkins, of course, made the correct decision. His turning point illustrates a consideration that every consultant must face—risk. There is no progress without risk; there is no business that can be built without risk.

Every one of the 10 was willing to risk everything. "If there is no risk involved, there is no opportunity," Van Den Berg says. "The greater the risk, the greater the rewards. In business, as in life, that is a truism."

For Van Den Berg, the turning point took five years to reach. "It was the day I hit a break-even point. From there, everything becomes easier. Every dollar you bring in turns into profit. You are able to buy things (for your business) that you were never able to afford. The whole business changes."

Turning points may only occur once, twice, perhaps three times. But ethical decisions are faced daily by consultants. Van Den Berg is in a position where he could profit handsomely. He controls millions of dollars of investment funds. All he would have to do is steer clients to certain stock buys and brokerage houses. His income could double overnight.

"You don't want to structure something that will prevent you from doing a good job," he cautions. "There is pressure, especially on the newcomer who may need money to feed his family, to bend certain rules. That's why I would recommend to anyone entering the field, to set aside capital so you can avoid the pressure."

BUILDING CREDIBILITY

Van Den Berg has another word of caution. "If you work for a broker-age house and are a money manager at the same time, avoid temptations. Do not put the client's money in a stock transaction—and through your brokerage house—simply for the commission. This business takes credibility and you can never build it that way."

Zdonek has a book of rules and ethics that is given to each employee. He summarizes it with one word: "Honesty. Honesty with the client. Do not con him about what can and cannot be done. And honesty with your billings. Don't fudge hours."

Zdonek has a section in his book on billing. Consultants deal in a subjective billing area. Sitting across from a client for an hour, there is, of course, no question about time.

"But when we send someone to audit or go through and evaluate a bookkeeping procedure, there is no check on the time we bill. The same is true of the time we might spend researching a client's case. The only check is the person doing the work. Ethics is important."

It is also important in Peters's field. Unscrupulous headhunters could re-recruit one of their placements six months after he or she has been placed. This is a temptation in the headhunting field that Peters strongly cautions against.

Although a headhunter may get away with it, "chances are you are going to get caught and ruin your business." Peters goes out of his way to assure companies he will not be coming in "the back door." He even "guarantees" engineers he places.

"We give the company a 90-day, money-back guarantee. We return 1/90th of the fee for each day under 90 days. If an engineer only works 30 days, we return two-thirds of the fee."

Peters goes beyond the money-back guarantee. If a placement leaves before the 90 days is up, he will replace him at no cost to the company. "In the years I have been in business, I have had to pay back only one fee."

ETHICAL CONSIDERATIONS

To some, the greatest ethical consideration rests with consultants' employees. They are privy to confidential information as well as being in a position to leave with a client and either open shop or join another firm.

Client confidentiality is critical to Senn. He guards against any breach by cautioning his employees not to drink at lunch, especially when they are with clients. "I don't think it is any secret what alcohol does. Numb brains and loose tongues are a disaster in the consulting business."

Senn maintains a relationship with clients and frequently goes to lunch with them. The alcohol rule applies in his case as well.

Hopkins seconds the alcohol motion. "It is easy to overeat and drink too much in this business. You're on stage and when you come off people want to talk to you, buy you a drink, slap you on the back, and socialize. Be careful. I've spent a long time building a reputation as an excellent trainer. What takes years to build can be torn down in no time."

Nickels and his employees see equipment and procedures at companies that rivals would be anxious to know about. "One word and our credibility would be destroyed. I remind everyone at our office before they go out on a job about the importance of confidentiality."

Where employees are concerned, Holbert cautions about relying too much on secretaries. "Some attorneys try to cut corners by hiring a secretary and having them fill out forms and file them. Then they charge the client for attorney's time. That's a mistake, not only from an ethical standpoint but from an operational one as well.

"On more than one occasion, I have seen secretaries fill those forms out incorrectly. It's easy to do. If you turn in the wrong thing to the court, it can be critical—and create a disaster for your client."

Zdonek found hiring a problem as his firm grew. "My first thoughts were to try and hire accountants from other firms, people with four and five years' experience. That's what we did but it was a mistake. Many had bad habits and they brought them to our firm."

What Zdonek eventually did was recruit at the college level. It took more time but "we could train them in our methods."

In 16-plus years of business, Senn has overcome numerous pitfalls, but the one that everyone "has to face and conquer is sales."

HOW TO SELL

"It did not hit me until we put out our shingle that if you cannot sell, you are dead in this business. You can be the greatest in the world at your profession, but you have to sell it to someone." Senn is the first to admit he was not a salesperson, "but I was willing to learn." He bought books on selling, attended seminars, and started to develop his own style. "Essentially, good selling is just answering someone's needs. Find out what the client needs. Don't try to sell him something you think he wants. Good salespeople satisfy needs."

Senn called prospects to find out why they had turned his services down. "It's amazing what you learn. And people are ready to talk and help you. All you have to do is ask. That's the beauty of this business . . . there is never a closed door for the consultant who tries."

CHAPTER 6

WHAT IT TAKES

Holland. The beginning of WW II. The young boy was barely old enough to attend kindergarten. When they came for him he had no understanding of where he was going or why. Where were his parents? Why had they left?

For the duration of the war Arnold spent his time in an orphanage. Nutritious food was scarce. By the time the Allies freed Europe, Arnold was nothing more than a shriveled youngster. His bones were weakened from a lack of calcium.

When he came to the United States he was a sick and angry young man. His life was in shambles, his health poor, and his attitude completely negative. Three years in high school were punctuated by gang fights and unruliness.

His only success was as a gymnast (rope climber) in high school. For three years he struggled with the event but nothing he did seemed to help. Then, in the 10th grade, the rope climb became an obsession. He dedicated himself to it and suddenly there was a transformation. He not only succeeded, but he broke the school record, became league champion and was second in the city finals. Years later he would look back on his gymnastic experience as one of the most important events in his life.

He graduated high school and drifted. He knew automobiles and landed a job at a gas station for a time. One day, while taking a break, he was fascinated by the figure of an aged man working beneath a car.

He stared at the man and realized in 30 years, if he kept doing the same thing, that would be him. The thought disturbed him and made him think. He was convinced he should be doing something else. He tried college, where he majored in sociology. It didn't last long, especially after an argument with the professor.

He was hired by Atlantic Richfield and worked in the printing department. From there he went to another company and worked in a similar capacity. In four years he became a supervisor. He looked at his boss, a relatively young man, and understood there was no future at this job either.

He saw an ad in the Sunday paper: "Be in your own business. Be an independent financial counselor." He had no idea as to what financial counselors did, but it sounded good, especially if he could help people.

To his surprise, the position was with an insurance company as a salesperson. They hired him and he worked hard. For the first time he began to focus on a goal. He wanted to become an investment advisor, a money manager. He knew nothing about the market and little about economics. But he had an inquiring mind and from his insurance experience knew that people needed help when it came to managing funds.

He started studying. He read books about investment and the economy. He moved to another insurance firm where he was able to sell mutual funds. He tried to parlay his experience into a job with a brokerage house but no one would hire him—he had neither an education or the background.

Finally a small, over-the-counter securities firm gave him a chance. They didn't care about his education. All they wanted was someone to move the product.

Arnold continued to study and work. He read books, attended seminars, researched at libraries. He became proficient and knowledgeable about the economy. His insight into money and inflation was superior to anyone's at the firm.

Then, one day he opened his own office. It was a hole-in-the-wall, an embarrassment he would later say. For five years, he struggled to make payments on books and buy research material. Along the way, he handled clients. A few were willing to risk it.

Arnold stuck to it. He started making money for his clients. It did not happen overnight, but by the late 1970s he was in the black. He could see his firm growing. He moved to new offices, hired help, brought in a computer.

By 1984 Century Management was a success story and Arnold Van Den Berg had attained at least part of his dream, financial independence. Van Den Berg looks back on those years of hardship as a honing process.

"If you put those five years on a balance sheet," he says, "there would be no profit. Some people would even say I was a failure. But there is no way to put a value on the knowledge and goodwill I accumulated. I grew and learned business skills. I developed confidence. I believe every consultant should keep those things in mind. The beginning is never easy but it is worth it.

"Life and business are punctuated by failures. The important thing is to learn from those failures and do not become discouraged by them. I was entering a profession where everyone had a formal education. I had none. But I wanted to be a successful money manager. If you want anything bad enough—and you are willing to work for it—there isn't anything that can stop you."

CONSULTANTS SHARE ONE CHARACTERISTIC

Obviously, Van Den Berg is a positive thinker. So are every one of the 10 consultants in this book. They share many common characteristics, but none is more evident than their positive outlook. Success did not come easy. Yet they all made it. Why?

The ability to stick to it. That statement was uttered over and over again by the 10. Fred Peters, the headhunter, put it this way: "I'm far from being a genius. The one thing I do is come in this office every day and plug away. Nothing happens quickly. If you keep pushing, before you know it you find yourself running a business that is growing daily."

Tenacity, says information systems consultant Joseph Izzo, is the key. "Go after what you believe in. Believe that you are capable of accomplishing what you set out to do. Too many people listen to others and allow themselves to be dissuaded from what they want. Consulting is an open opportunity.

"If we use our capabilities, there is no limit. We have the capacity to do anything we want, only few realize it."

One of the required ingredients is the "ability to handle pressure," says Ed Pearson. "Pressure comes in the form of deadlines and in a client's personality. Not all clients are the same. Some are conservative, others flamboyant. You have to be willing to adjust to the client's personality.

"It does not matter whether you are introverted or extroverted. If you are a hard worker, know how to react to the client, and can handle pressure, this business is for you," he says.

BUSINESS BUILDS BY AIDING OTHERS

You must have the ability to work with people, stresses Van Den Berg. "Every consultant comes in contact with people. You have to enjoy dealing with them. You can be successful without that attribute, but the business becomes difficult if you do not like who you are dealing with on a daily basis."

Larry Nickels, the soft-spoken electrical engineer who considers himself an introvert, says you cannot succeed without the desire to work with people. "I am not a bubbly, outgoing person. In fact, I'm not even a good PR-type person. But I try to help people. They recognize that and appreciate it."

Having the ability to work with people does not mean you have to play cards with them, go to the ball game, or to a nightclub. It infers that you are willing to share your knowledge. You are willing to sit down and explain to them what might be wrong and how you would solve the problem. That's working and dealing with people.

All 10 maintain that building a business does not require salesmanship; that is, salesmanship as people think of it.

NO PRESSURE IN SALES

"Anyone," says Peters, "can become a good salesperson. The key is to believe in your product. If you believe in your product—or service—you will sell it. The enthusiasm and belief come across."

Van Den Berg has his definition of salesmanship. "The ability to communicate ideas, be persuasive, and convince people of the merit of your approach. That has nothing to do with pressure."

Too many people have the misconception that sales is pressure. In the consulting business, it is educating and informing the client. If you can sit across from someone and ask them questions, get them to be vocal about their problem, and then explain what you do, that's selling.

Larry Senn says the important belief in consulting is to "believe in yourself. Believe that you have the ability to solve problems. The confidence comes across."

Senn's confidence comes from his fascination with the client's problem. "In school, I loved case studies. They were like mysteries. I loved the variety and challenge of trying to figure out how to improve a business organization. If you're a mystery fan, consulting is your business."

Both Senn and Van Den Berg recommend a steady "diet" of positive-thinking books. Van Den Berg is adamant about the subject. "We are constantly bombarded by negative thoughts. TV, radio, and newspapers dwell on the negative. If you listen to it enough, it begins to depress you. To overcome that influence, you should be reading and thinking about positive materials."

It all relates to mental attitude. Van Den Berg believes that success is "the result of attitude and how people see themselves.

"It is far more important than people realize. What you believe yourself to be, you will ultimately become. Those thoughts have been said many times, but in this business it is truer than most. We are in a people business. We relate to them daily. What we think comes across and causes them to either believe in us or reject our ideas."

Van Den Berg suggests thinking "aspiration, inspiration, and achievement." Every consultant must continually affirm the things that he is doing. "We deal in a business where many people say no. That can be demoralizing. Don't let it be. Certainly, you may be depressed when someone turns your service down, but if you pick yourself up and go on, you will find someone who accepts your service."

Jack Spahn echoes those thoughts. The most important characteristic is "self-esteem. You have to think well of yourself or you will never have any motivation in this business."

For that reason, Spahn endorses college, especially in his field. "It gives you goals and motivation. You accomplish things and it builds your self-esteem."

Tom Hopkins takes it a step further. "It is the confidence and self-esteem that gives consultants the ability to do the thing they fear most. If you do the distasteful things first, you will find yourself accomplishing the most difficult tasks with no trouble. When you get them out of the way, you feel good about yourself and your confidence grows."

Hank Zdonek has been reading positive-thinking books since he was a youngster. His initial investment as a youngster was a 25-cent Bible ("that tells you how old I am"). The Bible is replete with positive stories and lessons. *Psychocybernetics* is another mainstay in his library. "It taught me how to set goals."

Joseph Izzo learned about goals at an early age. He was one of six kids and he worked his way through Ohio State. He went to IBM school at night and by the time he was 21, he was managing data processing for the army.

Izzo is an ardent reader. There are two kinds of books he dwells upon —books about management and those that relate to positive thinking. He's read all of Ayn Rand's novels, *Megatrends,* and most of Peter Drucker's works. They answer the two educational requirements that are a must for every consultant: "knowing what is happening and what may happen in your field, and improving your attitude."

Senn has similar habits. He reads *Fortune, Forbes, Business Week,* and other business-oriented publications. As is the case with most, he has read *Megatrends* and *In Search of Excellence.* He spends time reading trade journals and believes the reading a consultant does is critical to success.

GETTING TO THE REAL PROBLEM

Izzo agrees with Senn in his assessment of the kind of thinking a consultant is required to have. "If you are a person who has the ability to see things, decipher problems, and see through a situation to the real problem, you will make an excellent consultant," he says. "In other words, can you see the entire picture and analyze it?"

A good consultant should always "look at a situation and try to think of a better way of doing it," says Senn. "When you stand in line at a bank, do you ever look at the flow and try to think of a better way. I do. That's a good consulting characteristic."

Senn's doctorate was in behavioral sciences and human relations. Both relate to understanding and motivating people. "In consulting you not only have to motivate yourself, but also those who may be working within companies that you have as a client."

Senn equates positive thinking with the Olympics. "Just think of the commitment and dedication each athlete had to have in order to qualify for the games. It takes belief in yourself and your ability. Every Olympic athlete would make a super consultant. In fact, I wouldn't mind hiring some for our firm.

"Athletes are similar to consultants. They have disappointments. Consultants do, too, in the form of a client saying no. Yet the superior athlete, the successful one, keeps coming back regardless of how many races or events they may lose.

"The superior consultant keeps pushing, too. He must constantly be looking for new business. One thing to remember—don't sit back and relax when you get a new client. Look for others. The consultant who does can't help becoming a success."

For Senn, reading of positive literature helps develop that Olympian attitude. Senn read Norman Vincent Peale, Napoleon Hill, and others.

Van Den Berg reads, rereads, underlines, categorizes, and even files pages from books and magazines. His office is a well-indexed library, with information ranging from the history of money to the impact outside influences have on the mind and motivation.

MONEY MANAGEMENT BEYOND THE UNITED STATES

Van Den Berg intended it to be that way. In his field "knowledge is everything. I cannot stress the need for continuous research when it comes to money management. In today's environment money management does not just relate to the United States. You have to be aware of what is going on in the rest of the world. I read the *Economist,* which gives us information on Europe, *Value Line, Standard and Poor's,* and a number of other magazines."

One of the things that is behind his quest for information is his lack of formal education. "It hindered me in the sense that there are things in a formal education, such as accounting and economics courses, that would have helped. Without the education, I was unable to land the brokerage job.

"The lack of formal education also made it difficult to get the business off the ground. In this business, you can't know too much. The more you know, the better your performance will be.

"Unlike some consulting fields, money management is measurable. Every three months the client gets a statement. He can see how well you have done. Results are tangible. If you do a good job you will find referrals coming in the door." In the past five years, Van Den Berg has not had to do any solicitation. It has all been referral, and all based upon his performance for others.

Hopkins spends up to four hours a week reading. Because he spends so much time "on stage"—lecturing nearly 50 weeks of the year—he looks for escape in the form of Robert Ludlum novels.

He recommends Varude's *Complete Speakers and Toastmasters Library* to anyone who is going to get into the area of training.

"Basically," he says, "I am a positive thinker. What good does it do to be negative? We can control our thoughts and in this business it is a must," Hopkins explains.

Peters is positive, too. He always regards the glass as half-full. Although he is not an ardent reader, he has made it a practice to stay away from down, negative people. "There are lots of them around. Don't waste your time with them. The nice thing about this profession is that most of the people you deal with on a daily basis are positive. We are the greatest!"

That attitude goes back to Peters's ball-playing days. He worked his way through college on a football scholarship. Peters had to be an optimist. When he graduated with a degree in speech, he was told he was "unemployable. I said, what do you mean? What's this degree for?"

In his search for a job, Peters went to a personnel agency. While waiting for an interview, it occurred to him that the agency might be a good place to work. After all, they had access to numerous jobs. Why not work for them, wait until a good job came along, take it, and leave. That's exactly what he did. Peters convinced the agency to hire him—and he never left the personnel field.

ENDLESS POSSIBILITIES IN CONSULTING

Eventually he wound up becoming the manager of an agency, partner, and finally owner. Peters's rise is an example of what can be done if someone puts their mind to it. For years he bounced around (always in the personnel field) and never took his job or career seriously. Ultimately when he began to concentrate on business he built a successful headhunting firm in a matter of a few years.

Part of Peters's motivation was defiance. He was told that he was unemployable and would never make it. Rejection can either make a person fall back or, as was the case with Peters, cause him to go forward.

One of the things that has made Peters's business successful is his attitude towards sales. He never gets discouraged. He spends half the day on the telephone. Rarely does he ever see his clientele.

Initially, Van Den Berg was motivated by defiance, too. While formulating plans for his consulting firm, a friend set up an interview with a college professor who was an expert in management. Van Den Berg outlined the plan to the professor and was shocked when he heard the man's response.

The professor castigated him, questioned his ability, and asked "what makes you think you can open a consulting firm? I've been thinking about it for years and I'm still not ready. And I have 10 times the qualifications that you have."

That taught Van Den Berg two lessons, each critical in business. "First, if you believe in something, go ahead and do it. Not everyone is going to agree with your ideas. There is nothing wrong with getting advice. You can learn from others. But don't take everything people say to be the gospel. Like the professor, not everyone knows what they are doing."

VALUE OF COMMITMENT

The second thing it taught him was a commitment lesson. "Some people talk about going into business incessantly. They never take the step. Why? It may be they do not want to take the risk. Or perhaps they do not have the confidence.

"The phenomenal thing about business in this country, is that everyone has the opportunity to get into one. So why not try it? The worst that can happen is you fail and, believe me, failing is part of life. You learn from mistakes."

Senn almost never went into business. Although he always had an entrepreneurial flair (he ran a carnival as a kid and started a chain of street-corner flower shops while in college), he was hesitant about taking the plunge.

"I was never sure that I could sell my services to someone for hundreds of dollars a day." He thought additional education would help. He went back to school for an MBA, then a doctorate. If it had not been for a professor who got him involved in consulting, Senn might still be thinking about it.

"Ultimately," he says, "it takes a decision. Expect to make mistakes when you open your business. The person who doesn't is not growing and his business will never expand."

Hesitancy prevented Izzo from entering business. He mulled the prospects constantly, always putting the decision off. Finally, one day he mustered the courage and made the move. "It was either go or forget it." After 25 years of working for someone, he thought the risk and mistakes he would make would be worth it.

Mistakes are one thing, but Van Den Berg had a disaster. His first venture in consulting led him into a business with a partner. Van Den Berg discovered he had philosophical differences with his partner and, as a result, they had a difficult time working together.

Eventually, their differences caused them to split and close the business. Van Den Berg personally assumed the liabilities and paid every one of them. It took him three years to pay off those debts, but, in his words, it was a valuable learning experience. While others may have been shattered, Van Den Berg used it to his advantage.

"Although I would certainly not want to go through it again, it taught me to be more cautious with those you do business with and to take a little time to check things out before you get into something."

Hopkins learned from failure, too. His first sales job was a disaster until he went to a sales training session. He not only learned why he was a flop at sales, but it opened his eyes as to the importance of sales training. From that moment, he could see the industry need.

WHAT CANNOT BE GUARANTEED

Izzo is a realist about consulting and the potential failures. "We can't guarantee results in this business. It is an intangible industry. It is in the perception of the CEO or whomever hired you whether or not you did a good job. Don't take it personally."

Zdonek's failing was in the accounts receivable area. It gave him insight into the importance of a client's credit rating and it showed him that certain industries were not advantageous for accountants to get into.

Nickels never pictured himself as a risk-taker. He spent a career working for someone else. He knew much about electrical engineering but little about business. He was in a position similar to many engineers. He was quietly confident, though.

"My background was research and development in the product department. With the experience I had I could see how the end product was used. I could also envision designs. If you are a research-and-development-type person with a math background, you have an excellent chance of success."

Surprisingly he found he had a great deal of business ability. "I had a talent for hiring and keeping books, and I shocked myself when I found I could sell. These were things I had been doing all my life but never realized it. I think similar doubts hold back other engineers."

THE RISK FACTOR

Pearson doesn't question that there is risk but says, "If you put in the time and effort, the opportunity is there. In the years we have been in business, I've seen numerous engineers use our company as a springboard for their own business. Certainly there is competition, but so is there opportunity."

Risk is part of business. Nothing ventured, nothing gained is a truism in consulting or any enterprise. Illustrative of that philosophy is the story of the young promoter who had the opportunity to promote a rock group in concert during the sixties. The group had never been to this country but it did have a hit single.

The group's manager approached established promoters. He asked if they would want to promote concerts in their cities. There was one catch—the manager wanted a $25,000, nonrefundable advance.

Few promoters were willing to put up that sum. Most turned it down. The young promoter decided this was his chance to get into the business. He did not have the $25,000, but he did own a house and he had friends. He borrowed as much as he could and raised the $25,000. He was taking a chance but, in his mind, it was worth the risk. Thus the newcomer, who had never been able to break into the concert field, became the promoter for the first Beatles concert to be held in Los Angeles.

Naturally, the event was a sellout. In appreciation the Beatles manager gave the promoter the rights to promote every Beatle concert held in the West. As a result that unknown disc jockey became a millionaire.

Risk means more than taking a chance. In business it also means sacrifice. Van Den Berg gave up a secure position in the insurance field to start his business. He had a few small clients, just enough to pay the rent. He gave up his nice insurance office for a hole in the wall. He sacrificed his social life for study and the purchase of books and literature.

Senn decided the only way he was going to expand his management consulting practice was to hire more expensive and skilled assistants. He needed capital and found it by cutting his income and living style. Spahn gave up a secure, high-paying job (as did Izzo) to start their own practices. There was no guarantee that they would make a go of it.

Zdonek left the comfort of an established firm, borrowed money, cut his living style, dropped the frills, and scrimped for several years. The tales could go on endlessly about what these 10 consultants gave up in order to build a business.

THE REQUIRED CHARACTERISTICS

"There isn't," says Van Den Berg, "an easy way. If you are going to get into business—whether it be consulting or something else—you must be willing to sacrifice and dedicate yourself."

"The problem," says Peters bluntly, "is that not many people are willing. They may like the idea, but they will not take the chance. Owning your own business takes work and sacrifice. There is no getting around it."

It also takes salesmanship. Peters is convinced you can make a good salesperson out of anyone. The key, according to Spahn, is the consultant (or salesperson) should enjoy people and what he or she is doing.

Pearson feels a critical characteristic is the consultant's ability to do his or her "homework. Consultants have to be willing to put in the hours it takes to study a client's case and come up with a solution."

Work involves service. When you earn thousands of dollars in retainers or generate hourly fees from $100–$200, the client expects good service.

And at times service means putting in hours and not always getting paid for it. Zdonek is ready to talk to a client and reassure him if he calls. He may spend time on the telephone going through something that has been previously explained. And he does it without compensation.

Spahn may evaluate a builder's plans. Then he may spend an hour or two trying to get the builder to change them because he knows they are not good enough to get through city hall. He could take the plans, his fee, and run.

When the plans are rejected, he could dump them back in the builder's lap. Instead, he chooses to spend his own, noncompensated time trying to get the builder to compromise before he takes the plans through city hall. Why? Because he wants a happy, satisfied client.

Perhaps Van Den Berg explains it best. "If you are in business strictly to make money and you do not want to help people, business is not for you. Forget the money and remember the service. With that philosophy, the money comes automatically."

CONSULTING IS PEOPLE BUSINESS

Consulting is a people business, adds Zdonek. Even in accounting, "where you deal with numbers, you deal with people. You have to have the ability to translate numbers into ideas so the client can understand and use them."

Nickels keeps the personal element in his job even after he finishes a particular project. He will call or write to see how things are going. It's all done at his expense. Once again, service. Service means that the consultant, if he or she is to build a successful practice, is going to put in many hours and not be fully compensated for every one of them.

Zdonek's office lights are on from early morning to evening. His work week runs from 55–65 hours. That's substantially less than he put in during his first few years in business. Back then he worked seven days a week, 10–12 hours a day. Vacations were nonexistent.

Those hours are typical of Zdonek's work ethic. When he was a youngster he lived on the outskirts of a Canadian farm community. He had two work options. He could work close to home for $4 a day or travel several miles and harvest crops, which was harder work, and earn $12 a day. He chose the latter.

THE HOURS IT TAKES

Most consultants are early risers. They are in their office by 7 A.M. Saturdays is a "clean-up" day. It is usually reserved for paperwork and leftovers. Peters uses it to work through resumés and send them out. Holbert is the one consultant who takes weekends off.

"When I close up shop on Friday night, I'm gone. I try not to think about business until Monday morning. That doesn't mean that I never work weekends. Occasionally I do." Part of that philosophy is due to the effect work has had on Holbert's personal life. He is divorced.

"For me it was difficult to be married and work as a consultant. I would start at 7 A.M. and go until midnight. I never took weekends off. That's tough on family life. If you get into this business, set aside time for your personal life."

The toughest schedule belongs to Hopkins. He is the perpetual traveler who is seldom home. His training sessions take him to every part of the country, 50 weeks of the year. With his income he can afford to take his wife along, but his kids stay home in school. He seldom is in a position to open a can of beer and sit back and watch Monday night football.

"I schedule things so I am home Friday night and don't have to leave until Sunday evening," he says. Those lengthy hours do not mean consultants are chained to their desks. They have the freedom to leave anytime, take off for a day, or have a long lunch. There's no boss to check on them. Each has made a conscious decision to put in the hours. "That's why," says Hopkins, "you have to love your business. You live with it all the time."

Drawing away from the TV and other diversions takes discipline, one of the most important characteristics of a consultant. "It is almost as if you have to put blinders on and shut everything else out," says Izzo. "It isn't the hours as much as the effort. You have to channel all your energy into your task. You must concentrate on what you are doing. The mind cannot wander. That takes discipline."

Zdonek regards discipline as something that helps him set his priorities. "I'll have 10 or 12 things listed that I want to accomplish on a specific day. Regardless of what happens I follow that list as closely as I can."

WHERE DISCIPLINE FITS

To Van Den Berg discipline is one of the two most important attributes of a consultant (the other is "character," or a person's honesty). "Discipline is everything. It relates to many things aside from just following a laundry list of things to do.

"It relates to the prices you set for your services. In money management, knowing when to sell stock may involve discipline. When the stock reaches a certain price level, your discipline (or guidelines) may dictate selling it off. If you start bending those rules, you will be a poor money manager."

Peters has an interesting view of discipline. "The one discipline I have is I come to work each day. But I have bad habits at work. If I do well one day, I may slack off the next. I think that is a human tendency. If consultants could get around that flaw, they could make twice as much money." (Despite his admitted "flaws," Peters has done quite well. His business has been in the six-figure range for the past three years.)

Spahn, although a believer in discipline, thinks there are other things equally as important. "I am well-disciplined; I have to be. Anyone in business who is going to be successful better be, too.

"But there are two other considerations—self-esteem and motivation. If you don't think highly of yourself, who will? And, if you don't have a good opinion of yourself, you will never be able to be motivated or have discipline. Consultants need an ego. Without one, they're going to find their sales won't nearly be as good as a competitor's."

THEORY OF SELF-ESTEEM

Nickels says "amen" to Spahn's theory of self-esteem. Although he was one of the finest engineers in the country, he always had doubts about his ability to face higher management. That was one of the reasons he had an outside salesperson working with him. One day, however, he did find himself in the office of a chief executive.

"Initially," he recalls, "it bothered me. It made me nervous. By the time the meeting was five minutes old, I found that people in higher management were quite nice. They were broad-minded, knowledgeable, and patient. I had no trouble communicating. It was a surprise and an eye-opener."

Regardless of how much discipline or self-esteem a consultant has, he or she will not generate a six-figure income overnight. It takes time. From one to three years is a period of establishment. From three to five, growth. Beyond five, the consultant, if he or she is successful, will have a flourishing business.

Consultants in highly specialized areas (Nickels, Pearson, Spahn, Holbert) were making money within months after they opened. For others, it was not easy.

Van Den Berg struggled for five years before his efforts bore fruit. Much of the difficulty he had was due to a lack of background. Nevertheless, he stuck to it and developed a phenomenally successful practice. "When it starts to happen it snowballs," he says. "For five years it was tough making ends meet. Then it grew rapidly."

Van Den Berg has watched many enter the business and drop out. He maintains that most dropped out "just at the wrong time. Just when things seem the most difficult, just when you begin to wonder what you are doing in business, it will all turn around. That seems to be true in businesses ranging from manufacturing to consulting.

"Some people can build a business overnight, others in five years—

like me. Whether it comes overnight or years down the road, be aware that everyone experiences periods of doubt. You will doubt yourself. But you can overcome anything. I have a saying: 'don't sweat the small stuff.' Put everything into the proper perspective. How important is business next to life? Not very. That's what I mean by saying don't worry.

"If you get into it, stick. That saying, 'it is always darkest before the dawn,' is certainly true in business. If you put in the effort, you will make it. Nothing can stop you."

Consulting is a business where there are highs and lows. It is not like a product, a bar of soap or box of cereal, that sells itself. It takes effort.

Hopkins is an example of someone who put in the effort. He gave free talks for more than a year before he was paid $50. Then, his fees began to skyrocket. Less than two years after he was paid that $50, he was generating more than $1,000 a talk. Senn spent three years building his snowball, and Zdonek an equal amount of time.

EFFORT PAYS OFF

Regardless of the time, effort, and sacrifice involved, each of the 10 say it has been worth it. Perhaps much of the reason for that statement is their background. All worked at an early age. None were ever given anything. Holbert grew up in lower-middle-class environment where fighting was a way of life. As a youngster, he lost the sight in one eye.

Peters struggled as a youngster, too. His efforts paid off in a scholarship and education. Hopkins was out hustling from the time he was a teenager. By the time he was 21, he was selected as one of the 10 top salesman in Los Angeles by the Sales and Marketing Association Executives Association.

Senn had trouble deciding what he wanted to do, but he always worked. From his early teens, when he ran a carnival, to his creation of a flower business in college. Izzo was one of six kids and worked his way through school.

Although their professions are far apart, they all share one unmistakable characteristic—they were always willing to work in order to get something.

ENVIABLE LIFE-STYLES

Today, that work has paid off with 10 enviable life-styles. The life-styles are as varied as their professions. Zdonek says "I enjoy many things I would never have if I worked for someone else. Among those things are a second home in the desert (Palm Springs), a nice car, and better clothes.

"Most important," he adds, "is the knowledge that if I want to go somewhere or do something, I can afford it. Despite the long work days I have more time with my family. I can indulge some of my hobbies. And it is amazing how good it feels to be free from the burden of financial budgeting. That's one of the most important elements of success."

Van Den Berg's life-style has changed little. He has moved into more comfortable offices, has help, and can take time off when he wants. He likes his neighborhood and will always live there. He has no desire for fancy cars, nor does he yearn for dining out or throwing parties. He likes his privacy and his family.

"It's ironic. I am a financial advisor and I am not that excited about material things. I never have been."

His hobby, he says, "has always been business." He does, however, have more than a passing interest in philosophy and in the mind. He spends countless hours studying mind-improvement techniques and he has developed an exceptional one for athletes.

"I want to grow and improve myself. As you grow, you automatically increase your level of success in business."

Although Hopkins is successful, his life-style remains the same. Pearson, however, has found great changes. "From a materialistic point of view, we are certainly more comfortable. In fact, I could retire today if I wanted.

"The greatest change is with people we deal with daily. I was a naive, quiet engineer before I got into business—business changes that. You not only become a sophisticated businessperson, but you also run across a great many powerful, influential people. That, in itself, changes the way you think and act. It has made life more fascinating."

Nickels now has two homes (Minnesota and Arizona), but his life-style has only changed in one way—"I spend more time at work. And

I enjoy it. I have the satisfaction of knowing that the hours I put in are going to pay dividends for me and my family."

Holbert laughs when you ask about life-style. He drives a nice car —"as do my ex-wives. Being single is different, too." He has owned several homes and is in the process of building his own.

Peters laughs, too. He has a nice home ("bigger payments") in an exclusive beach community, and his vacations have been extended. For the past six years, he has averaged two to two and a half months' time off for rest and relaxation.

Senn has utilized his success to become more active physically. He's a jogger and is preparing for a minitriathalon. He reserves his weekends for his hobbies and his family. Perhaps better than any consultant, Senn expresses what it means to own your own consulting business.

"I cannot think of anything that is more fulfilling, exciting, or creative than running your own consulting business. You constantly make things happen. It is creative because of the work you do with clients and the latitude you have with your company. You can move it any way you want. And it is financially rewarding.

"Most important, you are in charge of your life."

CHAPTER 7

CASE STUDIES
AND SITUATIONS

Listening to a consultant describe his or her operation is informative, but there is nothing more eye-opening than to follow the procedure utilized in approaching a case and/or situation by these professionals.

We have selected several situations. They are indicative of the problems and cases consultants encounter in these 10 fields.

CASE/SITUATION/INFORMATION SYSTEMS

Joseph Izzo did not generate the client in typical fashion. Usually it is a mailing or client referral that leads to business. This time it was a speech.

He was invited to address the members of a prestigious group that was composed of industry executives. Those in the audience were executives of major companies that were dependent upon data processing to keep things running smoothly.

Izzo's topic was appropriate: "it is time to break down the big computer centers and move responsibility closer to the user." Users, in data processing/information systems terminology, are the people who depend on DP for the information. They may be sales, production, or even shipping departments.

The topic hit home. Within minutes after he concluded, he was approached by an executive from a major company. His firm had run headlong into a dilemma. Users within the firm had been bitterly complaining about the poor performance of DP. They could not get the information they required in a timely manner.

The executive approached the DP manager. They spent several hours talking around the problem, and the executive was given everything but a solution. In the end the DP manager said he would handle it.

That never happened. The complaints continued and the friction between DP and the user units grew. Management could see that the organization, which was a multimillion-dollar-a-year established firm with thousands of employees, could not survive with its current system.

As a last resort, management scheduled a series of meetings between DP and the user units. They hoped problems would be aired and solutions developed.

The architecture for a new system began to develop through these meetings. How to move data more efficiently to the users was discussed. The value of the existing "centralized" system was questioned. The solution appeared to be decentralization. The suggestion emerged that perhaps not everything be done from DP.

This suggestion threatened DP. They saw it as a sign that the "company does not need us anymore." They resisted the changes.

Enter Joseph Izzo. The executive asked Izzo if he would be willing to attend the sessions. Izzo complied. In his business he frequently spent afternoons, even days, at a company analyzing problems. (It would, incidentally, cost the company nothing for Izzo's attendance.)

Question:

How would you handle the situation? Here's how Izzo did. The result was one of the largest consulting contracts ever awarded to his firm.

Izzo's attendance was an opportunity. He had three sessions in which to master the situation, offer input, and arrive at a solution. He also had to determine if this was the kind of case he wanted his firm to handle.

Izzo attended three meetings. He listened to the problems and complaints. It became obvious that the 18-year-old system was antiquated. DP was trying to protect its territory. They offered to remedy the situation by updating the system.

Izzo had heard similar stories. "Updating" meant "tweaking" the system. It indicates a modification or two, but it does not remedy the basic problem. The system, according to Izzo, had been tweaked many times previously.

It is similar to designing a rocket engine, Izzo explains. Initially the engine may be adequate for 200,000 pounds of thrust. By tweaking, the engine can get up to 275,000 pounds of thrust. Ultimately the engine becomes unstable and blows apart. The same is true of computers. With enough tweaking the entire system could collapse.

Izzo's approach at these meetings (and he recommends it to others) is to listen, then express your opinion. His policy is to be "strong and straightforward." And he was. After three meetings he recommended a complete redesign of the system.

That recommendation would not be considered if management did not realize the problem. Izzo sent a two-page proposal/agreement. It is his standard procedure. It spells out the fees and duties of the consulting firm and has space for management's signature. In contrast to other consultants, Izzo does not prepare lengthy agreements. His credibility —the articles he has published, speeches he has given, and references —do much of the speaking for him.

Izzo headed the redesign project. A project team was formed. It consisted of 15 employees and 2 from Izzo's firm. The 15 were employees from both the user units and DP. The project lasted for five months (Izzo estimated six). Izzo describes the five months as "living hell."

There were two initial problems. Some team members, especially those from DP, thought they would lose their jobs or, at the very least, their power. The second was the team looked upon the consultants as people who would tell them exactly what to do.

Izzo explains that is one of the fallacies encountered when consulting. Employees or supervisors look to the outsider for direction. In reality, the outsider is just as lost as the members of the team.

The object is to get everyone to attack "the marshmallow." The initial weeks are taken up with meetings of the project team. They sit around and have an open discussion. Various problems—and the causes of those problems—begin to surface.

As discussions continue, redesign suggestions are made. This is where Izzo's firm plays a major role. His people are familiar with the systems. The first redesign is put down on paper. It has to be approved by all the general managers. That means the DP chief as well as the user department heads have to agree.

Usually, that first redesign is only step one. The obstacle is breaking into "DP's culture." There is continued resistance. Eventually, with enough input from DP, the resistance is conquered. Another design is submitted to general managers.

The redesign will take three years and an expenditure in the millions. Once it is approved, Izzo's firm removes one of its employees. The second, the project team manager, remains. He spends about 70 percent of his time nurturing, guiding, and clarifying.

Izzo says that as the project gets further downstream, the value of the consulting firm diminishes. The project person, who is a degreed engineer, meets with Izzo every other week for about two hours. A summary is prepared. They examine "hot spots" and loose ends.

Izzo looks for things that are dangling. The more things out of place, the greater the chance the project will stall and fail. Izzo meets with the person who hired him about once every six weeks. He brings him up to date.

During one of these meetings, another department approaches Izzo. They want to develop a strategy for themselves that will tie into the company's overall system. The result is another assignment for Izzo's company.

Question:

What sold the company on Izzo's services? There are several distinct characteristics.

1. His knowledge of information systems. This was exhibited during his speech and at the sessions. Izzo did not just talk for the sake of talking. Whenever he spoke, he had specific questions and suggestions.

2. His ability to analyze the situation and offer a plan.

3. His ability to speak up without fearing management. At the same time he showed he could get along with those in the room. There were pointed questions but no sharp, degrading words aimed at anyone.

4. His ability, and that of his employees, to get along with the project team and the employees they dealt with in each department. Izzo's work is not confined to project meetings. There are sessions with employees within DP and the user units. He needs their cooperation and confidence. The solution to most problems develops from the interchange in this area.

5. The ability to implement a plan, back away, and slowly relinquish control.

6. References from previous clients.

These were all selling elements. Management could have "cut the cord" at any point if progress was not made. Izzo points out that getting the contract is only the beginning. Doing the work and getting along with a variety of different "company cultures" presents an entirely new set of problems.

Izzo's projects are not confined to consulting. He has one of the few, if not the only, information systems firm that does "turnaround management."

A turnaround situation arises where data processing is running so poorly that management asks Izzo to bring in a team, take over, and reposition the entire system and department. It is similar to a company going "Chapter 11" and asking for a court trustee. In management's eyes all hope is gone.

Izzo tackles these cases with the goal that his people will be replaced as soon as possible. He comes in with a team of three to four people. The existing DP employees are moved to other positions either within the department or somewhere else.

Retraining begins. An executive team is formed. Members of it come from Izzo's firm, management, DP, and user units. Izzo's job is to make the department function smoothly. The new system, if the old one requires revision, is left up to the management team.

Izzo's staff begins to implement professional standards. The users are asked to explain what needs they have. This usually ends in a presentation by the user departments, in which they outline what they need to improve performance.

The consultants participate during these sessions. Turnaround time, that is, the time it takes for Izzo to reverse the trend, retrain, and put the firm's regular employees back in charge, can run 12–14 months.

Izzo's firm is currently working on one of these projects. The DP department is spending $130,000 a month. Izzo can put in a replacement network at less than half the cost ($50,000), and it will outperform the current system.

Turnaround occurs when the system has developed significant cracks. Characteristic cracks range from information that does not reach the users in time to a move on the part of user departments to buy their own hardware/software.

Izzo explains turnaround is happening more frequently than before. Equipment is advancing rapidly. Demands on DP departments are accelerating. And department managers of user units have become familiar with computers and their capabilities. Many are tempted to bypass DP and bring in their own system.

Turnaround takes the same expertise as consulting. It also requires Izzo to come up with employees who have management skills. Whether it is turnaround or consulting, Izzo's contracts all commit him to deliver in a specified amount of time. They can also be cancelled at any time.

How does a consultant recognize these problems? Major signs are complaints from user departments. DP is a support unit. If it lags, complaints will surface. The sharp consultant not only acquaints management of companies with his services, but he familiarizes himself with heads of user departments. Should complaints surface, he will be among the first to know.

CASE/SITUATION/MANAGEMENT CONSULTING

Dr. Larry Senn met the new president while giving a talk to a service club. It was one of the many "nonpaying" engagements that paid off. The president had just taken over from his father. It was an extremely profitable business, but the new chief executive felt changes were needed.

The company produced a high-quality product, but the lower cost of foreign labor was beginning to make an impact. He wanted to make the company operate more efficiently (it was labor-intensive) and, at the same time, maintain quality in his product line.

He had a second desire as well. He wanted to change the management style of the organization. The president wanted to see a shift from "old school" to one that was more flexible, more open to change. He wanted to involve more people at different levels.

That was the problem he posed to Senn. Senn believed that management needed greater insight into the president and his thinking. If anything was going to be changed, the first move was to shift management styles.

Initially, Senn developed a management seminar. Attendees would be the president and his senior team. Senn custom-designed a seminar so that attendees could take a "historical" look at the culture of the organization. He talked a great deal about new age management skills, explored concepts from the Japanese style of management, and spent time having each manager explore his own style.

Senn also introduced the theories of *In Search of Excellence*. Senn designed a "behavioral matrix" so managers could examine their strengths and weaknesses. At first, the managers were cautious, hesitant. But by the time they left at the end of the third day they were enthusiastic and excited.

Senn planned the session so it would be off-site. In his opinion it is important to take people away from their work environment. They become more creative and there are no interruptions.

He expected the initial hesitancy, as should every consultant. The cause, as he explains, is managers have the mistaken belief that they "should have everything together, have all the answers." They feel, he continues, that they are not supposed to make mistakes.

What he created in the seminar was a "safe environment." There were no right or wrong answers. They were able to explore and discover more about their company without feeling threatened.

Complicating the sessions was the presence of the new president. Until managers relaxed and accepted the three days for what it was—an exploratory session—there could be little communication. These were all problems that fell into Senn's domain.

The end result of the seminar was the decision by the managers that the major payoff would come by improving their productivity. A hand-s-on consulting project was awarded to Senn's company.

Senn's first step was to conduct a survey of the facility. He studied its systems, supervisory techniques, and organizational structure, which are all part of his firm's surveying method. He came back with a written proposal.

The first part covered the findings: the firm's strengths and the opportunities for improvement. It concluded with the steps required in order to attain the objectives, while maintaining employee morale and quality.

The survey involved more than observations. There were interviews with the president and vice president of manufacturing. The survey related to productivity and the manufacturing VP would have critical input. The goals, of course, were to reduce unit cost, maintain quality, and keep employee morale high.

The proposal did not focus on productivity but rather on how employees and supervisors could work better together. From better working relationships would come the first steps in improved productivity.

The proposal also included a projected savings. The fee for the project was based upon the estimated return on investment. The survey took a week to complete. It took an additional few days to put the findings together and prepare the proposal. The cost to management was $3,000 for the survey/proposal.

The procedure is to leave the proposal with management. Usually they ask for time to think it over. They want to check references and discuss it among themselves. Senn makes sure the proposal has hit the mark. He asks what it is they like, what concerns or hesitation they may have.

Senn views the proposal presentation as an important part of the selling process. He does not want negative feedback, but he is anxious to address their concerns. Usually management shies away from criticizing the document.

They prefer to keep things running smoothly. If there is something that bothers them, they would rather talk about it among themselves at a later time. Senn may never know about it until he is turned down.

Thus, Senn attempts to have their concerns surface. He is willing to ask questions like "what would stand in your way or prevent you from going ahead with this proposal?" Or "what concerns do you have?" "what do you think about this part?"

Senn probes to get management's concerns in the open. Once they are, he can address them. Whenever possible he gets a conditional agreement (i.e., we would go ahead with this if . . .). Then he can meet that condition. There is no high-pressure convincing of management.

In this particular case, Senn got the go-ahead on the spot. He had one project manager assisted by a part-time consultant who put in time over a period of six months.

Senn operates in a similar manner to other consultants. Once they are brought in they tread lightly. The first thing they do is build a relationship with the employees and supervisors. They begin to ask questions as to what the employees and supervisors feel would benefit them. Sometimes the employees come up with ideas; at other times it is the supervisors.

An "action team" is formed consisting of employees, supervisors and Senn's people. They meet regularly to contribute ideas, study processes, print flow diagrams. Through the suggestions from the team and the observations, Senn's team begins to come up with ideas that will cut production interruptions and delays.

They look for better, simpler ways of doing things. It is like a sporting event. When people contribute something worthwhile, points are given, appreciation is shown. They are listened to, perhaps for the first time. Senn calls it "performance coaching."

Supervisors respond because they are learning skills that make their job easier. They begin to see how it can work. In the proposal, Senn includes a time and action calendar. It describes in bar graph, the different phases of the project and when it will be completed.

The chart shows where savings begin. There are revisions, but the graph is fairly accurate. Senn estimated the project to take six to seven months. It took seven. Goals were exceeded in terms of savings. He had projected a 20 percent increase in productivity and achieved 33 percent.

Senn does not leave the productivity gains to chance. He follows up after the program is completed. He checks with management to make sure the levels are maintained. In his view, a satisfied client is the best salesperson.

In Senn's case, the success of the project goes back to the survey.

Unless his team came in with a 90 to 95 percent confidence level that the goals could be attained, he would not take the job. Some companies bring him in for surveys and say they want change, but the bottom line is it cannot be done because of internal difficulties. If this is the case, he lets management know.

Senn's approach is such that he will often come up with machinery modification suggestions. Part of that is made possible because of his engineering background. At times, it is the people within the company who are responsible for the innovation.

Senn's people may say, "gee, if we could only get the employee to work on this side of the machine instead of that." The step may save time in the production process. In many cases, the workers stop and get a maintenance man to examine the machine and see if sides can be altered.

It's all part of Senn's team concept. He makes the employees and supervisors feel as if they are part of the solution; and they are. The changes take place in an evolutionary, not revolutionary, way. Consultants, says Senn, do not have all the answers when they start a project, much comes from the interaction with employees.

Senn does not leave the project to manager. Either he or a partner visits the project monthly. The team communicates on almost a daily and weekly basis to him. Senn tells management not to expect any results for the first two months. The only time problems develop is when communication slows. To keep feedback and communication ongoing, Senn's project supervisor does a number of little things—such as buying coffee and donuts for the team—to involve as many people as possible.

The production case is no different from Senn's other projects. Instead of a manufacturing facility, it could have been a department store and people handling goods in the back room. Or it could have involved another facility where people were selling.

The basis of Senn's program is to establish communication between managers, supervisors, employees, and the consultant. He believes this is a necessity in any case because of the "new age employee," the employee who wants to understand what is going on and how he or she fits into the company's plans.

Employees are more curious and they want to be more involved. They can be, he says, just as productive as those employees of 40 years ago. They have the same work ethic. That ethic has to be brought out, and it is up to the company to do it.

CASE/SITUATION/LAND-GOVERNMENT CONSULTANT

Jack Spahn's cases are not always cut-and-dried. At times they take wheeling and dealing. The county recommended him to a builder—and for good reason. The builder/client had a major problem, one that demonstrates the expertise and skills a land/government consultant needs.

The client owned 70 acres of agricultural land. He wanted it rezoned for commercial development. The homeowners in the area were anxious to find out what he planned to build. The client did not tell them anything, because he did not know.

In order to get the rezoning, the client had to appear before a commission. At that time, the commission reviews the client's plans, examines what he or she intends to build and then decides whether or not to grant the change.

Zone changes are not automatic. Agricultural-zoned land is "less valuable" than commercial. On agricultural, the owner can only graze cattle, grow crops, etc. On commercial, he or she can construct office buildings and increase his or her income tenfold.

The client's hearing date had been set for December 3. At this point, he called in Jack Spahn. He knew there were problems but he wasn't sure what or why.

Spahn knew the problems immediately. The zone change would never go through unless there was a plan. The county was not about to give the client/builder carte blanche. They always insist on a plan.

There was a second problem, the homeowners. In his haste and indecision, the client/builder had neglected to include them. Homeowners, Spahn knew, have changed the course of building and his profession completely around in the past decade. They have made "environment" a word to be concerned about.

If the client went to his hearing with homeowner opposition, he was bound to run into additional problems.

There was a third problem: the client. Spahn regards client/builders as more of a headache than the homeowners or government officials. "They are the toughest people to get to listen."

Spahn explored the case. (This exploratory process is something he does with every potential client. He does not bill for his time or services. If, however, he eventually accepts the case, this time is billed retroactively. If not, he absorbs the loss.)

He knew there would never be enough time to get plans prepared for the Dec. 3 meeting. He needed time. He went to the county and told the officials about his problem. They told him they were loaded and he could get a three-month extension. He would have to apply for it at the Dec. 3 meeting.

Next, he approached the homeowners. He found a surprised, receptive attitude. They had never heard from the client/builder. Spahn was the first person they had ever talked to who was connected with the builder.

Spahn told them the builders were planning a "fantastic" development, one the citizens would be proud to have in the neighborhood. It would not only enhance property values, but it would create additional commercial space; commercial space that would attract companies that wanted to relocate. There was a possibility that many of the homeowners in the area would end up working in the park.

Additionally, Spahn told them the client/builder wanted their input for the plan. Spahn would like to meet with them and get some of their ideas. Those ideas would then be given to the architect. In turn, would the homeowners join Spahn in asking for a postponement of the December 3 hearing?

Spahn went back to the client and explained the situation. The client protested. He did not want to be strapped into a plan. He might want to sell off parcels of the 70 acres to other developers. Spahn informed him that the law reads as long as the final building "plan substantially conforms to the one initially submitted" the builder can modify his plans.

Spahn proposed several other steps. When the plans were prepared, he wanted to invite the homeowners to a brunch and unveil them. He wanted the homeowners behind the project when it came up for the March hearing.

He also intended to take the plans to the local chamber of commerce for its blessings. The more groups behind the plan, the better chance of passage.

At the December 3 hearing, Spahn would walk in with homeowner backing for the postponement. In March, he planned to have homeowners, the chamber, and county officials behind it.

Spahn does not leave the opinions of officials to chance. He meets with them before plans are drawn and gets their input. He finds out what commercial features they like, dislike. He wants to make sure the development conforms to their desires before he presents it.

This is the plan Spahn presents to the client/builder. Spahn estimates he will spend 200 hours on the case in the next six months. Will the client commit? And, most important, will he listen to Spahn? If the answer is yes to those questions, Spahn works the project. If it is no, he walks away. He is not interested in representing losers.

CASE/SITUATION/ELECTRICAL ENGINEERING

Larry Nickels generates income from two kinds of clients: manufacturers and users. Manufacturers are the most lucrative client base. Seventy-five percent of Nickels's business emanates from them.

Nickels is an expert on power conversion and AC and DC motor drives are throughout industry. Manufacturers know his reputation and they call him for bids on designs. A typical call finds a manufacturer asking him to prepare a proposal for the design of a voltage and current regulator.

The caller will ask for Nickels's firm to include performance specifications of the regulator, the response time in milliseconds, and the cost to have it packaged into a printed circuit board.

The manufacturer will ask for delivery time as well. Nickels sends the proposal. Sometimes he may wait two to three months for an answer. Or he may be called within a few days. Either way, Nickels follows up. He will call the manufacturer to determine if he received the proposal and if there are questions.

The reason for the delay is that manufacturers change their minds frequently. If Nickels is told to go ahead with the project, there is either a purchase order or confirming letter sent to him. There are no other contracts/agreements involved. Projects for manufacturers can last five to six months.

From the user point of view, Nickels's services come into play when there is an equipment problem. The time frame is critical. They will call and ask if he can service a particular piece of equipment. If he can, they will want service within 24 hours. And Nickels has a man there within that period.

The user pays airfare, expenses, and per diem ($24 per day). The daily rate will be somewhere between $500 and $600 for Nickels's man.

CASE/SITUATION/INVESTMENT ADVISOR

Arnold Van Den Berg is in a profession that generates a variety of clients—and questions.

Everyone who comes through his office is from a referral. Some are cautious. They are not sure. They will sit with Van Den Berg and pick his brain. They want to know his philosophy on investment, what he thinks of stocks, bonds, the economy, inflation, the future. Why has he chosen to keep his investments liquid?

Others are far from cautious. Van Den Berg recalls the occasion when a prospective client walked in and asked if the consultant could handle his funds. He asked Van Den Berg if $300,000 would be sufficient to open the portfolio. Van Den Berg tried to explain his philosophy and how money management worked. The client stopped him, said he did not want to be discourteous, but he had a golf game he did not want to miss. Would Van Den Berg just take the $300,000 and explain the operation later?

Whether they are hesitant or anxious, Van Den Berg does not have to sell them. They are already sold. That's why they are in his office. That does not mean Van Den Berg sits there and takes their money. He is anxious to find out how significant the money in their portfolio is in relationship to their total financial picture.

How important are the funds? For someone who has $10 million, a portfolio with $250,000 may not be significant. But, for a person who has $500,000 in a portfolio and it represents his life savings, it can be significant. It may also determine Van Den Berg's investment strategy, that is, should he be conservative or not.

There are times when he turns down clients. Recently, a business-person who owned a company that was worth $10 million walked into his office. He had $200,000 cash of the company's money that he wanted Van Den Berg to handle.

Van Den Berg suggested the businessperson forget the portfolio and keep the money in the business, where it might be needed. Why invest cash and then have to borrow money if you run into a cash crunch?

From the day an investment advisor takes over a portfolio he is responsible for the holdings. There are two things that can be done. The consultant can sell everything and start over or he can hold onto it. Van Den Berg chooses the latter technique. He feels he should analyze the holdings first and hold what might be good.

This can create additional work. A client may have 300 shares in a stock that Van Den Berg's firm isn't following. He will not automatically sell it. He will research the stock first to determine if it is worth holding. His firm has clients invested in numerous stocks and it follows many more.

Money managers deal with numbers but it is actually a people business. Clients with more money are more realistic. They don't, according to Van Den Berg, expect their money to double overnight. They know there are ups and downs. It is the client with the lower-value portfolio who will call and question.

CHAPTER 8

CONTRACTS AND PROPOSALS

Proposals, contracts, and agreements can be deceptive. Consultants spend countless hours introducing and selling their services to potential clients. Ultimately, decisions are usually made on the basis of a proposal and contract.

Proposals can win—or lose—a job for a consultant. There are certain elements they should contain and others that they should not. For example, the good proposal addresses the client's needs. It does not just talk about previous experience but, rather, how the current problem can be solved.

At the same time, a consultant does not want to give "the store away" with a proposal. In other words, don't give the client a step-by-step set of instructions on how to solve the problem. If you do, you may find the potential client saying "thank you," keeping your proposal, and turning it over to another firm.

How do you know which firms will be honest and which will not? You don't. After awhile in business you get a "gut feel," explains Jack

Spahn. But, realistically, there will always be risk when preparing a proposal.

The 10 professionals in this book have been preparing proposals for years. They have supplied several as illustrations of the type of preparation and wording that goes into a proposal for a potential account.

They have also been preparing contracts, giving speeches, writing and reprinting articles and even preparing news releases and biographies. All of these materials are used to sell the consultant's services. They have graciously provided samples of each which you will find in this chapter.

Contracts should be simple and to the point. Avoid "legalese," says attorney Hugh Holbert. His standard letter of agreement follows. Most other consultants use a similar approach.

HUGH W. HOLBERT
A Professional Corporation
171 E. Thousand Oaks Boulevard
Suite 205
Thousand Oaks, California 91360
(805) 497-7088

FEE AGREEMENT

I understand that your fee for professional services is $150.00 per hour and that your minimum fee for any service rendered, including each telephone conversation, is $30.00.

I understand that I will be billed monthly for services rendered and costs advanced on my behalf during the month. I understand that your statement must be paid in full within thirty (30) days of your billing date. In the event that I fail to pay the balance of my account in full when due, I further understand that I will incur a monthly administrative charge of 2% of the unpaid balance or $5.00, whichever is greater, and that you reserve the right to withhold rendering additional services until my account is current.

I understand that a retainer or security for payment of your fees will be required prior to commencement of services beyond the initial interview where the services to be rendered are estimated to exceed $500.00.

I understand that you may find it necessary to increase your hourly rates and that any such increase will apply to my case. I will, however, be notified at least sixty (60) days in advance of such change and will, at that time, have the option to retain other counsel.

I understand that by signing this Agreement I accept direct personal responsibility for all legal fees and costs billed to my account regardless of the fact that a third party may ultimately agree or be ordered to pay some portion of said fees and costs. I agree to pay reasonable attorney's fees and costs in the event that litigation becomes necessary to collect any amounts pursuant to this Agreement.

I am aware that you have the right to associate any other attorney of your choice in the handling of my legal matter at your discretion. I further understand that your firm does not render advice pertaining to state or federal taxation and that you recommend only that such advice be obtained from a Certified Public Accountant.

I understand that any modification of this Agreement must be in writing.

DATED: _____

                                                              SIGNATURE

FIGURE 1. Fee agreement.

NEW CLIENT INFORMATION

Name of Client: _____

Home Address: (Street) _____

(City) _____ (Zip) _____ Own__ Rent__

Soc. Sec. # _____ Driver's License # _____

Phone: Residence ( ) _____ Business ( ) _____

Occupation: _____

Employer: _____

Work Address: (Street) _____

(City) _____ (Zip) _____

Name of Spouse: _____

Home Address: (Street) _____

(City) _____ (Zip) _____

Phone: Residence ( ) _____ Business ( ) _____

Occupation: _____

Employer: _____

Work Address: (Street) _____

(City) _____ (Zip) _____

For Dissolutions The Following Information Is Required:

Date of Marriage: _____ Date of Separation: _____

Place of Marriage: (City) _____ (State) ___

Children:

Name	Sex	Date of Birth
_____	_____	_____
_____	_____	_____
_____	_____	_____
_____	_____	_____

FIGURE 1. Continued.

Hank Zdonek has three different agreements that he provides to potential clients. The first confirms the client's retaining of Zdonek's firm as an independent consultant who will handle the company's accounting.

The second allows for a review of the corporation's various statements. Notice the explanation of the review procedure that the document provides.

The third agreement spells out terms and objectives of another short-term arrangement (the second agreement is a short-term arrangement as well). Interestingly, all three of these agreements have language that protects the accountant from potential liability should the CPA firm be given falsified information.

Zdonek & Lieb
ACCOUNTANCY CORPORATION

Date

Dear Mr. _____:

This letter is to confirm the arrangements we discussed for you retaining our firm as the independent certified public accountants for The Company. As we informed you, our acceptance of this engagement is subject to the results of our firm's investigatory and approval procedures.

We will examine the consolidated balance sheet of The Company, and subsidiaries as at December 31, 19__, and the related statements of income, retained earnings, and changes in financial position for the year then ended. Our examination will be in accordance with generally accepted auditing standards and will include such tests of the accounting records and such other auditing procedures as we consider necessary in the circumstances. Our examination will be for the purpose of expressing an opinion on the consolidated balance sheet as at December 31, 19__, and on the related statements of income, retained earnings, and changes in financial position for the year then ended. Since we were not the Company's auditors for the previous year, we will have to extend our procedures to satisy ourselves as to the opening balances for the current year, and the consistency of application of accounting principles and methods in the current year with those of the preceding year.

We are not considering a detailed examination of all transactions nor do we expect that we will necessarily discover fraud, should any exist. We will, however, inform you of findings that appear to be unusual or abnormal.

Your accounting department personnel will assist us to the extent practical in completing our engagement. They will provide us with the detailed trial balances and supporting schedules we deem necessary. A list of such schedules will be furnished you shortly after we begin the engagement.

25500 Hawthorne Boulevard / Torrance, CA 90505-6828 / (213) 540-8200 / 378-9911, (714) 638-2430

FIGURE 2.   Zdonek & Lieb's confirmation of the retention of an independent consultant.

We will also be available to assist you, either in person or by telephone, with accounting, business or tax problems, and with planning. We will prepare the 19__ Federal and State income tax returns for The Company, and its subsidiaries.

Since this is our first examination of The Company, you requested that we review the Company's accounting system and procedures in detail and submit a separate report, including our evaluation, comments and recommendations. We will also review copies of the Company's income tax returns for the preceding three years and submit to you any comments we feel appropriate.

Fees for these services are at our standard rates and will be billed to you, plus out-of-pocket costs, monthly. These invoices are payable on presentation.

If this letter correctly expresses your understanding, please sign the enclosed copy where indicated and return it to us.

Thank you for the confidence you have placed in us by engaging us as your independent certified public accountants. We hope this proves to be the beginning of a long and mutually beneficial association.

Sincerely,

H. Zdonek

HZ:bjp

APPROVED:

By: _____

Date: _____

Zdonek & Lieb Accountancy Corporation

FIGURE 2. Continued.

ACCOUNTANCY CORPORATION

                                                    Date

Dear Mr._____ :

    This letter will confirm our understanding of the nature
and limitations of the accounting and review services we are
to render to **The Corporation** with your needs   as   previously
discussed.

    Our engagement will consist of the following services:

    1) We will review the balance sheet of **The
    Corporation** as of June 30, 19__ and the related
    statements of income, retained earnings, and changes
    in financial position for the year then ended, in
    accordance with standards established by the
    American Institute of Certified Public Accountants.
    We will not perform an audit of such financial
    statements, the objective of which is the
    expression of an opinion regarding the financial
    statements taken as a whole and, accordingly,
    we will not express such an opinion on them. Our
    report on the financial statements is presently
    expected to read as follows:

        We have reviewed the accompanying balance
        sheet of **The Corporation** as of
        June 30, 19__, and the related statements of
        income, retained earnings, and changes in

FIGURE 3.   Zdonek & Lieb's agreement regarding review of a corporation's various statements.

174

financial position for the year then ended,
in accordance with standards established
by the American Institute of Certified
Public Accountants. All information
included in these financial statements
is the representation of the management
of **The Corporation**

A review consists principally of inquiries
of company personnel and analytical
procedures applied to financial data. It
is substantially less in scope than an
examination in accordance with generally
accepted auditing standards, the objective
of which is the expression of an opinion
regarding the financial statements taken as
a whole. Accordingly, we do not express such
opinion.

Based on our review, we are not aware of any
material modifications that should be made
to the accompanying financial statements in
order for them to be in conformity with
generally accepted accounting principles.

If, for any reason, we are unable to complete our
review of your financial statements, we will not
issue a report on such statements as a result of
this engagement.

2. We will provide your chief accountant with such
consultation on accounting matters as he may require
in adjusting and closing the books of account and in
drafting financial statements for our review. Your
chief accountant also will provide us with a detailed
trial balance and any supporting schedules we require.

3. We will also prepare the federal and California
income tax returns for **The Corporation** for
the fiscal year ended June 30, 19___.

Our engagement cannot be relied upon to disclose errors,
irregularities, or illegal acts, including fraud or
defalcations, that may exist. However, we will inform you
of any such matters that come to our attention.

Zdonek & Lieb Accountancy Corporation

FIGURE 3. Continued.

Our fees for these services will be based on our regular hourly rates and we will bill you monthly as work progresses. It is understood that the fee for our services will not exceed $0,000. Our invoices are due and payable upon presentation.

If these arrangements meet with your understanding and approval, please sign the duplicate copy of this letter in the space provided and return it to us.

Yours very truly,

H. Zdonek

HZ:lm

Encls. a/s

APPROVED:

THE CORPORATION

By:_____

Date:_____

FIGURE 3. Continued.

Date

Dear Mr. _____ :

This letter is to confirm our understanding of the terms and objectives of our engagement and the nature and limitations of the services we will provide.

We will perform the following services:

1. We will compile, from information you provide, the annual balance sheet and related statements of income, retained earnings, and changes in financial position of Company for the year 19 __. We will not audit or review the financial statements. Our report on the annual financial statements of Company is presently expected to read as follows:

    We have compiled the accompanying balance sheet of Company as of December 31, 19 __, and the related statements of income, retained earnings, and changes in financial position for the year then ended, in accordance with standards established by the American Institute of Certified Public Accountants.

    A compilation is limited to presenting in the form of financial statements information that is the representation of management. We have not audited or reviewed the accompanying financial statements and, accordingly, do not express an opinion or any other form of assurance on them.

25500 Hawthorne Boulevard / Torrance, CA 90505-6828 / (213) 540-8200/378-9911, (714) 638-2430

FIGURE 4. Zdonek & Lieb's standard agreement detailing duties and responsibilities.

Our engagement cannot be relied upon to disclose errors, irregularities, or illegal acts, including fraud or defalcations, that may exist; however, we will inform you of any such matters that come to our attention.

Our fees for these services will be computed at our standard hourly rates. Billings will be submitted monthly and are payable when due.

We would be pleased to discuss this letter with you at any time. If the foregoing is in accordance with your understanding, please sign the copy of this letter in the space provided and return it to us.

Sincerely,

H. Zdonek

HZ:bjp

APPROVED:

Company

_____
President

_____
Date

Zdonek & Lieb Accountancy Corporation
_____

FIGURE 4. Continued.

Ed Pearson has a standard agreement that details his duties and responsibilities. Notice how Pearson spells out hourly fees and payment schedules.

It's interesting to compare Pearson's agreement with one supplied by a client with whom he has worked. Compare what the client expects and how Pearson's contract—which is a combination contract/-proposal—answers those needs.

AGREEMENT BETWEEN

DEVELOPER AND ENGINEER FOR PROFESSIONAL SERVICES

THIS AGREEMENT, made and entered into this   day of
      , 19 , by and between
          hereinafter referred to as the "DEVELOPER",and
E. 1. PEARSON & ASSOCIATES, INC., hereafter referred to as
the "Engineer":

WITNESSETH

WHEREAS, the Developer proposes to develop a parcel of land
for single family residential purposes know as Tentative Tract
Number 32994, in the County of Los Angeles, located northerly of
                                        and comprising
approximately two hundred thirty-one acres;

WHEREAS, the Developer desires to engage the Engineer to
perform certain engineering services pertinent to above
development;

NOW, THEREFORE, in consideration of the premises and mutual
benefits which will accrue to the parties hereby in carrying out
the terms of this Agreement, it is mutually understood and agreed
as follows:
1. The engineer agree to furnish and perform the various
professional services, pertinent to above-named development
specifically outlined as follows:
   A. Prepare feasibility studies, tentative map, Environmental
       Impact Report and process for approval.
   B. Office Work
       1. Prepare formal tract maps and expedite to record
           (not to exceed three units).
       2. Prepare street and storm drain plans and quantities
           for bidding and final pay.
       3. Prepare sanitary sewer plans and quantities for
           bidding and final pay.
       4. Prepare water plans (preliminary design by water
           district not included).
       5. Prepare rough grading plan and quantities for bidding
           and final pay and prepare erosion control plan if
           winter grading contemplated.
       6. Provide engineering supervision and coordination to
           to accomplish recordation and construction of project.
   C. Field Work
       1. Furnish boundary and topographic survey.

FIGURE 5. Agreement between developer and engineer for professional services.

2. Furnish one (1) set of rough grade stakes and one (1) of fine grade (blue tops) stakes (vertical only, two° (2) per pad.
3. Furnish one (1) set of stakes for defining lot lines for building construction.
4. Furnish one (1) set of stakes for sanitary sewer construction.
5. Furnish one (1) set of stakes for storm drain construction.
6. Furnish one (1) set of stakes for curb construction (utilities) to be constructed from curb location.
7. Furnish one (1) set of final lot stakes, i.e. chisel cross on curb and rear property corner.
8. Furnish survey for centerline of street survey monuments and ties.

NOTE: Items B and C do not include revisions to plans and re-staking, which are a result of requirements of the Developer and or/its representatives subsequent to submission of said plans for first review by the County of Los Angeles, unless said revisions are required by the County of Los Angeles, nor do they include any prints, (including photographic enlargements and reductions) or fees.

II. The Engineer will notify the Developer ahead to time as to any conferences held between the Engineer and the governing body, so that the Developerr may attend.

III. A. The Developer or his authorized representative only shall notify the Engineer 48 hours in advance for field crews on Item I.C, and the Engineer agrees to furnish said field crews at the end of said 48 hours notification. The Developer agrees that the site shall be in a condition to permit staking without undue delay and in the event staking may not proceed due to site conditions, Developer shall pay for four (4) hours of survey, in accordance with Hourly Schedule herein.

B. The Engineer shall at all times carry, on all operations hereunder, Workmen's Compensation Insurance, Public Liability and Property Damage Insurance, and Automotive Public Liability and Property Damage Insurance.

C. Engineer shall pay and discharge and indemnify Owner and Developer against any and all liens and charges of every type, nature, kind or description which may at any time be filed or claimed against the real property of the Developer, or any portion

FIGURE 5. Continued.

181

thereof, as a consequence, direct or indirect, of
any act or omission of Engineer, his agents, servants,
and employees, except as set forth in this agreement.
D. The Developer agrees to pay the Engineer as compensation
for the above-named professional services, fees based
on the folowing schedules:

PAYMENT SCHEDULES

The following fees are to be paid as work is completed, due and
payable upon submission of invoices by Engineer.

CONTRACT SCHEDULES

Phase I - A. PRELIMINARY
 A fixed fee of   to be paid as work is completed.
Phase I - B. Office Work
 A fixed fee of $102,725.00 to be paid as work is
 completed, as follows:

Item B - 1.	$ 9,875.00
Item B - 2.	$ 36,210.00
Item B - 3.	$ 7,265.00
Item B - 4.	$ 5,485.00
Item B - 5.	$ 24,140.00
Item B - 6.	$ 19,750.00

Total Office Work $102,725.00

Phase I - C. Field Work
 A fixed fee of $ 137,445.00 to be paid as work is
 completed, seperated as follows:

Item C - 1.	$ 9,620.00
Item C - 2.	$ 41,230.00
Item C - 3.	$ 10,995.00
Item C - 4.	$ 11,260.00
Item C - 5.	$ 14,170.00
Item C - 6.	$ 27,370.00
Item C - 7.	$ 10,995.00
Item C - 8.	$ 10,805.00
Total field work	$137,445.00

Phase A.	$102,725.00
Phase B.	$137,445.00
Grand Total Contract	

FIGURE 5. Continued.

HOURLY SCHEDULE

Professional Consultation (Hearings) . . . . . . $ 55.00 per hour
Principales . . . . $ 35.00 per hour
Supervision, Design and Other office work . . . $ 29.00 per hour
3- Man Survey Party and Equipment . . . . $ 75.00 per hour

IV. Failure to meet any payment after an elapse of sixty days (60) from stipulated time as set forth in above schedules shall be sufficient cause for the Engineer to terminate this Agreement and demand payment based upon the work completed. Additional charges at the rate of 1% per month will be charged on all fees and invoices which are over sixty (60) days past due.

V. In the event of any increase of standard billing rates (Hourly Schedule) due to the granting of wage increases and/or other employee benefits, due to terms of any labor agreement during the lifetime of the Agreement, such increase shall be adjusted percentage-wise to above payment schedules. Contract Schedule and Hourly Schedule include all such increases up to August 1, 1977.

VI. In the event that any of the aforesaid stakes are removed by accident or otherwise, the cost of restaking shall be paid under Hourly Schedule as extra work. Critical survey markers shall be so marked as to be readily identifiable to the contractor.

VII. In the event all or any portion of the work performed, prepared or partially performed, or partially prepared by the Engineer be temporarily suspended, Developer shall pay in accordance with Contract Schedule for work performed to date. If abandoned, the Developer shall pay the Engineer on an Hourly Schedule.

VIII. The Developer shall pay the costs of all fees, permits, bond premiums, blueprints and reproductions, and all other charges not specifically covered by the terms of this Agreement. Engineer will provide all materials and equipment normally required in the prosecution of his work, including monuments and stakes.

IX. The Engineer and the Developer each binds himself, his partners, successors, executors, administrators and assigns, to the other party to this Agreement. Except as above, neither party shall assign, sublet or transfer his interest in this Agreement without the written consent of the other party hereto.

X. E.L. PEARSON & ASSOCIATES, INC., may retain all plans, working drawings, calculations and other papers as partial security for payment hereunder.

XI. Cost estimates are made in good faith and according to the best information available to engineers and surveyors. However, estimates which are made for the convenience of client, and estimates which are made for presentation to public bodies,

FIGURE 5. Continued.

whether or not in writing, are not intended to be relied upon by the client on predicting construction costs.

XII. Charges for items of work not specifically set forth in Item I will be charged in accordance with Hourly Schedule as extra work and are not to be included in Contract Schedule.

XIII. The Engineer agrees to begin work requested by the Developer as soon as reasonably possible, and to proceed with diligence to completion of said work. In the event the Engineer fails to diligently prosecute said work in accordance with accepted engineering standards the Developer, upon written notice to the Engineer, may cancel this contract. In the event of cancellation, the Developer shall pay the Engineer in accordance with Contract Schedule for percentage of work completed.

XIV. Any grace periods, or waiver of any terms of this Agreement, granted by Engineer, shall not constitute a waiver of future performance by Developer as to timely payment, or otherwise.

XV. In the event any litigation shall arise between Developer and Engineer involving any matter covered by the terms of this contract, the judgement in such litigation shall include an award of attorney's fees and Court costs to the prevailing party. The liability assumed by the Engineer in his performance under this contract is limitwed to the amount of compensation paid for the professional services named herein.

IN WITNESS WHEREOF, the parties hereto have affixed their hands this   day of   , 19

                                        BY _____
            "DEVELOPER"
                                        BY_____

                E.L. PEARSON AND ASSOCIATES, INC.
                1555 W. Redondo Beach Blvd.
                Garden, California   90247

                                        BY_____
            "ENGINEER"
                                        BY_____

FIGURE 5. Continued.

Agreement Between Developer and Engineer

SECTION 1: ENGINEER AGREES to furnish and perform the various professional services hereinafter listed. Further it is the intent of this Agreement that a complete professional engineering job shall be done, and to that extent the scope of work is not necessarily limited to the services hereinafter listed:

OFFICE

1. Prepare preliminary land planning studies of property.
2. Attend meetings as required with DEVELOPER and the City of_____and other involved public agencies.
3. Prepare formal tract maps and perform all work required for recordation.
4. Prepare street improvement plans for construction purposes, effect cprrections, and obtain approval by the City of _____.
5. Prepare domestic water and sanitary sewer plans for construction purposes, effect corrections and obtain approval by the City
6. Prepare storm drain plans for construction purposes, effect corrections, and obtain approvals by the City of _____ and any other involved agencies.
7. Prepare rough grading plans and obtain approval of the City of _____.
8. Prepare 20-foot scale plot plan in accordance with the mylar system; prepare composite plot and grading plan; prepare 20-scale master utility plan.
9. Prepare sales map.
10. Perform necessary coordination work with utility companies.
11. Furnish three (3) sets of quantity and cost estimates:
    a. A preliminary estimate from tentative map.
    b. A preliminary estimate from unsigned plans.
    c. A final estimate from signed plans.
12. Prepare legal description and plat for each recorded unit.
13. Perform normal inspection of site improvements, required certifications and prepare "as-built" plans.

FIELDS

1. Prepare necessary grade sheets for inspectors, developers, etc.
2. Furnish one (1) set of stakes for rough grading of lots and streets.
3. Furnish one (1) set of "blue top" stakes for finish grading as required.
4. After the rough grading has been completed, ENGINEER

FIGURE 6. Civil engineering contract.

shall verify that streets, pads, slopes, etc., have been graded in accordance with the approved plans. It shall be the responsibility of the grading contractor to protect the stakes until all verification work has been completed.

5. Furnish one (1) of stakes for sanitary sewer construction.
6. Furnish one (1) set of stakes for storm drain construction, drainage terraces and other drainage facilities as shown on the approved plans.
7. Furnish one (1) set of stakes defining building locations.
8. Furnish one (1) set of stakes for underground electrical and telephone utilities.
9. Furnish one (1) set of stakes for curb and gutter construction, cross gutters and any other improvements requird to complete the street construction.
10. After completion of improvements and landscaping, set final lot corners, tract boundary monuments, street centerline monuments and other survey controls as shown on the record map and required by the County of _____ and City of _____.
11. Prepare tie notes for street centerline monuments and furnish copies to the County of _____.
12. Prepare "as built" plans.

SECTION 2: DEVELOPER AGREES to pay ENGINEER as compensation for the above-named professional services as set forth in Section 1 a fee of:

$_____ per dwelling unit.

SECTION 3: THE DEVELOPER AGREES to pay ENGINEER interim compensation for work performed on the "Percentage-of-compensation" method. The attached Schedule "A" per unit cost estimate, based on an estimated _____ units, shall be used as a guide in determining the percentage of work completed by ENGINEER. The contract shall be adjusted for any changes in the number or recorded residential units. Progress billings will be made monthly by ENGINEER on forms supplied by DEVELOPER.

SECTION 4: Revisions, variances or change orders needed to meet the requirements of the various jurisdictional agencies or good engineering practices, shall not be deemed extra work. Only revisions, variances of change orders requested by DEVELOPER after completion of the plans to the satisfaction of said jurisdictional agencies, legal descriptions not called for in the scope of the work, and plans for pumping stations, bridges and similar construction, shall be considered extra work. It shall be

FIGURE 6. Continued.

the responsibility of ENGINEER to work with DEVELOPER and apprise
him of solutions to engineering problenms and the general details,
approach or technique to be used in preparing final improvement
plans. In any event, all orders for extra work shall be
authorized in writing by DEVELOPER and acknowledged by ENGINEER.
With respect to extra work authorized by DEVELOPER as provided
above, ENGINEER shall be entitled to charge for his services the
following rates:

Office Technical Personnel	$ _____	per hour
Three (3) Man Survey Party	$_____	per hour
Two (2) Man Party	$_____	per hour

SECTION 5: On August 1, 1984, and as appropriate thereafter,
the "per unit fee" as set forth in Section 2 and the rate for
"extra work" as set forth in Section 4 shall be increased by
eighty percent (80%) of the percentage of wage and/or other
employee benefits granted surveyors under the Master Agreement
between the California Council of Civil Engineers and Land
Surveyors and the International Union of Operating Engineers Local
No. 12, AFL-CIO. These increases shall apply only to the
furnished work as of the date of increase.

SECTION 6: ENGINEER shall coordinate the planning of all
structures, utilities and other facilities which will affect the
tract and the subdivision development, including existing as well
as proposed facilities and regardless of whether plans for said
facilities are prepared by ENGINEER of third parties.

SECTION 7: All sketches, tracings, drawings, computations,
details and other original documents and plans are and shall
become and/or required to be filed with a governmental agency and
become public property, in which case ENGINEER is to furnish
duplicates to DEVELOPER upon its request.

SECTION 8: DEVELOPER reserves the right to terminate this
Agreement upon thirty (30) days written notice to ENGINEER. In
such event, for completed stages of the work, ENGINEER shall
receive that percentage of the fee set forth in the Schedule "A";
and in the case of partially completed stage of work, ENGINEER
shall receive an appropriately prorated percentage of the fee.

SECTION 9: DEVELOPER shall pay the cost of all fees, permits,
bond premium and title company charges not specifically covered by
the terms of this Agreement. All blueprinting and Xerox costs
will be included in the per unit cost as outlined in Schedule "A"
attached hereto.

FIGURE 6. Continued.

SECTION 10: ENGINEER and DEVELOPER each binds himself, his partners, executors and administrators of such other party in respect to all covenants of this Agreement. Neither party shall assign, sublet, or transfer his interest in this Agreement without the written consent of the other party hereto.

SECTION 11: Progress billings will be made monthly by the ENGINEER in accordance with rates set forth in Section 3 and Section 4. DEVELOPER will pay these billing within ten (10) days after receipt.

ENGINEER: DEVELOPER:

_____   _____

BY:_____   BY:_____

FIGURE 6. Continued.

AGREEMENT BETWEEN DEVELOPER AND ENGINEER

SCHEDULE "A"
TOWNHOUSE PROJECT

OFFICE
1. Quantity and Preliminary Cost Estimate $_____
2. Preparation of 20-scale Plot Plan $_____
3. Praparation of Composite and Grading Plan $_____
4. Preparation of 20-scale Master Utility Plan $_____
5. Preparation of 20-scale Water and Sewer Plan $_____
6. Preparation of Rough Grading Plan $_____
7. Preparation of Street Improvement Plan $_____
8. Preparation of final Quantity and Cost $_____
   Estimate
9. Blueprinting and Xeroxing $_____

                              Subtotal $_____

FIELD
1. Rough Grade Staking $_____
2. Construction Corner Staking $_____
3. Curbs and Alley Cutter Staking $_____
4. Sewer Staking $_____
5. Undergroud Electrical Staking $_____
6. Storm Drain Staking $_____
7. Block Wall Staking $_____
8. Water Line Staking $_____

                              Subtotal $_____

                              GRANDTOTAL $_____

FIGURE 6. Continued.

Pearson is not the only one who combines a contract with a proposal. Joseph Izzo's proposals are structured to be a combination of both as well. They range from two-page proposal/agreements to detailed documents that spell out time frames and goals.

Izzo usually includes a rate schedule and a figure that the proposed job will not exceed. His approach is the same, whether he is writing a proposal for a $15,000 or $100,000 job.

Providing a timetable for the client is important, especially where a job is going to run for several months. During a lengthy project, consultants may be totally involved, but they sometimes forget that the results—the thing the client will ultimately judge them upon—may not be evident for months.

Therefore it is important to spell out various stages of the project in a proposal and communicate with the client on a regular basis. Notice Izzo's "Project Plan" on the last page of the following proposal.

The JIA Management Group, Inc.

December 7, 1984

Dear

Based on previous discussions with you and _____ the following
outlines our approach for assisting the _____ Company in
migrating the computing activities of the _____ Corporation into
the _____ computer center. The JIA Management Group will
accomplish this in two phases:

   Phase I - Review Current Environment and Migration Plan

   Phase II - Direction of the West Coast Computer Facility in
              Achieving the Migration Goals

This letter proposal only addresses Phase I. The approach and
degree of involvement if JIA related to Phase II will be determined at the conclusion of the Phase I activity. The review of
the current environment and migration plan will be designed to
accomplish the following objectives:

   * Gain an understanding of existing environments at both
     _____ and _____ computer centers

   * Review the overall migration plan to determine the role
     that _____ can best perform in achieving migration
     objectives

   * Identify areas of vulnerability that may exist related
     to the _____ computer center close-down or the
     migration process

   * Develop an implementation for Phase II

The accomplishment of the above will require review of current
activities, plans, and computer centers in _____ and in
_____. The cost of Phase I will not exceed $15,000 in
professional services, and will be billed per the attached rate
schedule. Additional costs for travel, living and report preparation will be billed as accrued.

1299 OCEAN AVENUE • SUITE 333 • SANTA MONICA, CALIFORNIA 90401 • (213) 451-3041

FIGURE 7.   Joseph Izzo's agreement dated December 7, 1983.

Page Two

We look forward to working with you and the _____ Company on this important endeavor.

                              Sincerely,

                              Joseph E. Izzo
                              President

JEI/bj
Attachment

cc:

Accepted:

_____

_____
Date

                    JIA PROFESSIONAL SERVICES

                         RATE SCHEDULE

        Managing Partner   _____ per hour

        Managing Principal   _____ per hour

        Principal Consultant   _____ per hour

        Consultant   _____ per hour

                    FIGURE 7. Continued.

The JIA Management Group, Inc.

April 7, 1984

Senior Vice President, Finance
and Administration

Dear

To evaluate the effectiveness of_____ MIS group, The JIA
Management Group, Inc. will peform the tasks listed below. The
objectives of the study are to:

* Assess the capability of the MIS group to support the
  business, both for the short-term and for the next several
  years. This is critical because of rapid business growth.

* Determine ways of improving communication between MIS
  and executive and user management to enhance the effectiveness of directing and controlling the MIS function at

<u>Approach</u>

After a brief orientation to acquaint study team memeber with the
operations and system environment, these activities will be under-
taken:

* <u>Interview the ten to twelve key users of MIS services</u> in
  order to understand their perception of the quality of
  service being delivered.

* <u>Conduct an MIS administration review</u> to include planning
  and budgeting processes, project approval and priority
  assignmemt procedures, use of standards and product quality
  reviews, and management reporting.

* <u>Conduct an MIS operations review</u> to examine service
  delivery; problem identification, tracking, and resolu-
  tion; production scheduling; library controls; production
  documentation and change control procedures; computer
  utilization, performance, capacity analysis and reporting.

1299 OCEAN AVENUE ● SUITE 333 ● SANTA MONICA, CALIFORNIA 90401 ● (213) 451-3041

FIGURE 8. Joseph Izzo agreement dated April 7, 1984.

* Perform communication network performance analysis,
  including system availability, response time, network
  monitoring capability, growth plans, and use of available hardware and software tools to enhance network
  performance.

* Perform a systems and programming review, encompass
  staff capability, performance, turnover, and compensation; project management processes, and workload
  management; use of standard system development methods;
  use of productivity tools; and the quality of installed
  applications.

* Assess factors which are causing difficulties in MIS's
  ability to support the business and perform to expecta-
  tions. These may include:

  - Communication with senior management
  - Management of the MIS resource
  - Organization of the MIS function
  - Staff quality and quantity
  - Equipment

* Identify short-term actions which should be taken to
  improve communication between MIS and executive and user
  management, and improve the quality of direction given
  to MIS.

* Develop a one year plan to address network performance,
  organization, procedures, and management control issues.

* Prepare and present a management report of findings and
  recommendations.

Study Plan and Cost

Project activities and their duration are shown on the following
chart. The estimated charge for professional services is $55,000.
There will be additional charges for any travel, living, and document preparation. Charges will be billed monthly.

FIGURE 8. Continued.

Page Three

We look forward to working with _____ on this assignment.

                              Sincerely,

                              Joseph E. Izzo
                              President

JEI/bi

Approved:_____

Date: _____

MIS REVIEW - PROJECT PLAN

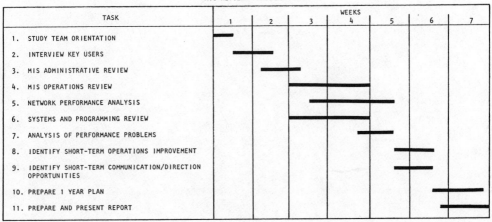

FIGURE 8. Continued.

In Izzo's third agreement, he refers to a discussion held with the client. At this meeting the duties, responsibilities, and fees were agreed upon before the proposal was ever put in writing.

This agreement is for a much larger sum ($120,000) than any of the previous two proposals. Izzo spent numerous hours researching the client's problem before the April 19 "conversation" ever took place.

This proposal illustrates the importance of knowing what the client needs before putting anything in writing. A boilerplate approach does not work for the successful consultant.

The JIA Management Group, Inc.

April 30, 1984

Dear

Based on our discussion of April 19, 1984, JIA submits the following proposal to assist _____ in developing an Office Automation/Business Data Service Strategy and Long-Range Plan. JIA proposes to work with the established _____ Steering Committee and its members in accomplishing the above goal.

The objectives of the plan are to:

* Identify and document the office automation and business data system needs of the _____ Group

* Determine the impact of the LOMM architecture on these needs, and identify the items that will be developed and supported by _____

* Develop a long-term office automation/business data services strategy and plan to support _____ current and future business requirements. This will include a strategy and plan for the following:

    - Business Applications
    - Office Automation Applications
    - Business Data Services Organization
    - Computer Hardware & Software

  The plan will also identify personnel resource requirements, costs, of the program, and the financial impact on _____ in the near-term, as well as over the long-term.

The approach recommended for the study was identified during our previous discussions and JIA's presentation to you on April 18, 1984 (Attachment I). The key ingredient in that presentation was a description of the proposed working relationship between JIA and members of the Committee and their staff: JIA 's role in the project is to assist the Committee in developing the future

1299 OCEAN AVENUE • SUITE 333 • SANTA MONICA, CALIFORNIA 90401 • (213) 451-3041

FIGURE 9. Office automation/business data services strategy and long-range plan proposal (April 18, 1984)

Page Two

strategy, not to develop a JIA recommended strategy for _____
which will then be presented to the Committee.

The implication of this approach is that the Committee members
must maintain significant involvement in all aspects of the study.
This does not necessarily imply a significant time commitment;
it does though require that the members provide the project with
guidance and ideas. A key element in this is the "three-day
strategy session" where the fundamental _____ office automa-
tion/business date services strategy will emerge and be agreed to.

Attachment II identifies study plan activities and schedule. We
estimate the effort to take approximately eleven weeks. Two and
a quarter JIA staff members will be involved in the study. The
schedule was developed assuming the availability of the Committee
members and their staff, including the possible involvement of a
new ___ hire who will be included as part of the study team.

The estimated cost for professional services is $120,000 based
on the attached rate schedule (Attachment III). Expenses for
necessary travel, living and document preparation will be charged
as incurred. Invoices for professional services and expenses will
be billed at the end of each month. Payment is expected within
15 days after receipt of invoice.

We look forward to the opportunity to work with you and the Committee on this important engagement.

                    Sincerely,

                    Joseph E. Izzo
                    President

JEI/en

Attachments

Approved:_____

Date:_____

FIGURE 9. Continued.

Strategic Planning Process

Develop an overall strategic direction for the use of computers by in support of office automation and business data services

Identify an overall technical architecture which integrates computer hardware, software, data communications, and the emerging LOMM concept in support of developed strategy

Determine long- and short-range implementation plans including organization approach, manpower and hardware requirements, costs, and policies and procedures

Provide a framework for executive control over future data processing activities

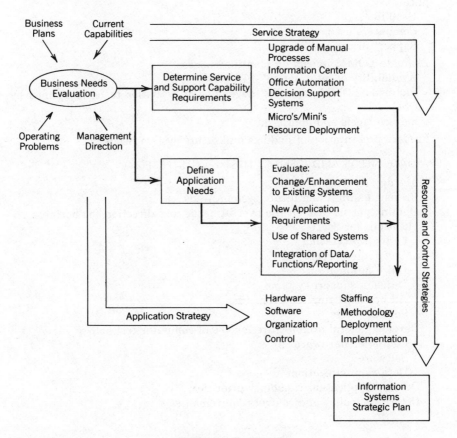

FIGURE 9. Continued.

199

IDENTIFY NEEDS

Establish system requirement—work with each of the task force business groupings to identify current and future business application needs:
Business management systems
Project management systems
Staff management systems
Pricing and estimating systems

Determine desired future capability requirements:
Office automation
Decision support systems
Ad hoc reporting requirements
Service levels

Review existing state of current business processes and computer-based applications:
Usability
Computers used
Support arrangements

Evaluate LOMM impact on identified needs:
Availability of information
Planned "LOMM common" development activities to be performed by OSG
Service levels and approach

Prepare presentation of findings and future system needs

EVALUATE NEEDS AND IDENTIFY FIRST LEVEL STRATEGY

Three day strategy session:
Present findings and future system needs
Obtain concurrence on the overall needs and direction for business applications for S&TG
Central processing
Distributed processing
Office automation
Decision support systems
Ad hoc reporting requirements
Service levels
Develop general architecture for use of computer technology
Computer hardware
Software
Data communications
Develop application/capability priorities
Determine policy and control requirements

FIGURE 9.   Continued.

ESTABLISH DETAIL COMPUTER HARDWARE/SOFTWARE STRATEGY

Computer processing
Personal computers
Word processing
Office automation
Decision support systems
Data communications systems

DEVELOP BUSINESS DATA SERVICES ORGANIZATION STRATEGY

Resource requirements
Reporting relationships
Deployment of personnel
Required skills and capabilities

FORMULATE CONTROL STRATEGY

Data processing executive policy committee
Decision control for requests for service
User responsibilities
Policies and procedures
Management visibility into data processing performance and resource utilization

DETERMINE IMPLEMENTATION STRATEGY

Near-term action plans
Long-term implementation plans
   Application development/acquisition
   Decision support systems
   Office automation
   Hardware/software/communications
   Resource requirements
   Financial impact

FIGURE 9. Continued.

Office Automation/Business Data Services Strategy

Study Plan

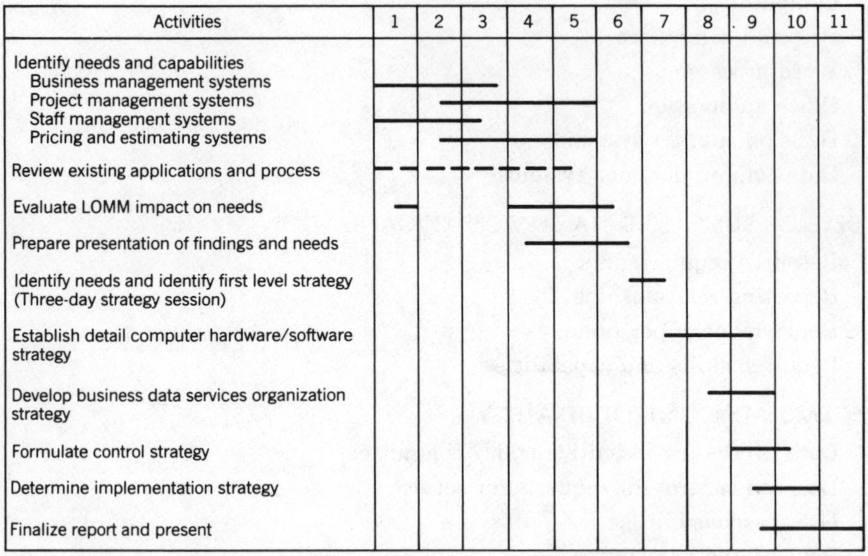

Activities
1
2
3
4
5
6
7
8
9
10
11
Identify needs and capabilities
Business management systems
Project management systems
Staff management systems
Pricing and estimating systems
Review existing applications and process
Evaluate LOMM impact on needs
Prepare presentation of findings and needs
Identify needs and identify first level strategy (Three-day strategy session)
Establish detail computer hardware/software strategy
Develop business data services organization strategy
Formulate control strategy
Determine implementation strategy
Finalize report and present

JIA Professional Services Rate Schedule

Managing partner	________	per hour
Managing principal	________	per hour
Principal consultant	________	per hour
Consultant	________	per hour

FIGURE 9. Continued.

Information Systems Implementation

	Months										
	1	2	3	4	5	6	7	8	9	10	11

Applications architecture
  Develop enterprise system requirements
  Develop departmental system requirements
  Develop detail office systems approach
  (PROFS, graphics, LAN, PC's, etc.)
  Develop interim needs
  Establish S&TG development requirements
  Develop two year plan
  Approval and implementation of plan
  Development, approval, and implementation
  of short-term preplan activities

Hardware/software
  Computer facilities selection
  Configuration selection
  Software selections
  Negotiation and acquisition
  Implementation and testing
  Develop long-term hardware plan
  Implement capabilities (office automation) plan
  Implement capacity planning and reporting

Present plan

Approved

Approved

Move to
two year plan

FIGURE 9. Continued.

Larry Nickels does more than service equipment. A good portion of his electrical engineering consulting practice is represented by design. In the following proposal, Nickels outlines what he is going to do and the monies involved. The company will usually respond verbally and then issue a purchase order. If Nickels does not hear from them within a reasonable amount of time (two to three weeks), he will call.

Subject: Proposal and Quotation for a New Line of Solid State Reduced
Voltage Starters

Dear

Attached is a proposal for the subject line of starters and options. The
proposal is based on our understanding of the submitted specifications,
, and meetings with key   people.
A meeting should be held after the proposal has been reviewed to resolve any
differences between   and NEI. Please note that the ambient temperature
range was changed and line voltage tolerances added to agree with the
existing   The values added are also consistent with
those of motor drive standards. The proposal also omits reference to UL
standards. NEI will design to any published U.L. standards, however the
prices quoted do not reflect any effort by NEI to obtain U.L. approval of
the starter line. Frequently, obtaining U.L. approval is a sole effort by
a manufacturer.

The proposal is arranged as follows:

 1.0 Power Circuit Packaging
 2.0 Electronics Packaging of Standard Starter Less the Firing Circuit
 3.0 180° Standard Firing Circuit
 4.0 Options
 5.0 System Testing at
 6.0 Acceleration and Plugging Printed Circuit Board for Existing
      General Motors Starter

The base pricing of all items except 6.0 is for functional design circuitry
only. Breadboard construction is included, as required, to check the operational capability of newly designed circuits. Included in the base price are
schematic sketches and Bills of Materials, using   part numbers where
applicable. Sufficient information will be provided for   to layout and
produce the printed circuit boards. Note the price of 6.0 includes this
information plus prototype PCB's (max. of 2) plus layout and silk screen
drawings.

FIGURE 10. Larry Nickels' agreement.

Each item, involving printed circuit boards, will have a price adder for furnishing the layout, silk screen drawings and PCB's as required to complete a starter. An advantage in having Nickels Engineering Inc. design the PCB's is that it will be accomplished as a fully tested complete board within the time frame of the scheduled project completion date. The PCB assemblies will be tested for circuit accuracy and functional performance. If required, the PCB's will be modified to correct for any deficiencies. The design and layout of PCB's can be time consuming and may add considerable time to the overall schedule if the work is accomplished after receiving the schematics and BOM's from NEI. We propose to integrate the design, layout, assembly and testing of the PCB's within the time frame of the schedule proposed for the project with the price adder option.

Quotations: The following is for the base price which includes schematic sketches, bills of material, test procedures and bread boards as required by NEI.

Item 1.0 - Power Circuit Packaging $

Item 2.0 - Electronics Packaging of Standard Starter $
           Less the Firing Circuit

Item 3.0 - 180° Standard Firing Circuit $

Item 4.1 thru 4.5 - All Options Except Power Factor $
           Control

Item 4.6 - Power Factor Control $

Item 5.0 - System Testing (Estimate 20 days) $

Item 6.0 - Acceleration and Plugging Printed Circuit $
           Board for Existing General Motors Starter

           Testing at   or   as required $ _____

           Total for all functions except system testing $

           Delivery 6 months after receipt of order.

Quotation for Adders: To provide prototype assembled printed circuit boards
           (using components as required and furnished by   ),
           layout drawings and silk screen drawings.

Item 1.0 - Snubber PCB's (if used) - quantity of 3 $

Item 2.0 - Power supply and accel. PCB plus backplane PCB $
           quantity of 1 each

Item 3.0 - 180° Firing PCB - quantity of 3 $

FIGURE 10. Continued.

```
Item 4.1 & 4.2 - Acceleration and P.S. PCB -                    $
                 quantity of 1 (if required)

Item 4.3 - Plugging PCB - quantity of 1                        $

Item 4.4 - Phase Failure and Phase Rev. PCB -                  $
           quantity of 1

Item 4.5 - Diagnostic Card - quantity of 1                    $

Item 4.6 - Power Factor PCB - quantity of 1                   $ _____
                    Total for all PCB's                       $
```

Delivery of total order, if placed with
circuits design order, is 8 months after
receipt of order.

I hope the attached proposal and the quotations meet with your approval.
If you have any questions regarding the subject, please contact me at your
convenience. We look forward to working with you on this project.

Sincerely,

L. E. Nickels, President
NICKELS ENGINEERING, INC.

LEN:pah
cc:

Encl.

FIGURE 10. Continued.

Izzo's firm provides clients with myriad brochures, however, he has also prepared a "company profile." Some consultants use the profile as background information for potential clients. It is a simple, factual document that states the firm's history, qualifications, and so forth.

Izzo has another use for it. He provides the profile to the media for background. He often writes stories for various publications and before they run one they want to know something about his firm. The profile supplies that information in a concise form.

BACKGROUNDER

In 1976, Joseph E. Izzo and several associates formed The JIA Management Group, Inc., a unique Santa Monica, California based management consulting firm specializing in data processing. Their premise in starting the company was that the computer would soon be the core of most businesses, and there would be an acute need for a new breed of consultant -- individuals who were technically knowledgeable but also had wide experience in management and business affairs. This premise proved true.

Today, JIA specialists work with corporations to help them use computer technology to improve the operation of their companies. They are expert problem solvers using tested and thorough analysis techniques; they are adept strategists and have the ability to re-direct data processing organizations to support the parent company's business goals.

Specifically, the firm does the following:

● Develops strategic plans for data processing

● Formulates office automation plans

● Establishes data processing executive policy
  committees to involve executives from key company
  functions in data processing policies and decisions

- MORE -

FIGURE 11. News backgrounder.

BACKGROUNDER
Page 2

- Educates clients in how to make the data processing
  department operate as a "business within a business"

- Performs a unique service, called "turnaround"
  management: JIA professionals go on-site to
  manage troubled data processing departments, then
  help select and train the company's employees to
  gradually reassume control.

JIA has worked with firms ranging from medium-sized companies to
huge conglomerates; highly integrated organizations as well as
geographically dispersed multi-industry corporations.   Some of
its clients are Coca Cola Bottling Company; Northrop Corporation;
Weyerhaeuser Company; Lockheed Corporation; Bergen Brunswig Corporation; Talley Industries; and Wickes Companies.

# # #

FIGURE 11.   Continued.

Many consultants generate potential clients by speaking to groups and industry associations. The successful speech dwells upon a common problem that those in the audience may have. It helps solve a need. Some time ago, Larry Senn developed a presentation about white-collar productivity—a subject of interest to every employer.

He uses an overhead projector ("Figure 1") to illustrate his points. Notice the speech does not dwell upon how "great his firm is" but rather on a problem that those in the audience have in common.

CREATING A WORK ENVIRONMENT
TO MAXIMIZE
CLERICAL AND WHITE COLLAR PRODUCTIVITY

Clearly America has been paying a price for not addressing productivity soon enough or aggressively enough. While much is being done to rectify that I fear that another mistake of equal magnitude may be made by many corporations. The next step in productivity improvement needs to more systematically embrace the clerical and white collar portion of our work force and to incorporate the Behavioral as well as the Technical aspects of productivity improvement.

The growth in white collar, service and clerical segments of our work force far exceeds blue collar growth. More than half of all workers in the United States are now white collar - over 50 million. Unless productivity in these areas is more adequately addressed corporate profits, national productivity and our overall standard of living will suffer.

As a nation we may have been lulled into thinking that the clerical productivity issue was solved because of the office automation boom now underway. What managers and administrators often discover all too late is that the equipment itself does not produce high productivity. Our firm was called in to a large clerical department that had recently been "automated". Because the productivity issue had not been addressed in a more holistic manner, the end result was an increase in the number of employees where a decrease had been forecast.

Even in a so called automated office - and most are far from that - the information that comprises the workload is still gathered by people, prepared for entry by people, input by people, interpreted by people, and distributed by people. In addition, the whole process of managing the work force from hiring to training and coaching is very much a human endeavor. When these issues in the clerical department described above were addressed by a comprehensive clerical productivity process output did go up by more than 30%.

All too often early attempts at white collar productivity improvement are erroneously patterned too closely after the early productivity work in manufacturing. It is true that most productivity improvement technology was developed in manufacturing environments. There, products are usually highly standardized and methods and procedures more precise. The most common techniques involve highly detailed methods improvement and engineered production standards.

FIGURE 12. Larry Senn's talk.

The clerical environment is different in many respects. The procedures are not as precise. The "runs" are often not as long and the employee often has to exercise more judgement in resolving paperwork problems.

All of these differences together with the shifting value systems of our "new age employees" require that the approach to clerical productivity improvement take on some different characteristics. The major ingredients that seem to be necessary in successful clerical productivity improvement include:

- Greater emphasis on employee involvement and participation.

- Supervisory training in the elements of productivity improvement.

- A comprehensive process which simultaneously addresses methods, systems, machines, and people.

FIGURE 12. Continued.

A Comprehensive Approach to Productivity Improvement

There is a science to productivity improvement that works well in clerical environments. It includes a series of technical and a series of behavioral elements. By blending physical improvements and uses of control systems with supervisory development, employee participation, and effective motivation, productivity of most any clerical group can typically be increased by 15% to 30%. In addition, because of the nature of the process, other benefits include:

- An improved quality of work life with more involved and fulfilled employees.

- An enhancement in the skills of managers and supervisors so they are better equipped to continue to develop improvement ideas in the future.

- Improved quality and controls via more concerned and conscientious employees.

The technical and behavioral elements in a comprehensive productivity effort are shown in Figure 1.

FIGURE 1

BEHAVIORAL IMPROVEMENTS
Motivational/Atttudinal

1. Overcome resistance to change.

2. Increase individual accountability for results.

3. Create involvement participation.(ie: Quality Circles)

4. Teach productivity skills to managers.

5. Teach managers PERFORMANCE COACHING (Employee Motivation)

TECHNICAL IMPROVEMENTS
Methods/Systems

1. Eliminate delays, interruptions, shortages.

2. Improve methods, systems layout, equipment.

3. Establish goals, standards, productivity targets.

4. Develop manpower planning and flexing systems.

5. Establish management reports to monitor and control.

FIGURE 12. Continued.

214

Creating a High Performance Environment

Increasing productivity is as much a motivational and behavioral process as it is a mechanical one. The best systems and the best design departments in the world will grind to a halt if the work force is unmotivated and resentful. The best sales or marketing plan does not ensure good customer service or effective selling. Results happen through people and while everyone acknowledges that, too few have done enough in equipping their supervisors to deal with today's "new age" employee.

Since most supervisors have come up through the ranks and have not been fully trained, they are not prepared to deal with the resistance that can occur in an improvement process.

The kinds of phenomenon they need to be equipped to deal with include the following:

1. Overcome resistance to change. Think back to the last change you wanted to initiate in a department or area. How many people jumped up and said, "Oh great, when can we change". Not many? What you encountered was a phenomenon called "Resistance to Change". There are techniques to overcome resistance to change and these can be taught to supervisors and managers.

    Some simple tips to avoiding resistance include:

    .   Don't surprise people with changes, give them plenty of forewarning and give them reasons why.

    .   Involve people in the change. The more they participate, the less they resist - the ideas coming out of quality circles are rarely resisted because the employees thought of them.

2. Create an attitude of accountability for improvement results at all levels by eliminating the tendency of people to make excuses and blame others for lack of performance.

    We estimate that upwards of 25%-30% of all managers and supervisor' time is spent in proving why lack of performance is not their fault. Sales blames manufacturing, manufacturing blames engineering, etc. Everyone has excuses for their own lack of performance - it's called Cover Your ___ (CYA). This time and energy needs to be redirected towards solutions and results.

FIGURE 12. Continued.

215

3. <u>Create better communications and mutual support between groups, departments, and functions</u>. There is a tendency for different departments to compete rather than support one another in improving performance. Improving productivity requires going beyond the "Four Walls". Unfortunately, all too often a "win-lose" philosophy operates not just with outside competitors but between groups within a company. Recognizing and minimizing this tendency is an important part of productivity improvement.

   In a recent project in a large accounts payable clerical area many of the solutions to higher productivity were found <u>outside the department</u>. Data could not be entered in the computer until paperwork "matched" and it could not be processed unless it was accurate. Solutions to these problems had to be found in other departments and with the vendors. When they were solved productivity improved dramatically.

4. <u>Train supervisors to be coaches and problem solvers</u>. People are most productive only when management creates an environment which encourages high performers. Such an environment includes:

   - Training in the best methods.
   - Appreciative feedback to employees for improvement or a job well done.
   - Constructive feedback on how to do better.
   - Coaching and problems solving by supervisors to eliminate roadblocks to higher output.
   - Good listening skills to "hear" employees' needs and ideas.

FIGURE 12. Continued.

Improvements That Go Beyond Automation

The purchase of the best and most cost effective data processing and word processing equipment is, of course, important. With the decrease in prices of such systems cost justification is becoming easier. However, it is important that managers recognize that any such system is merely a piece of equipment. It functions well only when a series of other "paperwork systems improvement" steps are taken. These include:

1. **Eliminate delays, interruptions, and shortages.** Our studies and observations confirm the tremendous loss in clerical productivity due to interruptions, delays and shortages. Invoice processors are "processing invoices" less than a third of the time, input operators are "inputing" a fraction of the time, and clericals are processing paper, at best, one third of the time. Productivity can be improved tremendously by merely analyzing all of the causes of interruptions and delays and working to reduce them. In one recent program in a large input department productivity was increased by more than 20%, largely by reducing the delays that existed in preparing the data for input.

2. **Improve Methods, layouts and systems.** All too often things are done a given way because the previous employee did them that way. Paperwork systems, in particular, tend to "grow like topsy". There are continual additions of changes and modifications which layer on inefficiencies.

    There is one resource that is commonly sadly neglected in clerical productivity improvement - and that is the employee who is doing the work. Who is most aware of the cause of delays and interruptions? Who is most familiar with the procedures which are most cumbersome and time consuming? The answer in both cases is, of course, the employee performing the task. Any program to improve productivity in a clerical environment which does not draw upon the ideas and suggestion of the work force is sadly lacking.

3. **Develop productivity measurement and provide feedback to managers and employees.** Few of us play a game to our potential unless we keep score and get some timely feedback on how we are doing. I would guess that most all of you have a variety of goals and targets you are continually striving for. Unless your company is atypical, I would guess that more than half the employees under you are playing in a game where no score is kept. It is virtually

FIGURE 12. Continued.

217

impossible to achieve high productivity levels without the use of goals and feedback at all levels. The process of establishing a goal and providing feedback and coaching can typically increase productivity from 15% - 25%.

In this day and age, it is important to recognize that goals and targets can no longer be used as "hammers" but instead, must be used in an enlightened process which both involves and motivates employees. Untrained supervisors can create employee resentment and fail to generate the available productivity gains.

Without an income statement and balance sheet Presidents couldn't get the best from their companies. Without targets, goals and standards at all levels managers can't get the best from their people as can be seen on the chart on the following page.

FIGURE 12. Continued.

THE INFLUENCE OF GOALS & FEEDBACK

Average % Performance

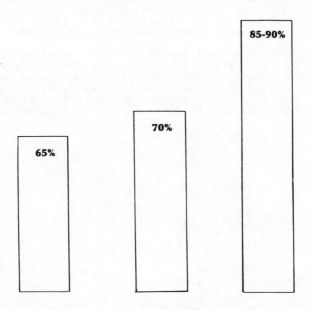

NO GOALS	GOALS	GOALS
NO MEASUREMENT	MEASUREMENT	MEASUREMENT
NO FEEDBACK	NO FEEDBACK	FEEDBACK
NO COACHING	NO COACHING	COACHING

FIGURE 12. Continued.

Summary

Productivity is still one of the most fruitful avenues to help get America back on track. Since one of the largest segments of our workforce is now in clerical and related white collar positions, this is an area which cannot be neglected.

A comprehensive clerical productivity program can yield many benefits for a company. Since the modern approach to productivity improvement includes better training of supervisors, overcoming resistance to change, and motivation of employees, additional benefits from such programs include improved employee morale, a higher quality product, and a stronger management team.

FIGURE 12. Continued.

One of the reasons why Izzo has been successful is his utilization of the media. He is interviewed and writes stories for publications as well. Then he reprints the articles and sends them out to present, as well as potential, clients.

The strength of the reprint is that it gives Izzo's firm credibility, that is, an independent third party (the media) is recognizing his firm and its expertise. They think enough about Izzo's ideas to give them editorial space.

The first three stories were written by Izzo. The next two were interviews. Notice the thrust of the stories. They talk about a subject that every potential Izzo client needs to know about. They are never self-serving.

Take Charge Of Your Computers

Most data processing problems are management problems. Get in control with these seven steps.

By Joseph E. Izzo

IF YOUR COMPANY is gnashing its collective teeth about problems with computers, it is not alone. Complaints about computers in business—what they produce and what they are doing to organization behavior—are as ubiquitous as the machines themselves.

A recent survey of major companies disclosed that two thirds of those responding were dissatisfied with their computer services. And business spends mind-boggling sums to straighten out computer-related difficulties.

Here we have a profound contradiction. Business people are well aware of the importance of computers to operations. Most executives can easily observe the impact of the computer on day-to-day activities. And increasingly, professional managers are not just observing the information revolution—they are enlisting in it by using personal computers.

Yet, for the most part, management and the computer people have not learned to live happily with one another. Why?

The answer, in my view, is simple: In many companies top management has not been sufficiently involved in data processing operations. Similarly, many data processing managers have not been adequately business-minded. They have been so enthralled with technology that they have failed to recognize that their function is to serve the company's business objectives.

As a result, there is frequently a serious communication barrier between senior executives and data processing people.

That barrier causes problems far more serious than the ordinary bugs that usually disrupt a computer system. The latter can easily be handled by a good programmer. But the bugs propagated by communication difficulties can be truly fearsome beasts, and it is a major task to banish them.

Here are seven prescriptions for extracting these formidable creatures from your computer operation.

1. Don't be intimidated by computers. There is no question that senior management has failed to come to grips with the computer because it has held the computer in awe.

Part of this is a language problem. Executives can talk knowledgeably about discounted cash flow, decision trees, cost per thousand and management by objectives, but they have found computer jargon largely impenetrable. As a result, computers are surrounded by mystery. So they have made executives uncomfortable—and even fearful.

Management should not be intimidated by the computer, though it often is.

But a manager does not have to be conversant with computer technology to make intelligent decisions about computers. Senior executives can learn quickly all they need to know to manage a computer operation. For example, translation of technical terms can be supplied by the data processing staff, managers with computer knowledge or consultants. The essential requirement is a determination to get control of the data processing organization.

2. Develop a strategy for data processing. Few executives need to be convinced of the virtues of planning. Yet even though a company may be highly sophisticated in other aspects of planning, it is likely to treat planning for data processing cursorily, if at all. That is a dangerous oversight for so vital and pervasive a function.

Strategic planning recommendations can be developed one of two ways. You can hire an outside consulting firm to work with your top-level executives, including a data processing representative. Or you can name a team from within the company to do the job. If you choose the latter approach, the head of the team should be someone with planning experience, whether or not he or she is from data processing, and the heads of each department should have input in the plan that is devised.

With either approach, the executives involved should be people who know your company well. It will be their task to bring data processing into accord with the objectives of your company.

Planning should be based on the fundamental question of what your business is now, what it will be in the future and what it should be.

In the context of these issues, the plan must address:

• Computer applications. Look at what systems exist in your company today. Are they adequate? Are your key business functions well supported by data processing? If not, why? What do you need to increase productivity, improve efficiency and gain a competitive edge?

• Organization and staffing. To whom should data processing report? What skills and capabilities should your data processing people have? Should they be housed in one department or assigned to specific operations throughout the company, such as marketing, finance or research and development?

• Monitoring and control. Finally, how can data processing be measured and controlled so it will be effective? Look at your present method. If it is not effective, it must be changed or your problems will persist.

Creating your strategic plan for data processing will be an arduous task. But it will be worth the effort.

3. Make sure your top data processing executive is a manager first and a technician second. He or she has one of the toughest jobs in the company. In addition to needing management skill and technical knowledge, your DP manager must be able to communicate well with top executives and other "customers" within the organization.

Reprinted From Nation's Business, September 1983

FIGURE 13. Joseph Izzo's feature from *Nation's Business* entitled "Take Charge of Your Computer."

The top data processing executive should be a manager first, a technician second.

Unfortunately, these attributes are not typical of data processing managers. Data processing is a young field—really only about 25 years old as a full-fledged business discipline—and its technical demands have always been so great that it has not yet developed a genuine managerial tradition.

As computers have become widespread, technicians rather than managers have been appointed data processing heads. And their careers have advanced through enhancement of technical, not managerial, skills. As a result, the business aspect of data processing management often gets short shrift. Do not let this happen in your company. Make sure your DP manager can talk the language of business as well as the language of computers.

And if your manager cannot or will not communicate clearly and work hard to make sure that DP acts as a service organization to your company, recognize that no one is indispensable. There have been too many instances where executives have been so fearful of losing their technical experts that they have put up with managerial incompetence. Now that the profession is maturing, you can find someone who is both a good manager and technically adept.

4. Demand documentation. Making a written record of what a computer program does and how to use it is a time-consuming and onerous task, so most computer professionals will avoid it like the plague. Do not let them. Missing documentation is an important reason why DP departments find themselves in difficulty. Lack of

Reprinted from Nation's Business

good written records puts a company at the mercy of a few individuals. If a key programer leaves or becomes ill and his or her work has not been well documented, it could take weeks or even months to make up the loss.

Good documentation also makes it easier to modify existing programs to meet new needs.

5. Establish controls. Set up a system to ensure that you get maximum benefit from your systems. Requests for new systems or modification of old ones, requisitions for personal computers—all must be evaluated to determine whether they will give a good return to your company. Will the requested item or activity improve productivity? Help you penetrate the marketplace? Yield added value?

When you set up controls, keep in mind that they should be effective, but not stifling—do not overcontrol. For instance, you should expect detailed documentation for a major application system, but do not require the same level of detail from managers who develop their own programs on personal computers (although some documentation is still needed even for personal computers).

6. Insist on executive involvement. The only way executives can get what they want from computers is to work closely with DP. The best way to involve executives in managing and controlling data processing is to set up a high-level committee for that purpose.

The tasks of the DP executive committee include setting overall data processing policy and formulating strategy, hiring top DP executives, approving the DP organizational structure, reviewing budgets and deciding on major expenditures. Committee membership should reflect the company's principal

The best way to get executives involved with data processing is to set up a high-level committee.

interests and functions. It should include the chief executive officer and a high executive from each line and staff function, including the top-ranking data processing person.

To be effective, the committee should hold monthly or bi-monthly meetings with formal agendas. Attendance must be mandatory. If a member cannot attend, an alternate should be given full voting authority.

A senior DP committee will represent a major commitment for your company; a lot of expensive people must prepare for and attend its meetings. But just as war is too important to be left to the generals, data processing is too important to be left solely to your DP department.

7. Exploit the changing technology—but beware. The inexorable growth of demand for speedily delivered information and the continuous development of computer technology have combined to distribute computer use ever more widely throughout corporations. The rise of word processing, networking, electronic mail, work stations and personal computers can be a tremendous boon to your company, but it can also cause severe headaches if appropriate policies are not established.

For example, a company that is a client of my firm thought it would be useful to link its personal computers in an interactive network. It discovered that it had so many incompatible brands of computers that forming a network was impossible without starting from scratch with compatible machines.

Or consider the companies whose executives, enamored of their PCs, write programs for important tasks that no one else can use because they have not been adequately documented.

Such glitches in computer systems are common. This does not mean you should not disperse computer power widely in your company. It means you should control it.

Computer technology need not be a mystery. It can be understood and managed. And business has a pressing responsibility to engage in that task. □

JOSEPH E. IZZO *is president of the JIA Management Group, a Santa Monica, Calif., consulting firm that helps companies solve data processing problems.*

FIGURE 13. Continued.

As Featured in

MIS STRATEGIES

Some Basic Concepts Of Strategic MIS Planning

By Joseph E. Izzo, president of The JIA Management Group, Inc., Santa Monica, California

The emergence of a pivotal role for MIS within corporations makes MIS planning crucial. Planning is always important for the survival of a business or organization, but when that organization — as is the case with MIS — has a great influence on the corporation it services, the process of planning becomes a necessity rather than a choice.

Four concepts are important to the understanding of MIS planning:

• The MIS organization is a business within a business. Like any enterprise, it has customers: the users; it sells products: computer-based systems and services, and like any other business, its performance should be measured by the application of the same business principles used elsewhere in the enterprise.

• The MIS organization is not the controller of the computer, it is the provider of computer service. Executive management is the controller.

• The planning process for MIS is similar to the planning process for any enterprise.

• Long-range MIS planning begins with the process of strategic planning.

Strategic planning is not a box of tricks or a bundle of techniques. It is analytical thinking that results in the commitment of resources to action. It is the application of thought, analysis, imagination, and judgment.

Strategic planning is not forecasting. The premise is that accurate forecasting is not possible; in fact, strategic planning is necessary because one cannot accurately forecast. Strategic planning does not deal with future decisions, it deals with the futurity of present decisions — the impact of the decisions we make now.

Lastly, a strategic plan is not a detailed plan specifying such things as hardware and software needs or personnel requirements, nor is it a formal commitment by management to spend money. (However, it usually does become the preliminary step to begin the expenditure of corporate resources.) A strategic plan provides the broad strokes from which the specifics are logically drawn.

Strategic planning is the process of deciding on the objectives of the organization, on changes in objectives, on resources used to attain those objectives, and on policies that

will govern the acquisition, use, and disposition of those resources. The idea behind strategic planning is a determination of *what a business should be*. This starts with addressing the question of *what a business currently is*.

MIS strategic planning involves setting objectives and directions. It is the vehicle used to arrive at concurrence with executive management on MIS directions, and it is the means by which the MIS organization begins to compete for scarce corporate resources in the form of money, staff and the most scarce resource of all — top management attention and time.

Every corporation is unique. Businesses vary widely in products, objectives, and management styles. Likewise, no two strategic plans can be identical. Most, however, are developed for a three-to-five-year period. In some businesses, such as banks and

airlines where the computer has long been an integral part of the business, the plan will extend beyond five years.

There are two critical factors in producing a good, business-oriented MIS Strategic Plan: a qualified study team, and informed, committed, and involved management.

The personnel assigned to the study team must be capable of understanding the business, data processing, and strategic planning. This requires them to possess entrepreneurial skills, analytical skills and, most of all, the ability to listen, assess, judge, and arrive at decisions that are compatible with corporate philosophies.

Since some of the information that will be gathered in developing the plan will be confidential in nature (such as a plan to divest Company X or close down a product line), the study team must also be highly trustworthy and discrete.

FIGURE 14. Joseph Izzo's feature from *Information System News* entitled "Some Basic Concepts of Strategic MIS Planning." Copyright© by CMP Publications, Inc., 600 Community Drive, Manhasset, N.Y. 11030. Reprinted with permission from Information Systems News.

No matter how good the study team is, the success and acceptance of an MIS Strategic Plan is closely tied to the degree of involvement and participation on the part of management — especially executive management. This cannot be overstated. At JIA, we have never known of an MIS Strategic Plan that was not implemented when there was deep involvement and counsel with executive management. Management must provide the raw material for the plan; the study team suggests, guides, and acts as a catalyst.

The actual planning process is performed in three steps: definition of needs, development of strategies, and development of an implementation approach.

At the completion of each step, there should be a presentation to management. Once the needs have been presented and there is agreement, there is a solid foundation for the development of strategies. Once the strategies are outlined and accepted there is a solid foundation for the preparation of an implementation approach. During each presentation, management will influence and modify the planning work; this is essential in the planning process.

The step-by-step presentation to management should never be short-circuited. That would severely jeopardize acceptance of the entire plan. Too often, if a strategic plan is presented as complete, an executive reviewing it focuses on one aspect, perhaps one or two of the stated needs with which he or she may disagree, and proceeds to discredit the entire report. Management's review and revision of each step of the process avoids this pitfall.

To accomplish the three planning steps, the study team engages in the following activities:

• Data and background information are gathered through a review and analysis of the corporate long-range plan (if one exists).

• In-depth interviews are conducted with corporate executives and with group, divisional, or functional management, to determine the management philosophy and business objectives; the effectiveness of current applications from the users' point of view; current and future information system needs; and the degree of satisfaction with the MIS organization, in terms of support and responsiveness.

• Existing and planned applications are reviewed in light of business objectives.

• A presentation of company information processing and technical computing needs is prepared and delivered.

• The MIS organization's overall ability to service the business' current and future needs is assessed, considering both organization and staff resources, and equipment/software/communications.

• Preliminary MIS strategy considerations are developed, taking into account equipment/software/communications; organization of staff resources; deployment of resources (people/equipment); management and control.

• A presentation of the proposed MIS strategy is prepared and delivered.

• An implementation strategy, schedule, and cost analysis are developed and presented to management.

• The MIS Strategic Plan is finalized.

Long-range planning will allow an MIS organization to enhance profitability and productivity in the corporation it serves, but it has several less obvious benefits as well. An MIS Strategic Plan allows the MIS organization to take on purpose and direction in its functioning; a pervasive sense of focus and coordination develops. This greatly reduces the amount of waste that occurs when the direction and role of the organization is absent or ambiguous.

A plan also bridges the gap between company executives and the MIS organization. Closer relationships develop between the MIS organization and top management as they join together in common objectives. Executive management begins to work with MIS to identify the future role information systems will play in the performance and growth of the business.

Finally, a plan educates executive management about the world of MIS. The planning process is a particularly appropriate vehicle for education because it provides a context that management understands. They gain insight about MIS by making the kinds of decisions they are accustomed to, setting objectives in the same manner they have used for years in the rest of their organization.

If the MIS community is going to help corporations reach their objectives, long-range planning must be implemented. Without it, MIS organizations will be working harder and harder while standing still, making little or no real progress toward satisfying their corporation's future information processing needs. With it, MIS can be instrumental in a company's business growth and profitability.

The JIA Management Group, Inc. does management and consulting in data processing with emphasis on bottom line results.

1299 Ocean Avenue
Suite 333
Santa Monica, California 90401
(213) 451-3041

Some of the material in this article was drawn from *Management*, P.F. Drucker; *Planning and Control Systems: A Framework for Analysis*, R.N. Anthony; and *Management Information Systems: A Framework for Planning and Development*, S.C. Blumenthal.

Reprinted with permission of Information Systems News

FIGURE 14. Continued.

Turnaround management

By Joseph E. Izzo

With turnaround management, a team of two to four highly qualified managers steps into key managerial posts within and atop the client company's data processing organization. The team's foremost objective is to turn around or reposition the DP organization so that it can move forward in aggressive support of the business.

Stuck with a problem data processing department? Let's get rid of the data processing manager!

No matter that he's working his tail off, never having learned how to say no to user requests. No matter that he's the kind of individual who seldom whimpers, even when his requisition for just one more programmer/analyst is turned down. No matter that he runs a business nearly as complex and demanding as the company it serves and that he may be tremendously overworked and underpaid.

Someone's got to take the rap for that three-year development backlog, that unforeseen 70% jump in hardware acquisition cost, the growing number of service complaints. We need a scapegoat, so let it be him.

Let me not imply that said manager is always without sin. He will, in fact, quite often lack the business skills to complement his technical know-how. To protect his domain, he may resort to high-tech jargon. He may even exude a holier-than-thou attitude. Maybe he should be let go.

In most cases though, the malfunctioning of in-house data processing organizations can be traced to more than one cause — often to a convolution of factors both trivial and significant. Terminating the silhouetted target is usually too simple a solution for a problem this complex.

Let's say that a serious problem does exist. This shouldn't surprise us because computers, despite their enormous propagation, still represent a comparatively adolescent technology and one for which economic use poses many as yet unanswered questions. How should the computer be applied? How should it be controlled? How should cost and benefit be measured to ensure a

FIGURE 15. Joseph Izzo's feature from *ComputerWorld* entitled "Turnaround Management."

This kind of attitude shift is not achieved overnight. When turnaround management is called for, it demands a considerable management commitment. In fact, it can easily take as long as a year or more to overcome initial resistance.

fair return? Few corporations have recognized that ascertaining valid answers to such questions may be absolutely prerequisite to development of a responsive data processing resource. Problems, therefore, are not that uncommon.

Available solutions — whether that means fixing a capability gone catastrophically awry or simply creating an environment in which an ailing service will flourish — are comparatively few and exhibit varying degrees of success.

We've found, for example, that the role of the sit-by-your-side consultant seldom carries sufficient authority to overcome the inertia of a major problem. A more drastic approach — that of selling off the existing capability to a facility management outfit — carries with it some more obvious worries.

"I had considered facilities management as a solution," one manager told us, "until I recognized that many of the very factors that fueled our information processing dilemma would very likely reconfront us when it came time to buy back the capability."

The remaining solution is what The JIA Management Group, Inc. calls "turnaround management." Under this concept, which we believe is unique, a team of two to four highly qualified managers literally steps into and assumes key managerial posts within and atop the client company's data processing organization.

These managers offer an average of 25 years of experience in business, computer technology and data processing management. And they come to the client company armed with systems and procedures, largely proprietary, that have been validated by repeated application.

The team's foremost objective is to turn around quickly or reposition the DP organization so that it can move forward in aggressive support of the business. Of course, that positioning must be accomplished in such a way that the department not only performs well during the turnaround team's residency, but also becomes sufficiently well organized, staffed, educated and motivated that a high level of service continues long after its departure.

A secondary objective is to reinforce strongly the credentials and acceptance of the data processing staff by adding to the staff's technical qualifications a familiarity with the principles of business planning and priorities as they might be viewed by the firm's executive offices — in short, giving data processing a business focus. Typically, the team leader, acting as department head and establishing an empathetic interface with the firm's user organizations, is the chief instrument of this achievement.

How well turnaround management can work was demonstrated a few years back at the Lincoln Telephone & Telegraph Co. in Lincoln, Neb. Lincoln Telephone is a utility whose data processing shop — despite the best of intentions — lacked the ability to implement the modern-day, online systems so necessary to customer service improvements. Yet after about 12 months of a turnaround management contract, the department proved its ability to design and develop major software systems, and the firm's customer service record improved dramatically.

So taken with its success, Lincoln Telephone recommended the concept to a major Midwest producer of high-fidelity equipment. The company hired JIA to turn around a data processing department that, despite some 50 people and millions of dollars worth of computer hardware, simply was not functioning.

When the turnaround was complete approximately 14 months later, JIA consultants had replaced themselves with a qualified internal management team, had instituted a major training program for the entire staff and had installed the company's first set of data processing standards and procedures covering everything from proposal format to quality assurance requirements.

One of the client firm's key executives found a changed company attitude. "When JIA arrived," he reported, "everyone in our company hated the DP department. It was not reliable, it fouled up and the like.

"By contrast, the department has now gained the confidence of our organization," he added. "Now there's dependability and good communications."

Not an overnight solution

This kind of attitude shift is not achieved overnight. When turnaround management is called for, it demands a considerable management commitment In fact, it can easily take as long as a year or more to overcome initial resistance, to educate the staff and to install new ideas, policies and procedures, while simultaneously maintaining and upgrading day-to-day operations. The greatest results are usually reaped toward the end of the contract, long after the JIA consultants are gone.

Turnaround management can also be effective on a more limited scale. In many instances, these same methods are applied to a single unit or function within the larger DP department: to systems development, to operations, to quality assurance or to business systems planning, for example.

One of the country's largest suppliers of private-label cheese had such a need. In this instance, the client's growth required major hard-

FIGURE 15. Continued.

ware additions coupled with state-of-the-art software and a new, more sophisticated operating environment. The operations staff, then about 30 people, couldn't meet the challenge and probably faced termination if an alternative solution could not be found.

Beginning with an effectiveness review, a JIA team of two individuals tackled the development of a data center operations improvement plan that ultimately established project request procedures, planning methodology and system turnover procedures among its several facets. The team also set up the documented methods to automate tape library management, automate software production and test, establish a viable recovery and restart procedure and implement other needed operational improvements. JIA also played a key role in procurement of a major software package.

Management involvement

True and lasting success of turnaround management almost invariably demands one very significant ingredient — the direct involvement of executive management: first to establish objectives for its data processing resource and then to monitor and control the operation to ensure continued attainment of the desired cost-benefit ratio and other goals.

Classically, top executives have more or less ignored data processing as they would never ignore engineering, marketing or finance — in many cases, simply because of uneasiness in dealing with the unfamiliar technology, compounded at times by the problems of technicians' jargon or aloofness. Yet in working with more than 100 client companies, we've learned that these executives can overcome this distance and learn to make correct decisions about data processing through the vehicle of the executive policy committee.

Properly framed, the data processing executive policy committee is not a discussion group, but a decision-making body made up of the firm's senior executives. Acting much as a corporation's board of directors does in serving and guiding the corporation, this group sets the data processing objectives and policies, appoints the top DP executives and approves their organizational structure, analyzes service responsiveness and reviews — for potential returns — major development projects and other proposed expenditures.

Believing that performance of the executive policy committee would depend largely on the quality of information on which it must act, JIA developed a number of innovative standards for reports and proposals to go before the committee. For proposed expenditures, the committee receives a document known as a decision package, which has proven to work primarily because it presents its case in business language rather than computer terminology. It also demands that the corporate user for whom the development is proposed participate fully in formulating the proposal.

Bergen Brunswig, a JIA client and a distributor of pharmaceutical and health-care products, had been heavily involved in data processing for many years, even operating a computerized inventory control system since 1955. Yet the company's president, Robert H. Martini, and other senior executives felt that until they had established the DP policy committee, they lacked the ability to manage or control the service properly.

"It seems easy to manage other parts of the business," Martini said, "but DP was always a mystical area."

As evidence of committee effectiveness, Bergen Brunswig has since reported about a 50% cut in backlog of DP projects from approximately 20 staff-years at $40,000 per year to about two staff-years . And the firm credits the committee with a drop in DP turnover from 35% to 8% in a single quarter.

Start-up situations

For the company that believes the best cure is prevention, JIA offers a start-up management service that employs many of the same principles of turnaround management. As with the turnaround service, the concepts can be applied to an entire DP department or just a new unit within the department.

In the typical situation (much like the separate case history of the Angeles Corp.), the client used outside services but reached the point where the bureau no longer seemed the most cost-effective or timely answer to data processing needs. In such a start-up, JIA can shoulder the entire burden, beginning with preparation of a detailed strategy plan for the changeover.

Subsequent functions include the actual hardware and software selection process, effecting the transfer from the service bureau, installing necessary standards and procedures, setting up an executive policy committee, designing the computer center, managing it until all the wrinkles are out and finally selecting and training the staff to replace JIA.

JIA's role in starting up a brand new unit within an existing data processing department is normally much more limited in scope. At Bergen Brunswig, JIA helped establish two new units — business systems planning and quality assurance — in addition to formation of the firm's executive policy committee.

For the most part, JIA's clients are firms undergoing a key transition of some sort — entering an exciting growth period, experiencing a product demand that's difficult to satisfy, reconsidering basic objectives or market strategies or even retrenching for one reason or another. In most cases, the transition demands samurai performance by data processing.

When it comes to developing specific solutions to the firm's problems, JIA consultants have been successful almost entirely because they are in a position to apply a vast amount of directly related experience and can do so in an objective way.

Experience level

For example, attaining improved personnel performance requires a well-stocked armory of reliable cause-and-effect experiences. From their work with many other clients, they know the results of adding people, adjusting salaries, reorganizing the department or units within it or even terminating people. And their actions are convincingly objective because their finite "reign" allows them a dispassionate, detached view.

FIGURE 15. Continued.

Moreover, their limited time in power demands that replacements be certifiable before that date. To ensure that happens, they begin to inform and educate the entire staff from the first day. Their initial objective is to alleviate the natural trepidation that occurs on arrival. A carefully orchestrated presentation, open to all DP personnel from managers to keypunch operators, explains precisely why they are there, what they propose to do and how long it should take.

Within the subsequent few weeks, the consultants conduct question-and-answer sessions with smaller groups. At one time or another, they talk privately with each individual about his goals and how they might best be achieved.

The consultants are always concerned about developing each staff member to his highest potential in line with the individual's goals. Naturally, those individual wishes sometimes conflict with the client's aims, making changes imperative. At worst, and this has applied to some department heads, it may be suggested that the employee seek another job.

Most often, however, shifting the person to a different function within the organization is the better solution and often benefits the employee directly. For example, switching a middle manager from programming

---

Most often, shifting the person to a different function within the organization is the better solution and often benefits the employee directly.

---

to quality assurance exposes that individual to a new overview of the system development cycle and the tools and techniques by which the cycle is best managed. That person then ends up with a depth of business experience to complement his technical qualifications.

To illustrate more specifically the firm's approaches to real problems, several brief case histories follow. Studies of the Lincoln Telephone & Telegraph Co. and Itel Corp. demonstrate the approach to turnaround management. A look at the Angeles Corp. shows how start-up management was accomplished.

Lincoln Telephone

About 80 years of age, the Lincoln Telephone & Telegraph Co. of Lincoln, Neb., is a sparkling example of Middle America's catch-up infatuation with contemporary data processing technology.

Here is a medium-size utility that offers local and long-distance services to 22 counties in southeastern Nebraska. Here's a regional firm that serves some 190,000 customers and 360,000 instruments. Here's a company whose data processing organization progressed in just a few years from operation of a semiarchaic batch-oriented accounting system to modern-day, on-line processing of customer and stockholder records, toll settlements (a major source of income) and sophisticated business

management tasks from what-if modeling to inventory control.

Yet in 1977, the DP outlook could not have appeared less promising. Lincoln Telephone's management — including Vice-President and Controller Laurence Connealy — had earlier recognized that the company's accelerating growth was demanding new and better ways to handle customer orders. "At that time," Connealy told us, "it took 3½ days to install service from the time a customer placed an order."

That was unacceptable to a firm that prided itself on service improvements and hold-the-line costs. So it attempted — starting in 1975 — to develop and implement a new computer-based order processing and billing system it called Cars (for Customer Automated Records System). It anticipated that Cars would be followed by other major DP developments.

But things didn't go according to plan. Off the beaten path and reflecting a somewhat provincial understanding of DP technology, the DP staff at Lincoln spent some 60 man-months in system development, forecast the need for an additional 60 and was finally judged short on system design know-how.

Desperate to solve the growing problem, Lincoln Telephone executive management considered its alternatives: the turnkey development of Cars by an outside firm, commitment to a five-year facilities management contract or simply extensive recruiting and training. The facilities management contract — under which both equipment and data processing staff would be legally absorbed by the contractor — was a drastic solution, but it looked like a front-runner in responsiveness.

"Although the facilities management approach seemed to be a good bet, it also featured some significant drawbacks," Connealy admitted. As he now recalls it, the dominant negatives were potential cost growth, lack of guarantees on return of the capability at contract termination and the utility's definite distaste for the idea of sandwiching a separate corporate entity between the utility and its customers.

Lincoln Telephone had heard of JIA and the turnaround management concept. It agreed to a one-year management services contract, with provisions for both cancellation and extension.

The contract's comprehensive work plan addressed the identified problems, called for the immediate insertion of qualified data processing management, defined a program to upgrade its employees and supervisors and specified month-by-month deliverables by which the utility could monitor and control the effort.

Connealy's recall is a bit more vivid. "JIA brought in five managers to run our shop. They moved our people aside temporarily, wrote standards, set up a project control system, prepared a personnel assessment and training plan and began a national search for a new DP manager."

Interestingly enough, while the JIA team had termination authority, no firings were found necessary. Even the displaced manager moved into a newly created quality assurance slot.

FIGURE 15. Continued.

Interestingly enough, while the JIA team had termination authority, no firings were found necessary. Even the displaced manager moved into a newly created quality assurance slot.

Steering committee

JIA also introduced Lincoln Telephone to the concept of the executive steering committee. According to Connealy, this group of top-level executives still meets quarterly to review DP status and proposals.

From the JIA viewpoint, the effort represented a repositioning of the data processing department and the turnaround of an intolerable situation. When the consultants went in, DP facilities could almost have been described as chaotic. Salaries lagged behind the industry, and morale was low.

When JIA left, about five years of learning had been jammed into one year; each employee had a prescribed route to education and advancement. And executive management had begun to understand and pay attention to the data processing operation.

Lincoln Telephone also whipped the order processing problem. With Cars, more than 50% of Lincoln Telephone's service orders are actually filled the day the order is received or, in the case of orders placed late in the day, within 24 hours.

Itel Corp.

Founded in 1967, San Francisco's Itel Corp. flourished in the next decade, earning Wall Street's favor for the booming revenue from the firm's equipment-leasing business — most notably in the leasing of low-cost alternatives to IBM computers.

But 1979 saw the company stagger enormously as IBM dropped some of its prices, making much of Itel's line uncompetitive. The company lost more than $400 million that year. In January 1981, it entered Chapter 11 bankruptcy.

Today, less than three years later, Itel has gained a new notoriety — this time for the apparent speed at which it has begun to recover. It has pared the number of business units from nearly 30 to only two — container leasing and rail-car operations. It cut its work force from 7,000 to 900.

Itel has installed what is considered to be a unique bankruptcy information support system — a data processing system that has, according to Itel management, contributed so much to the recovery process that it has already been marketed to at least three other Chapter 11 businesses.

However, getting that data processing system in gear was a struggle. JIA was eventually called in.

William Twomey, selected to preside over the firm during the later phases of reorganization, saw the basic problem as one of politics. "When we cut back our management staff in the fall of 1982, I — being the vice-president of finance and administration at that time — inherited several departments, including the Corporate Information Systems [CIS] Department. Unfortunately, the manager of the department held strong opinions of his own about the development and sale of the Chapter 11 software and threatened to quit."

Recognizing that the CIS manager's threat could have widespread impact on the struggling company, Twomey backed his own hand by planning, with JIA, for emergency management services. Sure enough, in a power play, three key CIS employees — including the manager — quit, giving only two weeks notice.

The task facing JIA was unusual in that the Chapter 11 reporting requirements were monumental. Itel was dealing with more than 50,000 creditors and shareholders. The reorganization involved 24,000 separate claims and more than 3,000 executory contracts.

Periodic documentation ordered by the bankruptcy court included statement of assets, statement of liabilities, statement of executory contracts and statement of affairs, also known as Information Schedule 1.

The computer was used to maintain a claims register, to handle mailings to the creditors and shareholders, to call for and tabulate votes on the reorganization plan and even to distribute newly issued stocks and bonds.

Primary tasks

JIA's primary tasks were to see the computer operation resume without a hitch, to improve service to the remaining operating companies, to develop an information systems strategic plan and to develop a business plan for the marketing of computer services to bankruptcy customers.

Recognizing that the CIS manager's threat could have widespread impact on the struggling company, Twomey backed his own hand by planning, with JIA, for emergency management services. Sure enough, three key CIS employees quit, giving only two weeks notice.

FIGURE 15. Continued.

On Angeles' behalf, the JIA team — which varied from two to five people during the contract period — evaluated equipment (eventually recommending an IBM System/38), centralized available DP resources and established a systems development methodology.

Another significant contribution by JIA has been a major reorganization of CIS. As recently as June 1983, the two operating companies and corporate headquarters were each serviced by a more or less independent section within CIS. Each group did its own development work, with a high probability of duplicated effort.

Under a department reorganization, all users are served by a unified group that offers several important new functions. A quality assurance and administration group, a business systems planning office and a customer support group were added. The small increase in total head count also accounts for a technical group concerned with network control.

In response to JIA recommendations, Itel formed a four-man executive steering committee that will soon begin to oversee CIS operations and proposed improvements.

Angeles Corp.

The Angeles Corp. is a nationwide financial services organization. Based in Los Angeles and employing about 275 people, it acts as general partner to a number of limited partnerships, investing primarily in real estate developments and motion picture productions. It also manages pension and profit-sharing funds for other corporations and for educational institutions.

As perhaps the best measure of the firm's recent suc-

cess, the past three years have seen its combined investments in stocks, bonds and other financial instruments soar to $2 billion from an already healthy $500 million.

Needed unified facility

But, according to Angeles President William H. Elliott, the firm had until recently been somewhat hampered by the lack of a professional, unified data processing facility.

"We were spending a good bit of money on service bureaus," Elliott said, "not too effectively, I might add. To keep up with our growth rate, we needed to significantly enhance our systems capabilities."

"I'm a great believer in systems," Elliott maintained. "And I'm convinced that data processing should be looked upon as a management tool, not simply an accounting tool."

Considered alternatives

The need for significant improvement led Angeles to the JIA group, but not before it considered a number of alternatives ranging from big-name consultants to equipment manufacturers.

"We were offered plenty of 'free' advice," Elliott recalled, also noting that most

such advice usually proves costly in the long run.

"We needed a sophisticated data center, with plenty of growth potential, and knew that we faced a painful, extremely challenging job because we were starting two or three years later than we should have."

JIA started to work early in 1980, beginning with development of a strategic data processing plan. On Angeles' behalf, the JIA team — which varied from two to five people during the contract period — evaluated equipment (eventually recommending a System/38 IBM minicomputer), centralized all the available DP resources and established a system development methodology.

Cost of the new facility ran to about $2 million.

The software task was one of implementing existing applications on the firm's new hardware and designing new applications. JIA also provided an extensive amount of training for the in-house staff.

As it does in the majority of instances, JIA also recommended and helped to implement an executive steering committee by which Angeles management can monitor and control the new centralized function.

FIGURE 15. Continued.

231

How the management contract works

The management contract is one way of quickly repositioning a data processing department and developing it into a professional, high-performance organization in a short period of time. This is accomplished by placing a JIA data processing management team in the department on a temporary basis to "turn around" the performance of the organization. During its tenure, the team's major responsibilities are:

■ To effect a quick turnaround in the performance of a data processing organization.

■ To develop within the client company a strong, reliable, enduring professional data processing organization, which includes finding the training replacements for the temporary management team.

■ To install methods and practices for ensuring an ongoing, quality organization with appropriate management reporting and control.

In bringing about the turnaround of a data processing organization, the management contract has some basic advantages over the more conventional methods of hiring a new management team or promoting managers from within.

The motivation is different. Under a management contract, the goal is to develop a lean but strong organization. Since the outside management team is there for only a relatively short period of time, the interest and focus is to put in place only what is needed; there is no tendency to build an "empire."

The contract management team has no personal ties to existing members of the organization and, therefore, can be objective in evaluating an individual's performance.

The JIA staff is experienced in working as a team to accomplish major DP objectives. In contrast, if a new manager is hired, it may take a minimum of six months before he can form and test a team that can move aggressively forward.

Many of the professional methods and practices required to effectively operate a data processing organization exist within JIA and have been tested and implemented in many organizations.

Therefore, the cost and time required to develop these methods and practices is minimized.

With a management contract, the team's success is measured by its ability to make the required changes on schedule and to select managers who will maintain a high level of performance for the organization in the future. There should be no need for outside management assistance when the management contract is completed.

A management contract is not designed to provide "hatchet men," but to serve as a means of enhancing the skills of in-house talent. Individuals will be replaced only in those cases in which capabilities are below acceptable standards.

Situation dictates size

Based on the size of the data processing installation, the number of JIA managers at the beginning of a management contract will range from 2½ to five, depending on the complexity of the situation. The contract's duration could be eight to 14 months. The time period is specified at the beginning of the engagement.

A brief scenario follows. For purposes of illustration, we will assume the requirement is for four members of the JIA management staff and the duration of the contract is 12 months.

During the first three to four months, four JIA team members would be assigned to the client site. At the conclusion of that period, one member would be replaced by a trained internal DP staff member, bringing the number down to three. At about the sixth month, an additional member of the JIA staff would be replaced by another staff member. At approximately the ninth month, the third member of the JIA staff would be replaced. The remaining JIA staff person would leave at the end of the 12th month.

This approach allows for the gradual shift from a JIA-managed organization back to a client-managed organization. The JIA management team brings about this shift and effects change while managing the daily activities of the organization.

Several other general features of the JIA management contract include:

■ The JIA staffing levels are reviewed formally each quarter to determine if reduction of JIA staff can be accelerated. An increase in JIA staff should never be considered since this defeats the purpose of the contract; the goal is to develop the people internally.

■ The contract can be canceled at any time, with 30 days' notice.

■ JIA will assume all responsibility for managing data processing within the client's policies and guidelines and report directly to the executive in charge. Outside advice and counsel will be provided to the contract management team by JIA executive management.

About the author

Joseph E. Izzo is president of The JIA Management Group, Inc., a Santa Monica, Calif.-based management consulting firm specializing in data processing.

FIGURE 15. Continued.

FEARED BUT EFFECTIVE:
JOE IZZO, THE DP DOCTOR

by Jack B. Rochester

*"Would you tell me, please, which way I
ought to walk from here?"*
*"That depends a good deal on where you
want to get to," said the Cat.*
"I don't much care where," said Alice.
*"Then it doesn't matter which way you
go," said the Cat.*
—Lewis Carroll's *Alice's Adventures
in Wonderland*

The Monday morning meeting had been in progress for nearly an hour, and the CEO was beginning to feel more and more like Alice. He certainly was trying not to look as uncomfortable and anxiety-ridden as he felt.

For one thing, the quarterly reports were late from data processing again, so three senior vice presidents had to waste time giving him a rundown of operations in person. And the corporation seemed to be in a mess in a lot of other ways. Order fulfillment was agonizingly slow. Departments were screaming for long-overdue assistance from data processing—and the DP department, more than frustrated, was screaming for a bigger computer. As he left the meeting, the CEO shook his head despondently, plagued by the thought that the company wouldn't make its business plan this time around.

When he got back to his office, he found a stack of mail on his desk, and on top was a small, elegant, red-velvet chapbook with gilt lettering that read, "Charting a Course for Management." Opening it, he saw Rockwell Kent's charming drawing of Alice, who was having her little tête-à-tête with the Cheshire Cat. The executive turned the page and read on.

"Unlike Alice, most managements recognize the importance of knowing their computer technology destinations," advised the booklet's author. The CEO read on and on until he reached the last page. And then he called Joseph E. Izzo, the man who had sent him the red-velvet solution to his problem.

Joe Izzo, known as The DP Doctor, specializes in helping companies whose data processing departments are ailing. And these days many are on the sick list. Virtually no one involved with corporate information systems can keep pace with all the new office technologies, and in many DP departments the task of completing applications for end users has reached Sisyphean proportions.

Enter Izzo and his computer paramedics, none with less than 15 years' experience, to help turn things around. Indeed, Izzo has coined the term *turnaround management* (see box p. 68) to describe the work his firm, JIA Management Group Inc. of Santa Monica, Calif., performs. Some data processing managers might describe his work in slightly less polite terms, for he has proved to be fairly brutal in bringing about "cures." Some DP managers or their assistants have lost their jobs along the way.

Izzo's tough treatment of clients comes directly out of his own experiences in data processing. For many years, he directed DP operations for such companies

---

**When he comes in the door,
your data processing department
will look different (and better)
within a few months.**

---

as North American Rockwell Corp. and Systems Development Corp. Then he became vice president of the commercial division of Computer Sciences Corp., where he managed systems development, consulting, and facilities management activities. Izzo kept coming across three critical DP situations.

• A company automating for the first time.
• A particular DP department that needs improvement or repositioning.
• An installation where work isn't getting done because of poor management, lack of high-level support, or poor utilization of technology.

A major difficulty, he found, was that although companies would bring in outside consultants to solve these problems, things would revert to an emergency-room atmosphere the minute the consultants left. Facilities management—hiring a firm to take over the

---

FIGURE 16. Joseph Izzo's feature from *Management Technology* entitled "Joe Izzo, The DP Doctor." Copyright© 1984 by Jack B. Rochester. Originally published in *Management Technology* magazine, Volume I, Number 9, January 1984, pp. 66–69. All rights reserved

JOHN SVOBODA

company is in trouble. They equally dislike the embarrassment of airing the trouble at, say, a board meeting. On top of all that, the task of getting half a dozen people to agree on a solution is taxing. Then there's the sticky problem of the DP manager's ego: The last thing he or she wants to hear is that things are so bad that someone else is coming in to run the installation.

So Izzo formulated a strategy for pushing the turnaround management pill:

• He decided JIA would report only to the president and senior-level executives of the company, for without their support his people couldn't make any real changes.

• He would bring in his own people to manage operations, but only for a short time. This would keep them out of internal politics and assure the corporate staff that things would soon return to normal.

• He would make changes in stages, each one carefully leading to the next, and provide all the training and support necessary to nurse the installation back to health.

This process puts the DP Doctor and JIA's computer clinic in a class by itself—but it does not make Izzo popular. When he's doing his job, it's the moment of truth for all concerned. "When you're working in a nonperformance or repositioning situation," says Izzo, "the fact is that usually 40 percent of the problem is the executive body itself. Management gets frustrated with DP and decides to put tight controls on expenditures. Then, all of a sudden they get nonperformance. Every DP problem is a management problem, too. You've got to solve both or you haven't done your job."

A hostile environment

One of JIA's clients, a large building-materials manufacturer, had a facility that had been trying for three or four years to gain approval for a manufacturing accounting control system. The first request was rejected because it wasn't clear where the hardware would be located. Then, one after another, the corporation put a lid on new capital expenditures, the study turned out to be too incomplete, the vendor analysis proved to be poor, and the specs were somewhat off.

The JIA team entered "a very hostile environment." The managers affected couldn't believe that Izzo and his consultants could succeed where they had failed. The two groups met to discuss ways the request could be made acceptable to corporate management. "We talked about it for three or four hours," the JIA team leader recalls, "and the clients started turning around right away. We discussed specifications and strategies—ways to save the company some money. They got excited, felt a challenge. Within two months we had approval. They didn't get the computer at their site, which they weren't really happy about, but they got the system. It works and we saved the company $320,000."

entire DP operation on a contract basis—worked, but wasn't the right Band-Aid for everyone. If an outsider could come in, help iron out problems, teach the staff better skills, and hand the reins back, Izzo reasoned, maybe the DP department could then manage on its own.

It was seven years ago that Joe Izzo put on his stethoscope and began practicing his particular brand of DP diagnosis. But he found that pioneering new ideas is rough work.

First, chief executives don't like to admit that their

FIGURE 16. Continued.

234

Blending strategy and business systems

Turnaround management is consultant Joseph Izzo's way of combining the best principles of strategic management with business systems planning to fix up embryonic or ailing data-processing organizations. Strategic management—a set of decisions, practices, and actions—aims at gaining a clear-cut advantage over the competition. Business systems planning prepares detailed blueprints for achieving the organization's objectives. Together, these principles are supposed to work to make a business successful and profitable.

The data processing department, says Izzo, should operate as a business within a business just like marketing, finance, or manufacturing. But a DP department can easily get off track because of an underachieving manager and an overburdened staff. Many managers rise through the ranks, from programmer to department head, and lack the necessary interpersonal and managerial skills. In many departments, project development backs up for so long—in some cases years—that the staff gets a feeling of hopelessness. High turnover continues to plague the DP profession. And many computer applications and uses such as office automation, word processing, and executive microcomputing are no longer the sole province of the DP manager.

Turnaround management aims at helping an organization develop a stable and professional DP department. Izzo's JIA Management Group teaches the DP department the textbook principles that, if generally followed, are supposed to make a staff invaluable.

Initially, the JIA team works with data processing in various ways by:
- Managing all daily technical work and business activities.
- Making changes in responsibilities and work assignments as needed.
- Pinpointing areas for improvement.
- Developing leadership and lateral support for systems development, quality assurance, operations, and software support functions.
- Setting up cost-effective standards for procedures, project management, and documentation.

With turnaround management, the data processing staff knows JIA will stay for only a short period of time—and is there to help, not to jockey for power. At a cost of between $300,000 and $1.2 million per contract, the cure isn't cheap, but it's probably right.

Clearly, it takes a strong, spirited person to do this kind of work. Izzo assumes a warrior-like attitude, and the other JIA principals act pretty much the same way. "When we come in, we're in command—absolute command. We have direct reporting relationships and hire/fire responsibilities. In an absolutely literal fashion, we become manager or director or vice president, whatever the title is, of the DP organization."

It's reminiscent of Akira Kurosawa's famous film *The Seven Samurai*, in which the roaming samurai warriors train a village to defend itself against bandits. Not only must the people be taught to use weapons, but they must learn to organize and manage themselves as well. Izzo's approach is no *Theory Z* technique of consensus management. His management Bible is *A Book of Five Rings*, a collection of principles and strategies for the life of a warrior written in the 17th century by Japan's most famous swordsman, Miyamoto Musashi.

A JIA Management Group turnaround project lasts anywhere from eight to 14 months—never longer. It's part of Izzo's "fast in and out" strategy. The team goes in, fixes things, trains people, gets out. "When we leave, we don't ever want to be asked back," says Izzo.

Hit the ground running

But before they actually begin, several things occur. First, as Izzo explains the process, management must acknowledge that it has an information systems problem and must realize that management itself may well be part of that problem. Next, in 90 percent of the cases, the JIA people conduct an effectiveness review, which identifies the trouble areas. "Then, when you walk in the door on Day One, you hit the ground running," says Izzo. The effectiveness review validates the problems that management felt it had and establishes the basis for the management contract.

The contract spells out what JIA intends to do, as well as what JIA expects from management. "Here are really detailed instructions for how to get where you want to go," says Izzo. "You find there are five or six things that will make an 80 percent improvement, then another hundred things that would be nice if you get to them. We try to live in the real world with our management contracts." Because of this realistic approach, one major aerospace company in Southern California whose computer expenditures amount to more than $100 million a year uses JIA to help prepare its strategic plans.

"In all our contracts we mandate forming an executive steering committee," Izzo continues. "The president must sit on it, and all executives must meet and report to him monthly. You see, while we begin working on three things—identify today's problems, manage today's problems, and manage today's process—we're also interested in an outcome that's a long-term strategic plan. But I believe top management has to learn what is actually happening in order to formulate

FIGURE 16. Continued.

that strategy. Sometimes a DP manager looks like he's performing terribly, but when you get in there, you learn he's done what he's supposed to. It's just not a workable strategy. He was doomed to failure from the beginning. Data processing goals must be tied to general business goals."

Concurrent with forming the steering committee, the JIA team leader takes over DP operations and reassigns—or, in some cases, terminates—the manager. While this may sound ruthless, often the problem person is in over his head, has an abrasive personality, or is unsuited for management. Any dismissals are handled through the firm's normal business procedures or the personnel department.

"To be very honest," says Izzo, "I move management around so I can get control. I might put the head of systems and programming in quality assurance for three months. You begin putting people where their shortcomings lie so you can start correcting them.

"Our people go in, one for three months, another for six, another for nine. We start having an impact, but we're also dropping off, letting the staff take charge gradually. We come in abruptly but we leave gradually, so if we've done an excellent job, by the time the last person leaves we are not missed. If you're missed, there's a weakness you've left them with."

Solving business problems

JIA has practiced its art for a wide range of companies, from bakeries and machine-tool producers to banks and insurance companies. The concept works well for companies with at least $30 million to $40 million in revenues that are starting their own DP operations or feeling the need for a "turnaround." "We get everything started, work with them on strategy, help select equipment and applications, hire and develop people, then disappear as they take over," says Izzo.

What seems to be the major problem with information systems today? Finance or marketing or distribution often must reassess its mission, as Izzo sizes up the situation, but that doesn't necessarily mean that something as drastic as turnaround management is the answer.

"Many data processing departments have a mistaken sense of their identity," he says. "They think they're an engineering facility or research and development lab, when in fact they're providing manufacturing services. There are no established practices and procedures in the industry. Data processing must come to terms with the fact that its mission is to solve business problems."

Otherwise, it's like the Cheshire Cat said: If you don't care where you're going, it doesn't matter which way you go. □

Jack B. Rochester, a contributing editor to Management Technology, *is co-author with John Gantz of a new book,* The Naked Computer, *published by William Morrow & Co. Inc.*

The true test is staying turned around

Gwen Myers, a managing principal at Joseph Izzo's JIA Management Group, tells about a particularly difficult turnaround.

It was an advertising firm that had been bought out and didn't want to go into the new organization the way they were. It was awful. Nothing worked. Every system was set for single-entry accounting. They would input profit and loss, and then print it out so it would look like an income statement on computer paper.

When we went in, there had been no preliminary effectiveness review. We tried to work with their systems and people, but pretty soon it became evident that there was no way to work with this data processing manager. She was forever going in and changing the figures, and there was no way to understand the system. Finally, with much fear, the chairman of the board let her go.

Then things really began falling apart, faster than you could count. People hated us because we fired one of them, and management kept wondering why they were paying us all this money when things weren't improving. We never missed a payroll, although we came close a few times.

Eventually, we threw out all their systems and put in packages. You know how packages are. They're supposed to be perfect, but someone always says, 'I don't like the screen.' So we made some changes. It's a rather difficult environment, but it turned out well.

We've been out of that client for three years now, and they can't say enough good about us. The people who bought them out point to them as their prize installation, the place that's running well.

We worked with the data processing manager until we recognized it wasn't going to work. Then we put a new foundation in place—it was a hard job at the time—but it's stayed in place. Turnaround means it's going to hell in a hand basket. I think the true test of turnaround management is if it stays turned around.

FIGURE 16. Continued.

How to get computers to speak your language

Executives are starting to take charge of data processing's direction

Gwyn Myers is a managing principal of The JIA Management Group, Inc., a Santa Monica-based management consulting firm specializing in data processing. The firm develops and implements management and control techniques, manages DP organizations, performs information needs and assessments, and manages new system development and quality assurance programs. Myers was formerly vice president of student affairs and director of the computer center at Rio Hondo College, and an IBM hardware/software consultant.

by Gwyn Myers

The question of how executive involvement is changing the computer and the computer is changing the executive is like the age-old question of which came first, the chicken or the egg? In the case of the executive and the computer, the changes and influences have actually gone in both directions.

It is important to look at some highlights from computer history, because we do things today based more on history than on tomorrow's needs.

The computer field began in 1890 when the Census Bureau invented the punch card to take the census. That was one of the first steps toward the development of computer technology.

In 1932, when the Social Security Department needed to keep up with the insurance administration, the tabulating machine was developed.

In 1940 the federal government needed a machine to assess military situations and forecast weather for military purposes and the first of the electronic, digital computers (Eniac) was developed in 1946.

In the mid-1950s the Department of Defense needed a system that would monitor and protect the air space of the United States; IBM developed a computer, the Q-7. In 1956 the Atomic Energy Commission needed a computer capable of handling nuclear code analysis; the Univac Lark was developed. In the late 1950s and early 1960s the aerospace industry needed computing capability to put a man on the moon; the IBM 700 series scientific computers were developed. From these demands, the current computer evolved.

First, there was the need, then the design was developed to support the need. However, this did not happen in the business world. No one said, "We need a system to help run our business." The Social Security Administration's tabulator was sold to business through the early 1950s as an accounting machine. In 1953, business finally got its own computer – the IBM 650 and the Univac I. This joined some scientific computer capabilities with business capabilities, but it was still predominantly used for accounting. In the late 1950s the development of disc storage and magnetic tape moved business from the punch card era into the computer storage era. The early 1960s brought the development of the larger and faster breed of computers – the IBM 1400 series and the Univac II's.

Gradually, salespeople and technologists convinced management it needed a computer, not only for accounting, but to control inventory and manufacturing processes, and to increase productivity. In the late 1960s and early 1970s, the merger finally began between the scientific computer and the business computer and evolved into today's computer. The need was still derived by the technologists, not by management. Management was being pushed by the technologists and sales people.

The executive today is becoming more aware of computers. One cannot pick up a business publication without seeing major articles. One can't even watch a TV football game without seeing Apple, Tandy and IBM advertising personal computers. And many books are being written on the computer's impact on business.

Another factor influencing executives simply is the overwhelming presence of computers, which now comprise a $75-billion industry with double digit-growth. It is claimed that 30% of all productivity gains result from the use of computers. The reduced cost of silicon chips has made the computer affordable to most businesses. In 1968 a large IBM 365 system cost $4 million. In 1982 dollars, that's about $8 million. Today a computer that will perform twice as fast as that $8-million computer costs $327,000. And as the cost has come down, the demand has risen. In 1975 there were 175,000 installed computers. In 1980 the number increased to 550,000. In 1985 it is estimated that 1.5 million computers will be installed in this country.

Soon executives no longer will need technologists. They will be able to have direct access to computers in the office systems of the future – systems with computer graphics, user-friendly languages, electronic mail and word processing.

Now, because executives are better educated about computers, and pressured by computer presence and potential to help in business, they are beginning to take control of data processing. They are fighting the "creeping legacy" of the technician telling management what it needs, when it needs it and how it needs it.

There are, however, half a million data processing people who still think that way. Unless their attitude is changed, the "creeping legacy" will keep management where it

FIGURE 17. "How to Get Computers to Speak Your Language," feature from *The Executive.*

is. There will be no changes until management realizes the company is not getting what it really needs or wants and begins to demand that those needs and wants be satisfied by the technologists.

One key to control is a DP board of directors. Such boards are run much like a corporate board of directors. Data processing is a business, just as the company is a business, except DP's clients are within the organization. Executives, through this board, can begin to deal with data processing as a business and apply basic business principles to its operation. Executives on DP boards are not dealing with technical questions but business questions that have always been there but were covered up with technology.

For example, during a recent business planning process, an executive in the drug distribution business asked each of his department managers, "What is the most critical element blocking you from reaching your objectives?" Without exception, every manager said, "Data processing. The DP department does not run well and if something is not changed, the firm will not be able to meet its business objectives."

Executive management, including the chairman, the president, all of the next level of executives, and the senior DP staff took an entire week to do nothing but address that problem, and to find methods to turn the department around. There it is — the executive starting to inch in and get control.

In another case, a large commercial bank wanted to study office automation, but its executives felt they could not turn to their own DP department because it was steeped in yesterday's way of thinking. Bank officials were forced to go outside the company for consultants to help define the office of the future and what it should be for the bank. They didn't use their own DP department because that organization started from this premise: "We have these systems in place. If you want office automation, we'll develop communication links tying all these pieces together." But office automation was a brand-new subject and the bank had to define what it needed, forgetting what exists, and define where to go and how to get there.

Executive involvement is now influencing the computer and, even more so, the delivery of computer applications and systems. Executives are beginning to dictate their "wants" and "don't wants." This has only been occurring for about five years. They also are beginning to understand that this is a productivity issue, not an information issue. Data processing is not the information czar, it is the productivity czar. The computer is there to achieve greater productivity for business.

If a company is going to have an efficient office automation system and one that supports executive decision-making, it has to recognize the first goal — to increase the productivity of the executive. Information alone may or may not be capable of this. Executives who operate from the premise that DP only involves information will never have a good system.

As hardware is coming out — and this is an interesting development — it is being tested on executives; experimental systems are being used by executives and executives can accept or reject them. Executives are making demands concerning design, approach, etc. with their own organizations. Their organizations, to support these demands, are influencing the manufacturer. For the first time, data processing organizations are being forced to think differently and in turn are pushing the manufacturers in different directions.

The last and most critical change that executives are making is the insistence that professionals are needed in DP and that these professionals must support the business. **E**

FIGURE 17. Continued.

Index